SAINT JOAN
THE APPLE CART

LONDON

PUBLISHED BY
Constable and Company Ltd.
10-12 Orange Street, W.C.2

CANADA
Longmans, Green and Company Ltd.
TORONTO

INDIA and PAKISTAN
Orient Longmans Private Ltd.
BOMBAY MADRAS CALCUTTA NEW DELHI

EAST AFRICA
Longmans, Green and Company Ltd.
NAIROBI

SOUTHERN AFRICA
Longmans Southern Africa (Pty.) Ltd.
CAPETOWN JOHANNESBURG SALISBURY

AUSTRALIA and NEW ZEALAND
Thomas C. Lothian Pty. Ltd.
MELBOURNE SYDNEY ADELAIDE BRISBANE
and AUCKLAND, N.Z.

SAINT JOAN A CHRONICLE AND THE APPLE CART A POLITICAL EXTRAVAGANZA BY BERNARD SHAW

LONDON

CONSTABLE AND COMPANY

LIMITED

Saint Joan first published 1924.   The Apple Cart 1930
Reprinted for this Standard Edition 1932
Reprinted 1933
Reprinted 1934
Reprinted 1936
Reprinted 1937
Reprinted 1938
Reprinted 1940
Reprinted 1949
Reprinted 1953
Reprinted 1961

PRINTED IN GREAT BRITAIN
BY R. & R. CLARK, LIMITED, EDINBURGH

CONTENTS

v

CONTENTS

SAINT JOAN

A CHRONICLE PLAY IN SIX SCENES
AND AN EPILOGUE

Saint Joan was performed for the first time by The Theatre Guild in the Garrick Theatre, New York City, on the 28th December 1923, with Winifred Lenihan in the title-part. Its first performance in London took place on the 26th March 1924 in the New Theatre in St Martin's Lane, with Sybil Thorndike as the Saint.

PREFACE TO SAINT JOAN

Joan the Original and Presumptuous

Joan of Arc, a village girl from the Vosges, was born about 1412; burnt for heresy, witchcraft, and sorcery in 1431; rehabilitated after a fashion in 1456; designated Venerable in 1904; declared Blessed in 1908; and finally canonized in 1920. She is the most notable Warrior Saint in the Christian calendar, and the queerest fish among the eccentric worthies of the Middle Ages. Though a professed and most pious Catholic, and the projector of a Crusade against the Husites, she was in fact one of the first Protestant martyrs. She was also one of the first apostles of Nationalism, and the first French practitioner of Napoleonic realism in warfare as distinguished from the sporting ransom-gambling chivalry of her time. She was the pioneer of rational dressing for women, and, like Queen Christina of Sweden two centuries later, to say nothing of Catalina de Erauso and innumerable obscure heroines who have disguised themselves as men to serve as soldiers and sailors, she refused to accept the specific woman's lot, and dressed and fought and lived as men did.

As she contrived to assert herself in all these ways with such force that she was famous throughout western Europe before she was out of her teens (indeed she never got out of them), it is hardly surprising that she was judicially burnt, ostensibly for a number of capital crimes which we no longer punish as such, but essentially for what we call unwomanly and insufferable presumption. At eighteen Joan's pretensions were beyond those of the proudest Pope or the haughtiest emperor. She claimed to be the ambassador and plenipotentiary of God, and to be, in effect, a member of the Church Triumphant whilst still in the flesh on earth. She patronized her own king, and summoned the English king to repentance and obedience to her commands. She lectured, talked down, and overruled statesmen and prelates. She pooh-poohed the plans of generals, leading their troops to victory on plans of her own. She had an unbounded and quite unconcealed

3

contempt for official opinion, judgment, and authority, and for War Office tactics and strategy. Had she been a sage and monarch in whom the most venerable hierarchy and the most illustrious dynasty converged, her pretensions and proceedings would have been as trying to the official mind as the pretensions of Caesar were to Cassius. As her actual condition was pure upstart, there were only two opinions about her. One was that she was miraculous: the other that she was unbearable.

Joan and Socrates

If Joan had been malicious, selfish, cowardly or stupid, she would have been one of the most odious persons known to history instead of one of the most attractive. If she had been old enough to know the effect she was producing on the men whom she humiliated by being right when they were wrong, and had learned to flatter and manage them, she might have lived as long as Queen Elizabeth. But she was too young and rustical and inexperienced to have any such arts. When she was thwarted by men whom she thought fools, she made no secret of her opinion of them or her impatience with their folly; and she was naïve enough to expect them to be obliged to her for setting them right and keeping them out of mischief. Now it is always hard for superior wits to understand the fury roused by their exposures of the stupidities of comparative dullards. Even Socrates, for all his age and experience, did not defend himself at his trial like a man who understood the long accumulated fury that had burst on him, and was clamoring for his death. His accuser, if born 2300 years later, might have been picked out of any first class carriage on a suburban railway during the evening or morning rush from or to the City; for he had really nothing to say except that he and his like could not endure being shewn up as idiots every time Socrates opened his mouth. Socrates, unconscious of this, was paralyzed by his sense that somehow he was missing the point of the attack. He petered out after he had established the fact that he was an old soldier and a man of honorable life, and that his accuser was a silly snob. He had no suspicion of the extent to which his mental superiority had roused fear and hatred against him in the hearts of men towards whom he was conscious of nothing but good will and good service.

CONTRAST WITH NAPOLEON

If Socrates was as innocent as this at the age of seventy, it may be imagined how innocent Joan was at the age of seventeen. Now Socrates was a man of argument, operating slowly and peacefully on men's minds, whereas Joan was a woman of action, operating with impetuous violence on their bodies. That, no doubt, is why the contemporaries of Socrates endured him so long, and why Joan was destroyed before she was fully grown. But both of them combined terrifying ability with a frankness, personal modesty, and benevolence which made the furious dislike to which they fell victims absolutely unreasonable, and therefore inapprehensible by themselves. Napoleon, also possessed of terrifying ability, but neither frank nor disinterested, had no illusions as to the nature of his popularity. When he was asked how the world would take his death, he said it would give a gasp of relief. But it is not so easy for mental giants who neither hate nor intend to injure their fellows to realize that nevertheless their fellows hate mental giants and would like to destroy them, not only enviously because the juxtaposition of a superior wounds their vanity, but quite humbly and honestly because it frightens them. Fear will drive men to any extreme; and the fear inspired by a superior being is a mystery which cannot be reasoned away. Being immeasurable it is unbearable when there is no presumption or guarantee of its benevolence and moral responsibility: in other words, when it has no official status. The legal and conventional superiority of Herod and Pilate, and of Annas and Caiaphas, inspires fear; but the fear, being a reasonable fear of measurable and avoidable consequences which seem salutary and protective, is bearable; whilst the strange superiority of Christ and the fear it inspires elicit a shriek of Crucify Him from all who cannot divine its benevolence. Socrates has to drink the hemlock, Christ to hang on the cross, and Joan to burn at the stake, whilst Napoleon, though he ends in St Helena, at least dies in his bed there; and many terrifying but quite comprehensible official scoundrels die natural deaths in all the glory of the kingdoms of this world, proving that it is far more dangerous to be a saint than to be a conqueror. Those who have been both, like Mahomet and Joan, have found that it is the conqueror who must save the saint, and that defeat and capture mean martyrdom. Joan was burnt without a hand lifted on her own side to save her. The comrades she had led to victory and the enemies she had disgraced and defeated, the French king she had crowned and the English king whose crown she had kicked into the Loire, were equally glad to be rid of her.

Was Joan Innocent or Guilty?

As this result could have been produced by a crapulous inferiority as well as by a sublime superiority, the question which of the two was operative in Joan's case has to be faced. It was decided against her by her contemporaries after a very careful and conscientious trial; and the reversal of the verdict twentyfive years later, in form a rehabilitation of Joan, was really only a confirmation of the validity of the coronation of Charles VII. It is the more impressive reversal by a unanimous Posterity, culminating in her canonization, that has quashed the original proceedings, and put her judges on their trial, which, so far, has been much more unfair than their trial of her. Nevertheless the rehabilitation of 1456, corrupt job as it was, really did produce evidence enough to satisfy all reasonable critics that Joan was not a common termagant, not a harlot, not a witch, not a blasphemer, no more an idolater than the Pope himself, and not ill conducted in any sense apart from her soldiering, her wearing of men's clothes, and her audacity, but on the contrary good-humored, an intact virgin, very pious, very temperate (we should call her meal of bread soaked in the common wine which is the drinking water of France ascetic), very kindly, and, though a brave and hardy soldier, unable to endure loose language or licentious conduct. She went to the stake without a stain on her character except the overweening presumption, the superbity as they called it, that led her thither. It would therefore be waste of time now to prove that the Joan of the first part of the Elizabethan chronicle play of Henry VI (supposed to have been tinkered by Shakespear) grossly libels her in its concluding scenes in deference to Jingo patriotism. The mud that was thrown at her has dropped off by this time so completely that there is no need for any modern writer to wash up after it. What is far more difficult to get rid of is the mud that is being thrown at her judges, and the whitewash which disfigures her beyond recognition. When Jingo scurrility had done its worst to her, sectarian scurrility (in this case Protestant scurrility) used her stake to beat the Roman Catholic Church and the Inquisition. The easiest way to make these institutions the villains of a melodrama was to make The Maid its heroine. That melodrama may be dismissed as rubbish. Joan got a far fairer trial from the Church and the Inquisition than any prisoner of her type and in her situation gets nowadays in any official secular court; and the decision was strictly according to law. And she was not a melodramatic heroine: that is, a physically beautiful lovelorn parasite on an equally beautiful hero, but a genius and a saint, about as completely the opposite of a melodramatic heroine as it is possible for a human being to be.

Let us be clear about the meaning of the terms. A genius is a person who, seeing farther and probing deeper than other people, has a different set of ethical valuations from theirs, and has energy enough to give effect to this extra vision and its valuations in whatever manner best suits his or her specific talents. A saint is one who having practised heroic virtues, and enjoyed revelations or powers of the order which The Church classes technically as supernatural, is eligible for canonization. If a historian is an Anti-Feminist, and does not believe women to be capable of genius in the traditional masculine departments, he

7

will never make anything of Joan, whose genius was turned to practical account mainly in soldiering and politics. If he is Rationalist enough to deny that saints exist, and to hold that new ideas cannot come otherwise than by conscious ratiocination, he will never catch Joan's likeness. Her ideal biographer must be free from nineteenth century prejudices and biases; must understand the Middle Ages, the Roman Catholic Church, and the Holy Roman Empire much more intimately than our Whig historians have ever understood them; and must be capable of throwing off sex partialities and their romance, and regarding woman as the female of the human species, and not as a different kind of animal with specific charms and specific imbecilities.

Joan's Good Looks

To put the last point roughly, any book about Joan which begins by describing her as a beauty may be at once classed as a romance. Not one of Joan's comrades, in village, court, or camp, even when they were straining themselves to please the king by praising her, ever claimed that she was pretty. All the men who alluded to the matter declared most emphatically that she was unattractive sexually to a degree that seemed to them miraculous, considering that she was in the bloom of youth, and neither ugly, awkward, deformed, nor unpleasant in her person. The evident truth is that like most women of her hardy managing type she seemed neutral in the conflict of sex because men were too much afraid of her to fall in love with her. She herself was not sexless: in spite of the virginity she had vowed up to a point, and preserved to her death, she never excluded the possibility of marriage for herself. But marriage, with its preliminary of the attraction, pursuit, and capture of a husband, was not her business: she had something else to do. Byron's formula, "Man's love is of man's life a thing apart: 'tis woman's whole existence," did not apply to her any more than to George Washington or any other masculine worker on the heroic scale. Had she lived in our time, picture postcards might have been sold of her as a general: they would not have been sold of her as a sultana. Nevertheless there is one reason for crediting her with a very remarkable face. A sculptor of her time in Orleans made a statue of a helmeted young woman with a face that is unique in art in point of being evidently not an ideal face but a portrait, and yet so uncommon as to be unlike any real woman one has ever seen. It is surmised that Joan served unconsciously as the sculptor's model. There is no proof of this; but those extraordinarily spaced eyes raise so powerfully the question "If this woman be not Joan, who is she?" that I dispense with further evidence, and challenge those who disagree with me to prove a negative. It is a wonderful face, but quite neutral from the point of view of the operatic beauty fancier.

Such a fancier may perhaps be finally chilled by the prosaic fact that Joan was the defendant in a suit for breach of promise of marriage, and that she conducted her own case and won it.

JOAN'S SOCIAL POSITION

By class Joan was the daughter of a working farmer who was one of the headmen of his village, and transacted its feudal business for it with the neighboring squires and their lawyers. When the castle in which the villagers were entitled to take refuge from raids became derelict, he organized a combination of half a dozen farmers to obtain possession of it so as to occupy it when there was any danger of invasion. As a child, Joan could please herself at times with being the young lady of this castle. Her mother and brothers were able to follow and share her fortune at court without making themselves notably ridiculous. These facts leave us no excuse for the popular romance that turns every heroine into either a princess or a beggarmaid. In the somewhat similar case of Shakespear a whole inverted pyramid of wasted research has been based on the assumption that he was an illiterate laborer, in the face of the plainest evidence that his father was a man of business, and at one time a very prosperous one, married to a woman of some social pretensions. There is the same tendency to drive Joan into the position of a hired shepherd girl, though a hired shepherd girl in Domrémy would have deferred to her as the young lady of the farm.

The difference between Joan's case and Shakespear's is that Shakespear was not illiterate. He had been to school, and knew as much Latin and Greek as most university passmen retain: that is, for practical purposes, none at all. Joan was absolutely illiterate. "I do not know A from B" she said. But many princesses at that time and for long after might have said the same. Marie Antoinette, for instance, at Joan's age could not spell her own name correctly. But this does not mean that Joan was an ignorant person, or that she suffered from the diffidence and sense of social disadvantage now felt by people who cannot read or write. If she could not write letters, she could and did dictate them and attach full and indeed excessive importance to them. When she was called a shepherd lass to her face she very warmly resented it, and challenged any woman to compete with her in the household arts of the mistresses of well furnished houses. She understood the political and military situation in France much better than most of our newspaper fed university women-graduates understand the corresponding situation of their own country today. Her first convert was the neighboring commandant at Vaucouleurs; and she converted him by telling him about the defeat of the Dauphin's troops at the Battle of Herrings so long before he had official news of it that he concluded she must have had a divine revelation. This knowledge of and interest in public affairs was nothing extraordinary among farmers in a war-swept countryside. Politicians came to the door too often sword in hand to be disregarded: Joan's people could not afford to be ignorant of what was going on in the feudal world. They were not rich; and Joan worked on the farm as her father did, driving the sheep to pasture and so forth; but there is no evidence or suggestion of sordid poverty, and no reason to believe that Joan had to work as a hired servant works, or indeed to work at all when she preferred to go to confession, or dawdle about waiting for visions and listening to the church bells to hear voices in them.

In short, much more of a young lady, and even of an intellectual, than most of the daughters of our petty bourgeoisie.

JOAN'S VOICES AND VISIONS

Joan's voices and visions have played many tricks with her reputation. They have been held to prove that she was mad, that she was a liar and impostor, that she was a sorceress (she was burned for this), and finally that she was a saint. They do not prove any of these things; but the variety of the conclusions reached shew how little our matter-of-fact historians know about other people's minds, or even about their own. There are people in the world whose imagination is so vivid that when they have an idea it comes to them as an audible voice, sometimes uttered by a visible figure. Criminal lunatic asylums are occupied largely by murderers who have obeyed voices. Thus a woman may hear voices telling her that she must cut her husband's throat and strangle her child as they lie asleep; and she may feel obliged to do what she is told. By a medico-legal superstition it is held in our courts that criminals whose temptations present themselves under these illusions are not responsible for their actions, and must be treated as insane. But the seers of visions and the hearers of revelations are not always criminals. The inspirations and intuitions and unconsciously reasoned conclusions of genius sometimes assume similar illusions. Socrates, Luther, Swedenborg, Blake saw visions and heard voices just as Saint Francis and Saint Joan did. If Newton's imagination had been of the same vividly dramatic kind he might have seen the ghost of Pythagoras walk into the orchard and explain why the apples were falling. Such an illusion would have invalidated neither the theory of gravitation nor Newton's general sanity. What is more, the visionary method of making the discovery would not be a whit more miraculous than the normal method. The test of sanity is not the normality of the method but the reasonableness of the discovery. If Newton had been informed by Pythagoras that the moon was made of green cheese, then Newton would have been locked up. Gravitation, being a reasoned hypothesis which fitted remarkably well into the Copernican version of the observed physical facts of the universe, established Newton's reputation for extraordinary intelligence, and would have done so no matter how fantastically he had arrived at it. Yet his theory of gravitation is not so impressive a mental feat as his astounding chronology, which establishes him as the king of mental conjurors, but a Bedlamite king whose authority no one now accepts. On the subject of the eleventh horn of the beast seen by the prophet Daniel he was more fantastic than Joan, because his imagination was not dramatic but mathematical and therefore extraordinarily susceptible to numbers: indeed if all his works were lost except his chronology we should say that he was as mad as a hatter. As it is, who dares diagnose Newton as a madman?

In the same way Joan must be judged a sane woman in spite of her voices because they never gave her any advice that might not have come to her from her mother wit exactly as gravitation came to Newton. We can all see now, especially since the late war threw so many of our women into military life, that Joan's campaigning could not have been carried on in petticoats. This was not only because she did a man's work, but because it was morally necessary that sex should be left out of the question as between her and her comrades-in-arms. She gave this reason herself when she was pressed on the subject; and the fact that this entirely reasonable necessity came to her imagination first as an order from God delivered through the mouth of Saint Catherine does not prove that she was mad. The soundness of the order proves that she was unusually sane; but its form proves that her dramatic imagination played tricks with her senses. Her policy was also quite sound: nobody disputes that the relief of Orleans, followed up by the coronation at Rheims of the Dauphin as a counterblow to the suspicions then current of his legitimacy and consequently of his title, were military and political masterstrokes that saved France. They might have been planned by Napoleon or any other illusionproof genius. They came to Joan as an instruction from her Counsel, as she called her visionary saints; but she was none the less an able leader of men for imagining her ideas in this way.

THE EVOLUTIONARY APPETITE

What then is the modern view of Joan's voices and visions and messages from God? The nineteenth century said that they were delusions, but that as she was a pretty girl, and had been abominably ill-treated and finally done to death by a superstitious rabble of medieval priests hounded on by a corrupt political bishop, it must be assumed that she was the innocent dupe of these delusions. The twentieth century finds this explanation too vapidly commonplace, and demands something more mystic. I think the twentieth century is right, because an explanation which amounts to Joan being mentally defective instead of, as she obviously was, mentally excessive, will not wash. I cannot believe, nor, if I could, could I expect all my readers to believe, as Joan did, that three ocularly visible well dressed persons, named respectively Saint Catherine, Saint Margaret, and Saint Michael, came down from heaven and gave her certain instructions with which they were charged by God for her. Not that such a belief would be more improbable or fantastic than some modern beliefs which we all swallow; but there are fashions and family habits in belief, and it happens that, my fashion being Victorian and my family habit Protestant, I find myself unable to attach any such objective validity to the form of Joan's visions.

But that there are forces at work which use individuals for purposes far transcending the purpose of keeping these individuals alive and prosperous and respectable and safe and happy in the middle station in life, which is all any good bourgeois can reasonably require, is established by the fact that men will, in the pursuit of knowledge and of social readjustments for which they will not be a penny the better, and are indeed often many pence the worse, face poverty, infamy, exile, imprisonment, dreadful hardship, and death. Even the selfish pursuit of personal power does not nerve men to the efforts and sacrifices which are eagerly made in pursuit of extensions of our power over nature, though these extensions may not touch the personal life of the seeker at any point. There is no more mystery about this appetite for knowledge and power than about the appetite for food: both are known as facts and as facts only, the difference between them being that the appetite for food is necessary to the life of the hungry man and is therefore a personal appetite, whereas the other is an appetite for evolution, and therefore a superpersonal need.

The diverse manners in which our imaginations dramatize the approach of the superpersonal forces is a problem for the psychologist, not for the historian. Only, the historian must understand that visionaries are neither impostors nor lunatics. It is one thing to say that the figure Joan recognized as St Catherine was not really St Catherine, but the dramatization by Joan's imagination of that pressure upon her of the driving force that is behind evolution which I have just called the evolutionary appetite. It is quite another to class her visions with the vision of two moons seen by a drunken person, or with Brocken spectres, echoes and the like. Saint Catherine's instructions were far too cogent for that; and the simplest French peasant who believes in apparitions of celestial personages to favored mortals is nearer to the scientific truth about Joan than the Rationalist and Materialist historians and essayists who feel obliged to set down a girl who saw saints and heard them talking to her as either crazy or mendacious. If Joan was mad, all Christendom was mad too; for people who believe devoutly in the existence of celestial personages are every whit as mad in that sense as the people who think they see them. Luther, when he threw his inkhorn at the devil, was no more mad than any other Augustinian monk: he had a more vivid imagination, and had perhaps eaten and slept less: that was all.

The Mere Iconography does not Matter

All the popular religions in the world are made apprehensible by an array of legendary personages, with an Almighty Father, and sometimes a mother and divine child, as the central figures. These are presented to the mind's eye in childhood; and the result is a hallucination which persists strongly throughout life when it has been well impressed. Thus all the thinking of the hallucinated adult about the fountain of inspiration which is continually flowing in the universe, or about the promptings of virtue and the revulsions of shame: in short, about aspiration and conscience, both of which forces are matters of fact more obvious than electro-magnetism, is thinking in terms of the celestial vision. And when in the case of exceptionally imaginative persons, especially those practising certain appropriate austerities, the hallucination extends from the mind's eye to the body's, the visionary sees Krishna or the Buddha or the Blessed Virgin or St Catherine as the case may be.

The Modern Education which Joan Escaped

It is important to everyone nowadays to understand this, because modern science is making short work of the hallucinations without regard to the vital importance of the things they symbolize. If Joan were reborn today she would be sent, first to a convent school in which she would be mildly taught to connect inspiration and conscience with St Catherine and St Michael exactly as she was in the fifteenth century, and then finished up with a very energetic training in the gospel of Saints Louis Pasteur and Paul Bert, who would tell her (possibly in visions but more probably in pamphlets) not to be a superstitious little fool, and to empty out St Catherine and the rest of the Catholic hagiology as an obsolete iconography of exploded myths. It would be rubbed into her that Galileo was a martyr, and his persecutors incorrigible ignoramuses, and that St Teresa's hormones had gone astray and left her incurably hyperpituitary or hyperadrenal or hysteroid or epileptoid or anything but asteroid. She would have been convinced by precept and experiment that baptism and receiving the body of her Lord were contemptible superstitions, and that vaccination and vivisection were enlightened practices. Behind her new Saints Louis and Paul there would be not only Science purifying Religion and being purified by it, but hypochondria, melancholia, cowardice, stupidity, cruelty, muckraking curiosity, knowledge without wisdom, and everything that the eternal soul in Nature loathes, instead of the virtues of which St Catherine was the figure head. As to the new rites, which would be the saner Joan? the one who carried little children to be baptized of water and the spirit, or the one who sent the police to force their parents to have the most villainous racial poison we know thrust into their veins? the one who told them the story of the angel and Mary, or the one who questioned them as to their experiences of the Œdipus complex? the one to whom the consecrated wafer was the very body of the virtue that was her salvation, or the one who looked forward to a precise and convenient regulation of her health and her desires by a nicely calculated diet of thyroid extract, adrenalin, thymin, pituitrin, and insulin, with pick-me-ups of hormone stimulants, the blood being first carefully fortified with antibodies against all possible infections by inoculations of infected bacteria and serum from infected animals, and against old age by surgical extirpation of the reproductive ducts or weekly doses of monkey gland?

It is true that behind all these quackeries there is a certain body of genuine scientific physiology. But was there any the less a certain body of genuine psychology behind St Catherine and the Holy Ghost? And which is the healthier mind? the saintly mind or the monkey gland mind? Does not the present cry of Back to the Middle Ages, which has been incubating ever since the pre-Raphaelite movement began, mean that it is no longer our Academy pictures that are intolerable, but our credulities that have not the excuse of being superstitions, our cruelties that have not the excuse of barbarism, our persecutions that have not the excuse of religious faith, our shameless substitution of successful swindlers and scoundrels and quacks for saints as objects of worship, and our deafness and blindness to the calls and visions of the inexorable power that made us, and will destroy us if we disregard it? To Joan and her contemporaries we should appear as a drove of Gadarene swine, possessed by all the unclean spirits cast out by the faith and civilization of the Middle Ages, running violently down a steep place into a hell of high explosives. For us to set up our condition as a standard of sanity, and declare Joan mad because she never condescended to it, is to prove that we are not only lost but irredeemable. Let us then once for all drop all nonsense about Joan being cracked, and accept her as at least as sane as Florence Nightingale, who also combined a very simple iconography of religious belief with a mind so exceptionally powerful that it kept her in continual trouble with the medical and military panjandrums of her time.

FAILURES OF THE VOICES

That the voices and visions were illusory, and their wisdom all Joan's own, is shewn by the occasions on which they failed her, notably during her trial, when they assured her that she would be rescued. Here her hopes flattered her; but they were not unreasonable: her military colleague La Hire was in command of a considerable force not so very far off; and if the Armagnacs, as her party was called, had really wanted to rescue her, and had put anything like her own vigor into the enterprise, they could have attempted it with very fair chances of success. She did not understand that they were glad to be rid of her, nor that the rescue of a prisoner from the hands of the Church was a much more serious business for a medieval captain, or even a medieval king, than its mere physical difficulty as a military exploit suggested. According to her lights her expectation of a rescue was reasonable; therefore she heard Madame Saint Catherine assuring her it would happen, that being her way of finding out and making up her own mind. When it became evident that she had miscalculated: when she was led to the stake, and La Hire was not thundering at the gates of Rouen nor charging Warwick's men at arms, she threw over Saint Catherine at once, and recanted. Nothing could be more sane or practical. It was not until she discovered that she had gained nothing by her recantation but close imprisonment for life that she withdrew it, and deliberately and explicitly chose burning instead: a decision which shewed not only the extraordinary decision of her character, but also a Rationalism carried to its ultimate human test of suicide. Yet even in this the illusion persisted; and she announced her relapse as dictated to her by her voices.

Joan a Galtonic Visualizer

The most sceptical scientific reader may therefore accept as a flat fact, carrying no implication of unsoundness of mind, that Joan was what Francis Galton and other modern investigators of human faculty call a visualizer. She saw imaginary saints just as some other people see imaginary diagrams and landscapes with numbers dotted about them, and are thereby able to perform feats of memory and arithmetic impossible to non-visualizers. Visualizers will understand this at once. Non-visualizers who have never read Galton will be puzzled and incredulous. But a very little inquiry among their acquaintances will reveal to them that the mind's eye is more or less a magic lantern, and that the street is full of normally sane people who have hallucinations of all sorts which they believe to be part of the normal permanent equipment of all human beings.

Joan's Manliness and Militarism

Joan's other abnormality, too common among uncommon things to be properly called a peculiarity, was her craze for soldiering and the masculine life. Her father tried to frighten her out of it by threatening to drown her if she ran away with the soldiers, and ordering her brothers to drown her if he were not on the spot. This extravagance was clearly not serious: it must have been addressed to a child young enough to imagine that he was in earnest. Joan must therefore as a child have wanted to run away and be a soldier. The awful prospect of being thrown into the Meuse and drowned by a terrible father and her big brothers kept her quiet until the father had lost his terrors and the brothers yielded to her natural leadership; and by that time she had sense enough to know that the masculine and military life was not a mere matter of running away from home. But the taste for it never left her, and was fundamental in determining her career.

If anyone doubts this, let him ask himself why a maid charged with a special mission from heaven to the Dauphin (this was how Joan saw her very able plan for retrieving the desperate situation of the uncrowned king) should not have simply gone to the court as a maid, in woman's dress, and urged her counsel upon him in a woman's way, as other women with similar missions had come to his mad father and his wise grandfather. Why did she insist on having a soldier's dress and arms and sword and horse and equipment, and on treating her escort of soldiers as comrades, sleeping side by side with them on the floor at night as if there were no difference of sex between them? It may be answered that this was the safest way of travelling through a country infested with hostile troops and bands of marauding deserters from both sides. Such an answer has no weight because it applies to all the women who travelled in France at that time, and who never dreamt of travelling otherwise than as women. But even if we accept it, how does it account for the fact that when the danger was over, and she could present herself at court in feminine attire with perfect safety and obviously with greater propriety, she presented herself in her man's dress, and instead of urging Charles, like Queen Victoria urging the War Office to send Roberts to the Transvaal, to send D'Alençon, De Rais, La Hire and the rest to the relief of Dunois at Orleans, insisted that she must go herself and lead the assault in person? Why did she give exhibitions of her dexterity in handling a lance, and of her seat as a rider? Why did she accept presents of armor and chargers and masculine surcoats, and in every action repudiate the con-

ventional character of a woman? The simple answer to all these
questions is that she was the sort of woman that wants to lead a
man's life. They are to be found wherever there are armies on
foot or navies on the seas, serving in male disguise, eluding detection for astonishingly long periods, and sometimes, no doubt,
escaping it entirely. When they are in a position to defy public
opinion they throw off all concealment. You have your Rosa
Bonheur painting in male blouse and trousers, and George Sand
living a man's life and almost compelling her Chopins and De
Mussets to live women's lives to amuse her. Had Joan not been
one of those "unwomanly women," she might have been canonized much sooner.

But it is not necessary to wear trousers and smoke big cigars
to live a man's life any more than it is necessary to wear petticoats to live a woman's. There are plenty of gowned and bodiced
women in ordinary civil life who manage their own affairs and
other people's, including those of their menfolk, and are entirely
masculine in their tastes and pursuits. There always were such
women, even in the Victorian days when women had fewer legal
rights than men, and our modern women magistrates, mayors,
and members of Parliament were unknown. In reactionary
Russia in our own century a woman soldier organized an effective regiment of amazons, which disappeared only because it was
Aldershottian enough to be against the Revolution. The exemp-
tion of women from military service is founded, not on any
natural inaptitude that men do not share, but on the fact that
communities cannot reproduce themselves without plenty of
women. Men are more largely dispensable, and are sacrificed
accordingly.

Was Joan Suicidal?

These two abnormalities were the only ones that were irre-
sistibly prepotent in Joan; and they brought her to the stake.
Neither of them was peculiar to her. There was nothing peculiar
about her except the vigor and scope of her mind and character,
and the intensity of her vital energy. She was accused of a sui-

cidal tendency; and it is a fact that when she attempted to escape
from Beaurevoir Castle by jumping from a tower said to be sixty
feet high, she took a risk beyond reason, though she recovered
from the crash after a few days fasting. Her death was deliberately chosen as an alternative to life without liberty. In battle she
challenged death as Wellington did at Waterloo, and as Nelson
habitually did when he walked his quarter deck during his battles
with all his decorations in full blaze. As neither Nelson nor Wellington nor any of those who have performed desperate feats,
and preferred death to captivity, has been accused of suicidal
mania, Joan need not be suspected of it. In the Beaurevoir affair
there was more at stake than her freedom. She was distracted by
the news that Compiègne was about to fall; and she was convinced that she could save it if only she could get free. Still, the
leap was so perilous that her conscience was not quite easy about
it; and she expressed this, as usual, by saying that Saint Catherine
had forbidden her to do it, but forgave her afterwards for her
disobedience.

Joan Summed Up

We may accept and admire Joan, then, as a sane and shrewd
country girl of extraordinary strength of mind and hardihood of
body. Everything she did was thoroughly calculated; and though
the process was so rapid that she was hardly conscious of it, and
ascribed it all to her voices, she was a woman of policy and not
of blind impulse. In war she was as much a realist as Napoleon:
she had his eye for artillery and his knowledge of what it could
do. She did not expect besieged cities to fall Jerichowise at the
sound of her trumpet, but, like Wellington, adapted her methods
of attack to the peculiarities of the defence; and she anticipated
the Napoleonic calculation that if you only hold on long enough
the other fellow will give in: for example, her final triumph at
Orleans was achieved after her commander Dunois had sounded
the retreat at the end of a day's fighting without a decision.
She was never for a moment what so many romancers and
playwrights have pretended: a romantic young lady. She was a

thorough daughter of the soil in her peasantlike matter-of-factness and doggedness, and her acceptance of great lords and kings and prelates as such without idolatry or snobbery, seeing at a glance how much they were individually good for. She had the respectable countrywoman's sense of the value of public decency, and would not tolerate foul language and neglect of religious observances, nor allow disreputable women to hang about her soldiers. She had one pious ejaculation "En nom Dé!" and one meaningless oath "Par mon martin"; and this much swearing she allowed to the incorrigibly blasphemous La Hire equally with herself. The value of this prudery was so great in restoring the self-respect of the badly demoralized army that, like most of her policy, it justified itself as soundly calculated. She talked to and dealt with people of all classes, from laborers to kings, without embarrassment or affectation, and got them to do what she wanted when they were not afraid or corrupt. She could coax and she could hustle, her tongue having a soft side and a sharp edge. She was very capable: a born boss.

Joan's Immaturity and Ignorance

All this, however, must be taken with one heavy qualification. She was only a girl in her teens. If we could think of her as a managing woman of fifty we should seize her type at once; for we have plenty of managing women among us of that age who illustrate perfectly the sort of person she would have become had she lived. But she, being only a lass when all is said, lacked their knowledge of men's vanities and of the weight and proportion of social forces. She knew nothing of iron hands in velvet gloves: she just used her fists. She thought political changes much easier than they are, and, like Mahomet in his innocence of any world but the tribal world, wrote letters to kings calling on them to make millennial rearrangements. Consequently it was only in the enterprises that were really simple and compassable by swift physical force, like the coronation and the Orleans campaign, that she was successful.

Her want of academic education disabled her when she had to deal with such elaborately artificial structures as the great ecclesiastical and social institutions of the Middle Ages. She had a horror of heretics without suspecting that she was herself a heresiarch, one of the precursors of a schism that rent Europe in two, and cost centuries of bloodshed that is not yet staunched. She objected to foreigners on the sensible ground that they were not in their proper place in France; but she had no notion of how this brought her into conflict with Catholicism and Feudalism, both essentially international. She worked by commonsense; and where scholarship was the only clue to institutions she was in the dark, and broke her shins against them, all the more rudely because of her enormous self-confidence, which made her the least cautious of human beings in civil affairs.

This combination of inept youth and academic ignorance with great natural capacity, push, courage, devotion, originality and oddity, fully accounts for all the facts in Joan's career, and makes her a credible historical and human phenomenon; but it clashes most discordantly both with the idolatrous romance that has grown up round her, and the belittling scepticism that reacts against that romance.

THE MAID IN LITERATURE

English readers would probably like to know how these idolizations and reactions have affected the books they are most familiar with about Joan. There is the first part of the Shakespearean, or pseudo-Shakespearean trilogy of Henry VI, in which Joan is one of the leading characters. This portrait of Joan is not more authentic than the descriptions in the London papers of George Washington in 1780, of Napoleon in 1803, of the German Crown Prince in 1915, or of Lenin in 1917. It ends in mere scurrility. The impression left by it is that the playwright, having begun by an attempt to make Joan a beautiful and romantic figure, was told by his scandalized company that English patriotism would never stand a sympathetic representation of a French conqueror of English troops, and that unless he at once introduced all the old charges against Joan of being a sorceress and a harlot, and assumed her to be guilty of all of them, his play could not be produced. As likely as not, this is what actually happened: indeed there is only one other apparent way of accounting for the sympathetic representation of Joan as a heroine culminating in her eloquent appeal to the Duke of Burgundy, followed by the blackguardly scurrility of the concluding scenes. That other way is to assume that the original play was wholly scurrilous, and that Shakespear touched up the earlier scenes. As the work belongs to a period at which he was only beginning his practice as a tinker of old works, before his own style was fully formed and hardened, it is impossible to verify this guess. His finger is not unmistakeably evident in the play, which is poor and base in its moral tone; but he may have tried to redeem it from downright infamy by shedding a momentary glamor on the figure of The Maid.

When we jump over two centuries to Schiller, we find Die Jungfrau von Orleans drowned in a witch's caldron of raging romance. Schiller's Joan has not a single point of contact with the real Joan, nor indeed with any mortal woman that ever walked this earth. There is really nothing to be said of his play but that it is not about Joan at all, and can hardly be said to pretend to be; for he makes her die on the battlefield, finding her burning unbearable. Before Schiller came Voltaire, who burlesqued Homer in a mock epic called La Pucelle. It is the fashion to dismiss this with virtuous indignation as an obscene libel; and I certainly cannot defend it against the charge of extravagant indecorum. But its purpose was not to depict Joan, but to kill with ridicule everything that Voltaire righteously hated in the institutions and fashions of his own day. He made Joan ridiculous, but not contemptible nor (comparatively) unchaste; and as he also made Homer and St Peter and St Denis and the brave Dunois ridiculous, and the other heroines of the poem very unchaste indeed, he may be said to have let Joan off very easily. But indeed the personal adventures of the characters are so outrageous, and so

Homerically free from any pretence at or even possibility of historical veracity, that those who affect to take them seriously only make themselves Pecksniffian. Samuel Butler believed The Iliad to be a burlesque of Greek Jingoism and Greek religion, written by a hostage or a slave; and La Pucelle makes Butler's theory almost convincing. Voltaire represents Agnes Sorel, the Dauphin's mistress, whom Joan never met, as a woman with a consuming passion for the chastest concubinal fidelity, whose fate it was to be continually falling into the hands of licentious foes and suffering the worst extremities of rapine. The combats in which Joan rides a flying donkey, or in which, taken unaware with no clothes on, she defends Agnes with her sword, and inflicts appropriate mutilations on her assailants, can be laughed at as they are intended to be without scruple; for no sane person could mistake them for sober history; and it may be that their ribald irreverence is more wholesome than the beglamored sentimentality of Schiller. Certainly Voltaire should not have asserted that Joan's father was a priest; but when he was out to écraser l'infâme (the French Church) he stuck at nothing.

So far, the literary representations of The Maid were legendary. But the publication by Quicherat in 1841 of the reports of her trial and rehabilitation placed the subject on a new footing. These entirely realistic documents created a living interest in Joan which Voltaire's mock Homerics and Schiller's romantic nonsense missed. Typical products of that interest in America and England are the histories of Joan by Mark Twain and Andrew Lang. Mark Twain was converted to downright worship of Joan directly by Quicherat. Later on, another man of genius, Anatole France, reacted against the Quicheratic wave of enthusiasm, and wrote a Life of Joan in which he attributed Joan's ideas to clerical prompting and her military success to an adroit use of her by Dunois as a *mascotte*: in short, he denied that she had any serious military or political ability. At this Andrew saw red, and went for Anatole's scalp in a rival Life of her which should be read as a corrective to the other. Lang had no difficulty in shewing that Joan's ability was not an unnatural fiction to be explained away as an illusion manufactured by priests and soldiers, but a straight-forward fact.

It has been lightly pleaded in explanation that Anatole France is a Parisian of the art world, into whose scheme of things the able, hardheaded, hardhanded female, though she dominates pro-vincial France and business Paris, does not enter; whereas Lang was a Scot, and every Scot knows that the grey mare is as likely as not to be the better horse. But this explanation does not con-vince me. I cannot believe that Anatole France does not know what everybody knows. I wish everybody knew all that he knows. One feels antipathies at work in his book. He is not anti-Joan; but he is anti-clerical, anti-mystic, and fundamentally unable to be-lieve that there ever was any such person as the real Joan.

Mark Twain's Joan, skirted to the ground, and with as many petticoats as Noah's wife in a toy ark, is an attempt to combine Bayard with Esther Summerson from Bleak House into an unim-peachable American school teacher in armor. Like Esther Sum-merson she makes her creator ridiculous, and yet, being the work of a man of genius, remains a credible human goodygoody in spite of her creator's infatuation. It is the description rather than the valuation that is wrong. Andrew Lang and Mark Twain are equally determined to make Joan a beautiful and most ladylike Victorian; but both of them recognize and insist on her capacity for leadership, though the Scots scholar is less romantic about it than the Mississippi pilot. But then Lang was, by lifelong pro-fessional habit, a critic of biographies rather than a biographer, whereas Mark Twain writes his biography frankly in the form of a romance.

PROTESTANT MISUNDERSTANDINGS OF THE MIDDLE AGES

They had, however, one disability in common. To understand Joan's history it is not enough to understand her character: you must understand her environment as well. Joan in a nineteenth-twentieth century environment is as incongruous a figure as she would appear were she to walk down Piccadilly today in her fifteenth century armor. To see her in her proper perspective you must understand Christendom and the Catholic Church, the Holy Roman Empire and the Feudal System, as they existed and were understood in the Middle Ages. If you confuse the Middle Ages with the Dark Ages, and are in the habit of ridiculing your aunt for wearing "medieval clothes," meaning those in vogue in the eighteen-nineties, and are quite convinced that the world has progressed enormously, both morally and mechanically, since Joan's time, then you will never understand why Joan was burnt, much less feel that you might have voted for burning her yourself if you had been a member of the court that tried her; and until you feel that you know nothing essential about her.

That the Mississippi pilot should have broken down on this misunderstanding is natural enough. Mark Twain, the Innocent Abroad, who saw the lovely churches of the Middle Ages without a throb of emotion, author of A Yankee at the Court of King Arthur, in which the heroes and heroines of medieval chivalry are guys seen through the eyes of a street arab, was clearly out of court from the beginning. Andrew Lang was better read; but, like Walter Scott, he enjoyed medieval history as a string of Border romances rather than as the record of a high European civilization based on a catholic faith. Both of them were baptized as Protestants, and impressed by all their schooling and most of their reading with the belief that Catholic bishops who burnt heretics were persecutors capable of any villainy; that all heretics were Albigensians or Husites or Jews or Protestants of the highest character; and that the Inquisition was a Chamber of Horrors invented expressly and exclusively for such burnings. Accordingly we find them representing Peter Cauchon, Bishop of Beauvais, the judge who sent Joan to the stake, as an unconscionable scoundrel, and all the questions put to her as "traps" to ensnare and destroy her. And they assume unhesitatingly that the two or three score of canons and doctors of law and divinity who sat with Cauchon as assessors, were exact reproductions of him on slightly less elevated chairs and with a different headdress.

Comparative Fairness of Joan's Trial

The truth is that Cauchon was threatened and insulted by the English for being too considerate to Joan. A recent French writer denies that Joan was burnt, and holds that Cauchon spirited her away and burnt somebody or something else in her place, and that the pretender who subsequently personated her at Orleans and elsewhere was not a pretender but the real authentic Joan. He is able to cite Cauchon's pro-Joan partiality in support of his view. As to the assessors, the objection to them is not that they were a row of uniform rascals, but that they were political partisans of Joan's enemies. This is a valid objection to all such trials; but in the absence of neutral tribunals they are unavoidable. A trial by Joan's French partisans would have been as unfair as the trial by her French opponents; and an equally mixed tribunal would have produced a deadlock. Such recent trials as those of Edith Cavell by a German tribunal and Roger Casement by an English one were open to the same objection; but they went forward to the death nevertheless, because neutral tribunals were not available. Edith, like Joan, was an arch heretic: in the middle of the war she declared before the world that "Patriotism is not enough." She nursed enemies back to health, and assisted their prisoners to escape, making it abundantly clear that she would help any fugitive or distressed person without asking whose side he was on, and acknowledging no distinction before Christ between Tommy and Jerry and Pitou the *poilu*. Well might Edith have wished that she could bring the Middle Ages back, and have fifty civilians, learned in the law or vowed to the service of God, to support two skilled judges in trying her case according to the Catholic law of Christendom, and to argue it out with her at sitting after sitting for many weeks. The modern military Inquisition was not so squeamish. It shot her out of hand; and her countrymen, seeing in this a good opportunity for lecturing the enemy on his intolerance, put up a statue to her, but took particular care not to inscribe on the pedestal "Patriotism is not enough," for which omission, and the lie it implies, they will need Edith's intercession when they are themselves brought to judgment, if any heavenly power thinks such moral cowards capable of pleading to an intelligible indictment.

The point need be no further labored. Joan was persecuted essentially as she would be persecuted today. The change from burning to hanging or shooting may strike us as a change for the better. The change from careful trial under ordinary law to recklessly summary military terrorism may strike us a change for the worse. But as far as toleration is concerned the trial and execution in Rouen in 1431 might have been an event of today; and we may charge our consciences accordingly. If Joan had to be dealt with by us in London she would be treated with no more toleration than Miss Sylvia Pankhurst, or the Peculiar People, or the parents who keep their children from the elementary school, or any of the others who cross the line we have to draw, rightly or wrongly, between the tolerable and the intolerable.

JOAN NOT TRIED AS A POLITICAL OFFENDER

Besides, Joan's trial was not, like Casement's, a national political trial. Ecclesiastical courts and the courts of the Inquisition (Joan was tried by a combination of the two) were Courts Christian: that is, international courts; and she was tried, not as a traitress, but as a heretic, blasphemer, sorceress and idolater. Her alleged offences were not political offences against England, nor against the Burgundian faction in France, but against God and against the common morality of Christendom. And although the idea we call Nationalism was so foreign to the medieval conception of Christian society that it might almost have been directly charged against Joan as an additional heresy, yet it was not so charged; and it is unreasonable to suppose that the political bias of a body of Frenchmen like the assessors would on this point have run strongly in favor of the English foreigners (even if they had been making themselves particularly agreeable in France instead of just the contrary) against a Frenchwoman who had vanquished them.

29

The tragic part of the trial was that Joan, like most prisoners tried for anything but the simplest breaches of the ten commandments, did not understand what they were accusing her of. She was much more like Mark Twain than like Peter Cauchon. Her attachment to the Church was very different from the Bishop's, and does not, in fact, bear close examination from his point of view. She delighted in the solaces the Church offers to sensitive souls: to her, confession and communion were luxuries beside which the vulgar pleasures of the senses were trash. Her prayers were wonderful conversations with her three saints. Her piety seemed superhuman to the formally dutiful people whose religion was only a task to them. But when the Church was not offering her her favorite luxuries, but calling on her to accept its interpretation of God's will, and to sacrifice her own, she flatly refused, and made it clear that her notion of a Catholic Church was one in which the Pope was Pope Joan. How could the Church tolerate that, when it had just destroyed Hus, and had watched the career of Wycliffe with a growing anger that would have brought him, too, to the stake, had he not died a natural death before the wrath fell on him in his grave? Neither Hus nor Wycliffe was as bluntly defiant as Joan: both were reformers of the Church like Luther; whilst Joan, like Mrs Eddy, was quite prepared to supersede St Peter as the rock on which the Church was built, and, like Mahomet, was always ready with a private revelation from God to settle every question and fit every occasion.

The enormity of Joan's pretension was proved by her own unconsciousness of it, which we call her innocence, and her friends called her simplicity. Her solutions of the problems presented to her seemed, and indeed mostly were, the plainest commonsense, and their revelation to her by her Voices was to her a simple matter of fact. How could plain commonsense and simple fact seem to her to be that hideous thing, heresy? When rival prophetesses came into the field, she was down on them at once for liars and humbugs; but she never thought of them as heretics. She was in a state of invincible ignorance as to the Church's view; and the Church could not tolerate her pretensions without either waiving its authority or giving her a place beside the Trinity during her lifetime and in her teens, which was unthinkable. Thus an irresistible force met an immovable obstacle, and developed the heat that consumed poor Joan.

Mark and Andrew would have shared her innocence and her fate had they been dealt with by the Inquisition: that is why their accounts of the trial are as absurd as hers might have been could she have written one. All that can be said for their assumption that Cauchon was a vulgar villain, and that the questions put to Joan were traps, is that it has the support of the inquiry which rehabilitated her twentyfive years later. But this rehabilitation was as corrupt as the contrary proceeding applied to Cromwell by our Restoration reactionaries. Cauchon had been dug up, and his body thrown into the common sewer. Nothing was easier than to accuse him of cozenage, and declare the whole trial void on that account. That was what everybody wanted, from Charles the Victorious, whose credit was bound up with The Maid's, to the patriotic Nationalist populace, who idolized Joan's memory. The English were gone; and a verdict in their favor would have been an outrage on the throne and on the patriotism which Joan had set on foot.

We have none of these overwhelming motives of political convenience and popularity to bias us. For us the first trial stands valid; and the rehabilitation would be negligible but for the mass of sincere testimony it produced as to Joan's engaging personal character. The question then arises: how did The Church get over the verdict at the first trial when it canonized Joan five hundred years later?

The Church Uncompromised by its Amends

Easily enough. In the Catholic Church, far more than in law, there is no wrong without a remedy. It does not defer to Joan-esque private judgment as such, the supremacy of private judgment for the individual being the quintessence of Protestantism; nevertheless it finds a place for private judgment *in excelsis* by admitting that the highest wisdom may come as a divine revelation to an individual. On sufficient evidence it will declare that individual a saint. Thus, as revelation may come by way of an enlightenment of the private judgment no less than by the words of a celestial personage appearing in a vision, a saint may be defined as a person of heroic virtue whose private judgment is privileged. Many innovating saints, notably Francis and Clare, have been in conflict with the Church during their lives, and have thus raised the question whether they were heretics or saints. Francis might have gone to the stake had he lived longer. It is therefore by no means impossible for a person to be excommunicated as a heretic, and on further consideration canonized as a saint. Excommunication by a provincial ecclesiastical court is not one of the acts for which the Church claims infallibility. Perhaps I had better inform my Protestant readers that the famous Dogma of Papal Infallibility is by far the most modest pretension of the kind in existence. Compared with our infallible democracies, our infallible medical councils, our infallible astronomers, our infallible judges, and our infallible parliaments, the Pope is on his knees in the dust confessing his ignorance before the throne of God, asking only that as to certain historical matters on which he has clearly more sources of information open to him than anyone else his decision shall be taken as final. The Church may, and perhaps some day will, canonize Galileo without compromising such infallibility as it claims for the Pope, if not without compromising the infallibility claimed for the Book of Joshua by simple souls whose rational faith in more important things has become bound up with a quite irrational faith in the chronicle of Joshua's campaigns as a treatise on physics. Therefore the Church will probably not canonize Galileo yet awhile, though it might do worse. But it has been able to canonize Joan without any compromise at all. She never doubted that the sun went round the earth: she had seen it do so too often.

Still, there was a great wrong done to Joan and to the conscience of the world by her burning. *Tout comprendre, c'est tout pardonner*, which is the Devil's sentimentality, cannot excuse it.

When we have admitted that the tribunal was not only honest and legal, but exceptionally merciful in respect of sparing Joan the torture which was customary when she was obdurate as to taking the oath, and that Cauchon was far more self-disciplined and conscientious both as priest and lawyer than any English judge ever dreams of being in a political case in which his party and class prejudices are involved, the human fact remains that the burning of Joan of Arc was a horror, and that a historian who would defend it would defend anything. The final criticism of its physical side is implied in the refusal of the Marquesas islanders to be persuaded that the English did not eat Joan. Why, they ask, should anyone take the trouble to roast a human being except with that object? They cannot conceive its being a pleasure. As we have no answer for them that is not shameful to us, let us blush for our more complicated and pretentious savagery before we proceed to unravel the business further, and see what other lessons it contains for us.

Cruelty, Modern and Medieval

First, let us get rid of the notion that the mere physical cruelty of the burning has any special significance. Joan was burnt just as dozens of less interesting heretics were burnt in her time. Christ, in being crucified, only shared the fate of thousands of forgotten malefactors. They have no pre-eminence in mere physical pain: much more horrible executions than theirs are on record, to say nothing of the agonies of so-called natural death at its worst.

Joan was burnt more than five hundred years ago. More than three hundred years later: that is, only about a hundred years before I was born, a woman was burnt on Stephen's Green in my native city of Dublin for coining, which was held to be treason. In my preface to the recent volume on English Prisons under Local Government, by Sidney and Beatrice Webb, I have mentioned that when I was already a grown man I saw Richard Wagner conduct two concerts, and that when Richard Wagner was a young man he saw and avoided a crowd of people hastening to see a soldier broken on the wheel by the more cruel of the two ways of carrying out that hideous method of execution. Also that the penalty of hanging, drawing, and quartering, unmentionable in its details, was abolished so recently that there are men living who have been sentenced to it. We are still flogging criminals, and clamoring for more flogging. Not even the most sensationally frightful of these atrocities inflicted on its victim the misery, degradation, and conscious waste and loss of life suffered in our modern prisons, especially the model ones, without, as far as I can see, rousing any more compunction than the burning of heretics did in the Middle Ages. We have not even the excuse of getting some fun out of our prisons as the Middle Ages did out of their stakes and wheels and gibbets. Joan herself judged this matter when she had to choose between imprisonment and the stake, and chose the stake. And thereby she deprived The Church of the plea that it was guiltless of her death, which was the work of the secular arm. The Church should have confined itself to excommunicating her. There it was within its rights: she had refused to accept its authority or comply with its conditions; and it could say with truth "You are not one of us: go forth and find the religion that suits you, or found one for yourself." It had no right to say "You may return to us now that you have recanted; but you shall stay in a dungeon all the rest of your life." Unfortunately, The Church did not believe that there was any genuine soul saving religion outside itself; and it was deeply corrupted, as all the Churches were and still are, by primitive Calibanism (in Browning's sense), or the propitiation of a dreaded deity by suffering and sacrifice. Its method was not cruelty for cruelty's sake, but cruelty for the salvation of Joan's soul. Joan, however, believed that the saving of her soul was her own business, and not that of *les gens d'église*. By using that term as she did, mistrustfully and contemptuously, she announced herself as, in germ, an anti-Clerical as thoroughgoing as Voltaire or Anatole France. Had she said in so many words "To the dustbin with the Church Militant and its blackcoated officials: I recognize only the

Church Triumphant in heaven," she would hardly have put her view more plainly.

CATHOLIC ANTI-CLERICALISM

I must not leave it to be inferred here that one cannot be an anti-Clerical and a good Catholic too. All the reforming Popes have been vehement anti-Clericals, veritable scourges of the clergy. All the great Orders arose from dissatisfaction with the priests: that of the Franciscans with priestly snobbery, that of the Dominicans with priestly laziness and Laodiceanism, that of the Jesuits with priestly apathy and ignorance and indiscipline. The most bigoted Ulster Orangeman or Leicester Low Church bourgeois (as described by Mr Henry Nevinson) is a mere Gallio compared to Machiavelli, who, though no Protestant, was a fierce anti-Clerical. Any Catholic may, and many Catholics do, denounce any priest or body of priests, as lazy, drunken, idle, dissolute, and unworthy of their great Church and their function as the pastors of their flocks of human souls. But to say that the souls of the people are no business of the Churchmen is to go a step further, a step across the Rubicon. Joan virtually took that step.

CATHOLICISM NOT YET CATHOLIC ENOUGH

And so, if we admit, as we must, that the burning of Joan was a mistake, we must broaden Catholicism sufficiently to include her in its charter. Our Churches must admit that no official organization of mortal men whose vocation does not carry with it extraordinary mental powers (and this is all that any Church Militant can in the face of fact and history pretend to be), can keep pace with the private judgment of persons of genius except when, by a very rare accident, the genius happens to be Pope, and not even then unless he is an exceedingly overbearing Pope. The Churches must learn humility as well as teach it. The Apostolic Succession cannot be secured or confined by the laying on of hands: the tongues of fire have descended on heathens and outcasts too often for that, leaving anointed Churchmen to scandalize History as worldly rascals. When the Church Militant behaves as if it were already the Church Triumphant, it makes these appalling blunders about Joan and Bruno and Galileo and the rest which make it so difficult for a Freethinker to join it; and a Church which has no place for Freethinkers: nay, which does not inculcate and encourage freethinking with a complete belief that thought, when really free, must by its own law take the path that leads to The Church's bosom, not only has no future in modern culture, but obviously has no faith in the valid science of its own tenets, and is guilty of the heresy that theology and science are two different and opposite impulses, rivals for human allegiance.

I have before me the letter of a Catholic priest. "In your play," he writes, "I see the dramatic presentation of the conflict of the Regal, sacerdotal, and Prophetical powers, in which Joan was crushed. To me it is not the victory of any one of them over the others that will bring peace and the Reign of the Saints in the Kingdom of God, but their fruitful interaction in a costly but noble state of tension." The Pope himself could not put it better; nor can I. We must accept the tension, and maintain it nobly without letting ourselves be tempted to relieve it by burning the thread. This is Joan's lesson to The Church; and its formulation by the hand of a priest emboldens me to claim that her canonization was a magnificently Catholic gesture as the canonization of a Protestant saint by the Church of Rome. But its special value and virtue cannot be apparent until it is known and understood as such. If any simple priest for whom this is too hard a saying tells me that it was not so intended, I shall remind him that the Church is in the hands of God, and not, as simple priests imagine, God in the hands of the Church; so if he answers too confidently for God's intentions he may be asked "Hast thou entered into the springs of the sea? or hast thou walked in the recesses of the deep?" And Joan's own answer is also the answer of old: "Though He slay me, yet will I trust in Him; *but I will maintain my own ways before Him.*"

The Law of Change is the Law of God

When Joan maintained her own ways she claimed, like Job, that there was not only God and the Church to be considered, but the Word made Flesh: that is, the unaveraged individual, representing life possibly at its highest actual human evolution and possibly at its lowest, but never at its merely mathematical average. Now there is no deification of the democratic average in the theory of the Church: it is an avowed hierarchy in which the members are sifted until at the end of the process an individual stands supreme as the Vicar of Christ. But when the process is examined it appears that its successive steps of selection and election are of the superior by the inferior (the cardinal vice of democracy), with the result that great popes are as rare and accidental as great kings, and that it has sometimes been safer for an aspirant to the Chair and the Keys to pass as a moribund dotard than as an energetic saint. At best very few popes have been canonized, or could be without letting down the standard of sanctity set by the self-elected saints.

No other result could have been reasonably expected; for it is not possible that an official organization of the spiritual needs of millions of men and women, mostly poor and ignorant, should compete successfully in the selection of its principals with the direct choice of the Holy Ghost as it flashes with unerring aim upon the individual. Nor can any College of Cardinals pray effectively that its choice may be inspired. The conscious prayer of the inferior may be that his choice may light on a greater than himself; but the sub-conscious intention of his self-preserving individuality must be to find a trustworthy servant for his own purposes. The saints and prophets, though they may be accidentally in this or that official position or rank, are always really self-selected, like Joan. And since neither Church nor State, by the secular necessities of its constitution, can guarantee even the recognition of such self-chosen missions, there is nothing for us but to make it a point of honor to privilege heresy to the last bearable degree on the simple ground that all evolution in thought and conduct must at first appear as heresy and misconduct. In short, though all society is founded on intolerance, all improvement is founded on tolerance, or the recognition of the fact that the law of evolution is Ibsen's law of change. And as the law of God in any sense of the word which can now command a faith proof against science is a law of evolution, it follows that the law of God is a law of change, and that when the Churches set themselves against change as such, they are setting themselves against the law of God.

CREDULITY, MODERN AND MEDIEVAL

When Abernethy, the famous doctor, was asked why he indulged himself with all the habits he warned his patients against as unhealthy, he replied that his business was that of a direction post, which points out the way to a place, but does not go thither itself. He might have added that neither does it compel the traveller to go thither, nor prevent him from seeking some other way. Unfortunately our clerical direction posts always do coerce the traveller when they have the political power to do so. When the Church was a temporal as well as a spiritual power, and for long after to the full extent to which it could control or influence the temporal power, it enforced conformity by persecutions that were all the more ruthless because their intention was so excellent. Today, when the doctor has succeeded to the priest, and can do practically what he likes with parliament and the press through the blind faith in him which has succeeded to the far more critical faith in the parson, legal compulsion to take the doctor's prescription, however poisonous, is carried to an extent that would have horrified the Inquisition and staggered Archbishop Laud. Our credulity is grosser than that of the Middle Ages, because the priest had no such direct pecuniary interest in our sins as the doctor has in our diseases: he did not starve when all was well with his flock, nor prosper when they were perishing, as our private commercial doctors must. Also the medieval cleric believed that something extremely unpleasant would happen to him after death if he was unscrupulous, a belief now practically extinct among persons receiving a dogmatically materialist education. Our professional corporations are Trade Unions without souls to be damned; and they will soon drive us to remind them that they have bodies to be kicked. The Vatican was never soulless: at worst it was a political conspiracy to make the Church supreme temporally as well as spiritually. Therefore the question raised by Joan's burning is a burning question still, though the penalties involved are not so sensational. That is why I am probing it. If it were only an historical curiosity I would not waste my readers' time and my own on it for five minutes.

TOLERATION, MODERN AND MEDIEVAL

The more closely we grapple with it the more difficult it becomes. At first sight we are disposed to repeat that Joan should have been excommunicated and then left to go her own way, though she would have protested vehemently against so cruel a deprivation of her spiritual food; for confession, absolution, and the body of her Lord were first necessaries of life to her. Such a spirit as Joan's might have got over that difficulty as the Church of England got over the Bulls of Pope Leo, by making a Church of her own, and affirming it to be the temple of the true and original faith from which her persecutors had strayed. But as such a proceeding was, in the eyes of both Church and State at that time, a spreading of damnation and anarchy, its toleration involved a greater strain on faith in freedom than political and ecclesiastical human nature could bear. It is easy to say that the Church should have waited for the alleged evil results instead of assuming that they would occur, and what they would be. That sounds simple enough; but if a modern Public Health Authority were to leave people entirely to their own devices in the matter of sanitation, saying, "We have nothing to do with drainage or your views about drainage; but if you catch smallpox or typhus we will prosecute you and have you punished very severely like the authorities in Butler's Erewhon," it would either be removed to the County Asylum or reminded that A's neglect of sanitation may kill the child of B two miles off, or start an epidemic in which the most conscientious sanitarians may perish.

We must face the fact that society is founded on intolerance. There are glaring cases of the abuse of intolerance; but they are quite as characteristic of our own age as of the Middle Ages. The typical modern example and contrast is compulsory inoculation replacing what was virtually compulsory baptism. But compulsion to inoculate is objected to as a crudely unscientific and mischievous anti-sanitary quackery, not in the least because we think it wrong to compel people to protect their children from disease. Its opponents would make it a crime, and will probably succeed in doing so; and that will be just as intolerant as making it compulsory. Neither the Pasteurians nor their opponents the Sanitarians would leave parents free to bring up their children naked, though that course also has some plausible advocates. We may prate of toleration as we will; but society must always draw a line somewhere between allowable conduct and insanity or crime, in spite of the risk of mistaking sages for lunatics and saviors for blasphemers. We must persecute, even to the death; and all we can do to mitigate the danger of persecution is, first, to be very careful what we persecute, and second, to bear in mind that unless there is a large liberty to shock conventional people, and a well informed sense of the value of originality, individuality, and eccentricity, the result will be apparent stagnation covering a repression of evolutionary forces which will eventually explode with extravagant and probably destructive violence.

Variability of Toleration

The degree of tolerance attainable at any moment depends on the strain under which society is maintaining its cohesion. In war, for instance, we suppress the gospels and put Quakers in prison, muzzle the newspapers, and make it a serious offence to shew a light at night. Under the strain of invasion the French

Government in 1792 struck off 4000 heads, mostly on grounds that would not in time of settled peace have provoked any Government to chloroform a dog; and in 1920 the British Government slaughtered and burnt in Ireland to persecute the advocates of a constitutional change which it had presently to effect itself. Later on the Fascisti in Italy did everything that the Black and Tans did in Ireland, with some grotesquely ferocious variations, under the strain of an unskilled attempt at industrial revolution by Socialists who understood Socialism even less than Capitalists understand Capitalism. In the United States an incredibly savage persecution of Russians took place during the scare spread by the Russian Bolshevik revolution after 1917. These instances could easily be multiplied; but they are enough to shew that between a maximum of indulgent toleration and a ruthlessly intolerant Terrorism there is a scale through which toleration is continually rising or falling, and that there was not the smallest ground for the self-complacent conviction of the nineteenth century that it was more tolerant than the fifteenth, or that such an event as the execution of Joan could not possibly occur in what we call our own more enlightened times. Thousands of women, each of them a thousand times less dangerous and terrifying to our Governments than Joan was to the Government of her day, have within the last ten years been slaughtered, starved to death, burnt out of house and home, and what not that Persecution and Terror could do to them, in the course of Crusades far more tyrannically pretentious than the medieval Crusades which proposed nothing more hyperbolical than the rescue of the Holy Sepulchre from the Saracens. The Inquisition, with its English equivalent the Star Chamber, are gone in the sense that their names are now disused; but can any of the modern substitutes for the Inquisition, the Special Tribunals and Commissions, the punitive expeditions, the suspensions of the Habeas Corpus Act, the proclamations of martial law and of minor states of siege, and the rest of them, claim that their victims have as fair a trial, as well considered a body of law to govern their cases, or as conscientious a judge to insist on strict legality of procedure as Joan had from the Inquisition and from the spirit of the Middle Ages even when her country was under the heaviest strain of civil and foreign war? From us she would have had no trial and no law except a Defence of The Realm Act suspending all law; and for judge she would have had, at best, a bothered major, and at worst a promoted advocate in ermine and scarlet to whom the scruples of a trained ecclesiastic like Cauchon would seem ridiculous and ungentlemanly.

The Conflict between Genius and Discipline

Having thus brought the matter home to ourselves, we may now consider the special feature of Joan's mental constitution which made her so unmanageable. What is to be done on the one hand with rulers who will not give any reason for their orders, and on the other with people who cannot understand the reasons when they are given? The government of the world, political, industrial, and domestic, has to be carried on mostly by the giving and obeying of orders under just these conditions. "Dont argue: do as you are told" has to be said not only to children and soldiers, but practically to everybody. Fortunately most people do not want to argue: they are only too glad to be saved the trouble of thinking for themselves. And the ablest and most independent thinkers are content to understand their own special department. In other departments they will unhesitatingly ask for and accept the instructions of a policeman or the advice of a tailor without demanding or desiring explanations.

Nevertheless, there must be some ground for attaching authority to an order. A child will obey its parents, a soldier his officer, a philosopher a railway porter, and a workman a foreman, all without question, because it is generally accepted that those who give the orders understand what they are about, and are duly authorized and even obliged to give them, and because, in the practical emergencies of daily life, there is no time for lessons and explanations, or for arguments as to their validity. Such obediences are as necessary to the continuous operation of our social system as the revolutions of the earth are to the succession of night and day. But they are not so spontaneous as they seem: they have to be very carefully arranged and maintained. A bishop will defer to and obey a king; but let a curate venture to give him an order, however necessary and sensible, and the bishop will forget his cloth and damn the curate's impudence. The more obedient a man is to accredited authority the more jealous he is of allowing any unauthorized person to order him about.

With all this in mind, consider the career of Joan. She was a village girl, in authority over sheep and pigs, dogs and chickens, and to some extent over her father's hired laborers when he hired any, but over no one else on earth. Outside the farm she had no authority, no prestige, no claim to the smallest deference. Yet she ordered everybody about, from her uncle to the king, the archbishop, and the military General Staff. Her uncle obeyed her like a sheep, and took her to the castle of the local commander, who, on being ordered about, tried to assert himself, but soon collapsed and obeyed. And so on up to the king, as we have seen. This would have been unbearably irritating even if her orders had been offered as rational solutions of the desperate difficulties in which her social superiors found themselves just then. But they were not so offered. Nor were they offered as the expression of Joan's arbitrary will. It was never "I say so," but always "God says so."

JOAN AS THEOCRAT

Leaders who take that line have no trouble with some people, and no end of trouble with others. They need never fear a luke-warm reception. Either they are messengers of God, or they are blasphemous impostors. In the Middle Ages the general belief in witchcraft greatly intensified this contrast, because when an apparent miracle happened (as in the case of the wind changing at Orleans) it proved the divine mission to the credulous, and proved a contract with the devil to the sceptical. All through, Joan had to depend on those who accepted her as an incarnate angel against those who added to an intense resentment of her presumption a bigoted abhorrence of her as a witch. To this abhor-

43

rence we must add the extreme irritation of those who did not believe in the voices, and regarded her as a liar and impostor. It is hard to conceive anything more infuriating to a statesman or a military commander, or to a court favorite, than to be overruled at every turn, or to be robbed of the ear of the reigning sovereign, by an impudent young upstart practising on the credulity of the populace and the vanity and silliness of an immature prince by exploiting a few of those lucky coincidences which pass as miracles with uncritical people. Not only were the envy, snobbery, and competitive ambition of the baser natures exacerbated by Joan's success, but among the friendly ones that were clever enough to be critical a quite reasonable scepticism and mistrust of her ability, founded on a fair observation of her obvious ignorance and temerity, were at work against her. And as she met all remonstrances and all criticisms, not with arguments or persuasion, but with a flat appeal to the authority of God and a claim to be in God's special confidence, she must have seemed, to all who were not infatuated by her, so insufferable that nothing but an unbroken chain of overwhelming successes in the military and political field could have saved her from the wrath that finally destroyed her.

Unbroken Success essential in Theocracy

To forge such a chain she needed to be the King, the Archbishop of Rheims, the Bastard of Orleans, and herself into the bargain; and that was impossible. From the moment when she failed to stimulate Charles to follow up his coronation with a swoop on Paris she was lost. The fact that she insisted on this whilst the king and the rest timidly and foolishly thought they could square the Duke of Burgundy, and effect a combination with him against the English, made her a terrifying nuisance to them; and from that time onward she could do nothing but prowl about the battlefields waiting for some lucky chance to sweep the captains into a big move. But it was to the enemy that the chance came: she was taken prisoner by the Burgundians fighting before

Compiègne, and at once discovered that she had not a friend in the political world. Had she escaped she would probably have fought on until the English were gone, and then had to shake the dust of the court off her feet, and retire to Domrémy as Garibaldi had to retire to Caprera.

MODERN DISTORTIONS OF JOAN'S HISTORY

This, I think, is all that we can now pretend to say about the prose of Joan's career. The romance of her rise, the tragedy of her execution, and the comedy of the attempts of posterity to make amends for that execution, belong to my play and not to my preface, which must be confined to a sober essay on the facts. That such an essay is badly needed can be ascertained by examining any of our standard works of reference. They give accurately enough the facts about the visit to Vaucouleurs, the annunciation to Charles at Chinon, the raising of the siege of Orleans and the subsequent battles, the coronation at Rheims, the capture at Compiègne, and the trial and execution at Rouen, with their dates and the names of the people concerned; but they all break down on the melodramatic legend of the wicked bishop and the entrapped maiden and the rest of it. It would be far less misleading if they were wrong as to the facts, and right in their view of the facts. As it is, they illustrate the too little considered truth that the fashion in which we think changes like the fashion of our clothes, and that it is difficult, if not impossible, for most people to think otherwise than in the fashion of their own period.

HISTORY ALWAYS OUT OF DATE

This, by the way, is why children are never taught contemporary history. Their history books deal with periods of which the thinking has passed out of fashion, and the circumstances no longer apply to active life. For example, they are taught history about Washington, and told lies about Lenin. In Washington's time they were told lies (the same lies) about Washington, and taught history about Cromwell. In the fifteenth and sixteenth centuries they were told lies about Joan, and by this time might very well be told the truth about her. Unfortunately the lies did not cease when the political circumstances became obsolete. The Reformation, which Joan had unconsciously anticipated, kept the questions which arose in her case burning up to our own day (you can see plenty of the burnt houses still in Ireland), with the result that Joan has remained the subject of anti-Clerical lies, of specifically Protestant lies, and of Roman Catholic evasions of her unconscious Protestantism. The truth sticks in our throats with all the sauces it is served with: it will never go down until we take it without any sauce at all.

The Real Joan not Marvellous Enough for Us

But even in its simplicity, the faith demanded by Joan is one which the anti-metaphysical temper of nineteenth century civilization, which remains powerful in England and America, and is tyrannical in France, contemptuously refuses her. We do not, like her contemporaries, rush to the opposite extreme in a recoil from her as from a witch self-sold to the devil, because we do not believe in the devil nor in the possibility of commercial contracts with him. Our credulity, though enormous, is not boundless; and our stock of it is quite used up by our mediums, clairvoyants, hand readers, slate writers, Christian Scientists, psycho-analysts, electronic vibration diviners, therapeutists of all schools registered and unregistered, astrologers, astronomers who tell us that the sun is nearly a hundred million miles away and that Betelgeuse is ten times as big as the whole universe, physicists who balance Betelgeuse by describing the incredible smallness of the atom, and a host of other marvel mongers whose credulity would have dissolved the Middle Ages in a roar of sceptical merriment. In the Middle Ages people believed that the earth was flat, for which they had at least the evidence of their senses: we believe it to be round, not because as many as one per cent of us could give the physical reasons for so quaint a belief, but because modern science has convinced us that nothing that is obvious is true, and that everything that is magical, improbable, extraordinary, gigantic, microscopic, heartless, or outrageous is scientific.

I must not, by the way, be taken as implying that the earth is flat, or that all or any of our amazing credulities are delusions or impostures. I am only defending my own age against the charge of being less imaginative than the Middle Ages. I affirm that the nineteenth century, and still more the twentieth, can knock the fifteenth into a cocked hat in point of susceptibility to marvels and miracles and saints and prophets and magicians and monsters and fairy tales of all kinds. The proportion of marvel to immediately credible statement in the latest edition of the Encyclopædia Britannica is enormously greater than in the Bible. The medieval doctors of divinity who did not pretend to settle how many angels could dance on the point of a needle cut a very poor figure as far as romantic credulity is concerned beside the modern physicists who have settled to the billionth of a millimetre every movement and position in the dance of the electrons. Not for worlds would I question the precise accuracy of these calculations or the existence of electrons (whatever they may be). The fate of Joan is a warning to me against such heresy. But why the men who believe in electrons should regard themselves as less credulous than the men who believed in angels is not apparent to me. If they refuse to believe, with the Rouen assessors of 1431, that Joan was a witch, it is not because that explanation is too marvellous, but because it is not marvellous enough.

The Stage Limits of Historical Representation

For the story of Joan I refer the reader to the play which follows. It contains all that need be known about her; but as it is for stage use I have had to condense into three and a half hours a series of events which in their historical happening were spread over four times as many months; for the theatre imposes unities of time and place from which Nature in her boundless wastefulness is free. Therefore the reader must not suppose that Joan really put Robert de Baudricourt in her pocket in fifteen minutes, nor that her excommunication, recantation, relapse, and death at the stake were a matter of half an hour or so. Neither do I claim more for my dramatizations of Joan's contemporaries than that some of them are probably slightly more like the originals than those imaginary portraits of all the Popes from Saint Peter onward through the Dark Ages which are still gravely exhibited in the Uffizi in Florence (or were when I was there last). My Dunois would do equally well for the Duc d'Alençon. Both left descriptions of Joan so similar that, as a man always describes himself unconsciously whenever he describes anyone else, I have inferred that these goodnatured young men were very like one another in mind; so I have lumped the twain into a single figure, thereby saving the theatre manager a salary and a suit of armor. Dunois' face, still on record at Châteaudun, is a suggestive help. But I really know no more about these men and their circle than Shakespear knew about Falconbridge and the Duke of Austria, or about Macbeth and Macduff. In view of the things they did in history, and have to do again in the play, I can only invent appropriate characters for them in Shakespear's manner

A Void in the Elizabethan Drama

I have, however, one advantage over the Elizabethans. I write in full view of the Middle Ages, which may be said to have been rediscovered in the middle of the nineteenth century after an eclipse of about four hundred and fifty years. The Renascence of antique literature and art in the sixteenth century, and the lusty growth of Capitalism, between them buried the Middle Ages; and their resurrection is a second Renascence. Now there is not a breath of medieval atmosphere in Shakespear's histories. His John of Gaunt is like a study of the old age of Drake. Although he was a Catholic by family tradition, his figures are all intensely Protestant, individualist, sceptical, self-centred in everything but their love affairs, and completely personal and selfish even in them. His kings are not statesmen: his cardinals have no religion: a novice can read his plays from one end to the other without learning that the world is finally governed by forces expressing themselves in religions and laws which make epochs rather than by vulgarly ambitious individuals who make rows. The divinity which shapes our ends, rough hew them how we will, is mentioned fatalistically only to be forgotten immediately like a passing vague apprehension. To Shakespear as to Mark Twain, Cauchon would have been a tyrant and a bully instead of a Catholic, and the inquisitor Lemaître would have been a Sadist instead of a lawyer. Warwick would have had no more feudal quality than his successor the King Maker has in the play of Henry VI. We should have seen them all completely satisfied that if they would only to their own selves be true they could not then be false to any man (a precept which represents the reaction against medievalism at its intensest) as if they were beings in the air, without public responsibilities of any kind. All Shakespear's characters are so: that is why they seem natural to our middle classes, who are comfortable and irresponsible at other people's expense, and are neither ashamed of that condition nor even conscious of it. Nature abhors this vacuum in Shakespear; and I have taken care to let the medieval atmosphere blow through my play freely. Those who see it performed will not mistake the startling event it records for a mere personal accident. They will have before them not only the visible and human puppets, but the Church, the Inquisition, the Feudal System, with divine inspiration always beating against their too inelastic limits: all more terrible in their dramatic force than any of the little mortal figures clanking about in plate armor or moving silently in the frocks and hoods of the order of St Dominic.

TRAGEDY, NOT MELODRAMA

There are no villains in the piece. Crime, like disease, is not interesting: it is something to be done away with by general consent, and that is all about it. It is what men do at their best, with good intentions, and what normal men and women find that they

E

must and will do in spite of their intentions, that really concern us. The rascally bishop and the cruel inquisitor of Mark Twain and Andrew Lang are as dull as pickpockets; and they reduce Joan to the level of the even less interesting person whose pocket is picked. I have represented both of them as capable and eloquent exponents of The Church Militant and The Church Litigant, because only by doing so can I maintain my drama on the level of high tragedy and save it from becoming a mere police court sensation. A villain in a play can never be anything more than a *diabolus ex machina*, possibly a more exciting expedient than a *deus ex machina*, but both equally mechanical, and therefore interesting only as mechanism. It is, I repeat, what normally innocent people do that concerns us; and if Joan had not been burnt by normally innocent people in the energy of their righteousness her death at their hands would have no more significance than the Tokyo earthquake, which burnt a great many maidens. The tragedy of such murders is that they are not committed by murderers. They are judicial murders, pious murders; and this contradiction at once brings an element of comedy into the tragedy: the angels may weep at the murder, but the gods laugh at the murderers.

THE INEVITABLE FLATTERIES OF TRAGEDY

Here then we have a reason why my drama of Saint Joan's career, though it may give the essential truth of it, gives an inexact picture of some accidental facts. It goes almost without saying that the old Jeanne d'Arc melodramas, reducing everything to a conflict of villain and hero, or in Joan's case villain and heroine, not only miss the point entirely, but falsify the characters, making Cauchon a scoundrel, Joan a prima donna, and Dunois a lover. But the writer of high tragedy and comedy, aiming at the innermost attainable truth, must needs flatter Cauchon nearly as much as the melodramatist vilifies him. Although there is, as far as I have been able to discover, nothing against Cauchon that convicts him of bad faith or exceptional severity in his judicial relations with Joan, or of as much anti-prisoner, pro-police, class and sectarian bias as we now take for granted in our own courts, yet there is hardly more warrant for classing him as a great Catholic churchman, completely proof against the passions roused by the temporal situation. Neither does the inquisitor Lemaître, in such scanty accounts of him as are now recoverable, appear quite so able a master of his duties and of the case before him as I have given him credit for being. But it is the business of the stage to make its figures more intelligible to themselves than they would be in real life; for by no other means can they be made intelligible to the audience. And in this case Cauchon and Lemaître have to make intelligible not only themselves but the Church and the Inquisition, just as Warwick has to make the feudal system intelligible, the three between them having thus to make a twentieth-century audience conscious of an epoch fundamentally different from its own. Obviously the real Cauchon, Lemaître, and Warwick could not have done this: they were part of the Middle Ages themselves, and therefore as unconscious of its peculiarities as of the atomic formula of the air they breathed. But the play would be unintelligible if I had not endowed them with enough of this consciousness to enable them to explain their attitude to the twentieth century. All I claim is that by this inevitable sacrifice of verisimilitude I have secured in the only possible way sufficient veracity to justify me in claiming that as far as I can gather from the available documentation, and from such powers of divination as I possess, the things I represent these three exponents of the drama as saying are the things they actually would have said if they had known what they were really doing. And beyond this neither drama nor history can go in my hands.

Some Well-meant Proposals for the Improvement of the Play

I have to thank several critics on both sides of the Atlantic, including some whose admiration for my play is most generously enthusiastic, for their heartfelt instructions as to how it can be improved. They point out that by the excision of the epilogue and all the references to such undramatic and tedious matters as the Church, the feudal system, the Inquisition, the theory of heresy and so forth, all of which, they point out, would be ruthlessly blue pencilled by any experienced manager, the play could be considerably shortened. I think they are mistaken. The experienced knights of the blue pencil, having saved an hour and a half by disembowelling the play, would at once proceed to waste two hours in building elaborate scenery, having real water in the river Loire and a real bridge across it, and staging an obviously sham fight for possession of it, with the victorious French led by Joan on a real horse. The coronation would eclipse all previous theatrical displays, shewing, first, the procession through the streets of Rheims, and then the service in the cathedral, with special music written for both. Joan would be burnt on the stage, as Mr Matheson Lang always is in The Wandering Jew, on the principle that it does not matter in the least why a woman is burnt provided she is burnt, and people can pay to see it done. The intervals between the acts whilst these splendors were being built up and then demolished by the stage carpenters would seem eternal, to the great profit of the refreshment bars. And the weary and demoralized audience would lose their last trains and curse me for writing such inordinately long and intolerably dreary and meaningless plays. But the applause of the press would be unanimous. Nobody who knows the stage history of Shakespear will doubt that this is what would happen if I knew my business so little as to listen to these well intentioned but disastrous counsellors: indeed it probably will happen when I am no longer in control of the performing rights. So perhaps it will be as well for the public to see the play while I am still alive.

The Epilogue

As to the epilogue, I could hardly be expected to stultify myself by implying that Joan's history in the world ended unhappily with her execution, instead of beginning there. It was necessary by hook or crook to shew the canonized Joan as well as the incinerated one; for many a woman has got herself burnt by carelessly whisking a muslin skirt into the drawing room fireplace, but getting canonized is a different matter, and a more important one. So I am afraid the epilogue must stand.

To the Critics, lest they should feel Ignored

To a professional critic (I have been one myself) theatre-going is the curse of Adam. The play is the evil he is paid to endure in the sweat of his brow; and the sooner it is over, the better. This would seem to place him in irreconcilable opposition to the paying playgoer, from whose point of view the longer the play, the more entertainment he gets for his money. It does in fact so place him, especially in the provinces, where the playgoer goes to the theatre for the sake of the play solely, and insists so effectively on a certain number of hours' entertainment that touring managers are sometimes seriously embarrassed by the brevity of the London plays they have to deal in.

For in London the critics are reinforced by a considerable body of persons who go to the theatre as many others go to church, to display their best clothes and compare them with other people's; to be in the fashion, and have something to talk about at dinner parties; to adore a pet performer; to pass the evening anywhere rather than at home: in short, for any or every reason except interest in dramatic art as such. In fashionable centres the number of irreligious people who go to church, of unmusical people who go to concerts and operas, and of undramatic people who go to the theatre, is so prodigious that sermons have been cut down to ten minutes and plays to two hours; and, even at that, congregations sit longing for the benediction and audiences for the final curtain, so that they may get away to the lunch or supper they really crave for, after arriving as late as (or later than) the hour of beginning can possibly be made for them.

Thus from the stalls and in the Press an atmosphere of hypocrisy spreads. Nobody says straight out that genuine drama is a tedious nuisance, and that to ask people to endure more than two hours of it (with two long intervals of relief) is an intolerable imposition. Nobody says "I hate classical tragedy and comedy as I hate sermons and symphonies; but I like police news and divorce news and any kind of dancing or decoration that has an aphrodisiac effect on me or on my wife or husband. And whatever superior people may pretend, I cannot associate pleasure with any sort of intellectual activity; and I dont believe anyone else can either." Such things are not said; yet nine-tenths of what is offered as criticism of the drama in the metropolitan Press of Europe and America is nothing but a muddled paraphrase of it. If it does not mean that, it means nothing.

I do not complain of this, though it complains very unreasonably of me. But I can take no more notice of it than Einstein of the people who are incapable of mathematics. I write in the classical manner for those who pay for admission to a theatre because they like classical comedy or tragedy for its own sake, and like it so much when it is good of its kind and well done that they tear themselves away from it with reluctance to catch the very latest train or omnibus that will take them home. Far from arriving late from an eight or half-past eight o'clock dinner so as to escape at least the first half-hour of the performance, they stand in queues outside the theatre doors for hours beforehand in bitingly cold weather to secure a seat. In countries where a play lasts a week, they bring baskets of provisions and sit it out. These are the patrons on whom I depend for my bread. I do not give them performances twelve hours long, because circumstances do not at present make such entertainments feasible; though a performance beginning after breakfast and ending at sunset is as possible physically and artistically in Surrey or Middlesex as in Ober-Ammergau; and an all-night sitting in a theatre would be at least as enjoyable as an all-night sitting in the House of Commons, and much more useful. But in St Joan I have done my best by going to the well-established classical limit of three and a half hours practically continuous playing, barring the one interval imposed by considerations which have nothing to do with art. I know that this is hard on the pseudo-critics and on the fashionable people whose playgoing is a hypocrisy. I cannot help feeling some compassion for them when they assure me that my play, though a great play, must fail hopelessly, because it does not begin at a quarter to nine and end at eleven. The facts are overwhelmingly against them. They forget that all men are not as they are. Still, I am sorry for them; and though I cannot for their sakes undo my work and help the people who hate the theatre to drive out the people who love it, yet I may point out to them that they have several remedies in their own hands. They can escape the first part of the play by their usual practice of arriving late. They can escape the epilogue by not waiting for it. And if the irreducible minimum thus attained is still too painful, they can stay away altogether. But I deprecate this extreme course, because it is good neither for my pocket nor for their own souls. Already a few of them, noticing that what matters is not the absolute length of time occupied by a play, but the speed with which that time passes, are discovering that the theatre, though purgatorial in its Aristotelian moments, is not necessarily always the dull place they have so often found it. What do its discomforts matter when the play makes us forget them?

AYOT ST LAWRENCE,
May 1924.

SAINT JOAN

SCENE I

A fine spring morning on the river Meuse, between Lorraine and Champagne, in the year 1429 A.D., in the castle of Vaucouleurs.

Captain Robert de Baudricourt, a military squire, handsome and physically energetic, but with no will of his own, is disguising that defect in his usual fashion by storming terribly at his steward, a trodden worm, scanty of flesh, scanty of hair, who might be any age from 18 to 55, being the sort of man whom age cannot wither because he has never bloomed.

The two are in a sunny stone chamber on the first floor of the castle. At a plain strong oak table, seated in chair to match, the captain presents his left profile. The steward stands facing him at the other side of the table, if so deprecatory a stance as his can be called standing. The mullioned thirteenth-century window is open behind him. Near it in the corner is a turret with a narrow arched doorway leading to a winding stair which descends to the courtyard. There is a stout fourlegged stool under the table, and a wooden chest under the window.

ROBERT. No eggs! No eggs!! Thousand thunders, man, what do you mean by no eggs?

STEWARD. Sir: it is not my fault. It is the act of God.

ROBERT. Blasphemy. You tell me there are no eggs; and you blame your Maker for it.

STEWARD. Sir: what can I do? I cannot lay eggs.

ROBERT [*sarcastic*] Ha! You jest about it.

STEWARD. No, sir, God knows. We all have to go without eggs just as you have, sir. The hens will not lay.

ROBERT. Indeed! [*Rising*] Now listen to me, you.

STEWARD [*humbly*] Yes, sir.

ROBERT. What am I?

STEWARD. What are you, sir?

ROBERT [*coming at him*] Yes: what am I? Am I Robert, squire of Baudricourt and captain of this castle of Vaucouleurs; or am I a cowboy?

STEWARD. Oh, sir, you know you are a greater man here than the king himself.

ROBERT. Precisely. And now, do you know what you are?

STEWARD. I am nobody, sir, except that I have the honor to be your steward.

ROBERT [*driving him to the wall, adjective by adjective*] You have not only the honor of being my steward, but the privilege of being the worst, most incompetent, drivelling snivelling jibbering jabbering idiot of a steward in France. [*He strides back to the table*].

STEWARD [*cowering on the chest*] Yes, sir: to a great man like you I must seem like that.

ROBERT [*turning*] My fault, I suppose. Eh?

STEWARD [*coming to him deprecatingly*] Oh, sir: you always give my most innocent words such a turn!

ROBERT. I will give your neck a turn if you dare tell me, when I ask you how many eggs there are, that you cannot lay any.

STEWARD [*protesting*] Oh sir, oh sir—

ROBERT. No: not oh sir, oh sir, but no sir, no sir. My three Barbary hens and the black are the best layers in Champagne. And you come and tell me that there are no eggs! Who stole them? Tell me that, before I kick you out through the castle gate for a liar and a seller of my goods to thieves. The milk was short yesterday, too: do not forget that.

STEWARD [*desperate*] I know, sir. I know only too well. There is no milk: there are no eggs: tomorrow there will be nothing.

ROBERT. Nothing! You will steal the lot: eh?

STEWARD. No, sir: nobody will steal anything. But there is a spell on us: we are bewitched.

ROBERT. That story is not good enough for me. Robert de Baudricourt burns witches and hangs thieves. Go. Bring me four dozen eggs and two gallons of milk here in this room before noon, or Heaven have mercy on your bones! I will teach you to make a fool of me. [*He resumes his seat with an air of finality*].

STEWARD. Sir: I tell you there are no eggs. There will be none —not if you were to kill me for it—as long as The Maid is at the door.

ROBERT. The Maid! What maid? What are you talking about?

STEWARD. The girl from Lorraine, sir. From Domrémy.

ROBERT [*rising in fearful wrath*] Thirty thousand thunders! Fifty thousand devils! Do you mean to say that that girl, who had the impudence to ask to see me two days ago, and whom I told you to send back to her father with my orders that he was to give her a good hiding, is here still?

STEWARD. I have told her to go, sir. She wont.

ROBERT. I did not tell you to tell her to go: I told you to throw her out. You have fifty men-at-arms and a dozen lumps of able-bodied servants to carry out my orders. Are they afraid of her?

STEWARD. She is so positive, sir.

ROBERT [*seizing him by the scruff of the neck*] Positive! Now see here. I am going to throw you downstairs.

STEWARD. No, sir. Please.

ROBERT. Well, stop me by being positive. It's quite easy: any slut of a girl can do it.

STEWARD [*hanging limp in his hands*] Sir, sir: you cannot get rid of her by throwing me out. [*Robert has to let him drop. He squats on his knees on the floor, contemplating his master resignedly*]. You see, sir, you are much more positive than I am. But so is she.

ROBERT. I am stronger than you are, you fool.

STEWARD. No, sir: it isnt that: it's your strong character, sir. She is weaker than we are: she is only a slip of a girl; but we cannot make her go.

ROBERT. You parcel of curs: you are afraid of her.

STEWARD [*rising cautiously*] No, sir: we are afraid of you; but she puts courage into us. She really doesnt seem to be afraid of anything. Perhaps you could frighten her, sir.

ROBERT [*grimly*] Perhaps. Where is she now?

STEWARD. Down in the courtyard, sir, talking to the soldiers as usual. She is always talking to the soldiers except when she is praying.

ROBERT. Praying! Ha! You believe she prays, you idiot. I know the sort of girl that is always talking to soldiers. She shall talk to me a bit. [*He goes to the window and shouts fiercely through it*] Hallo, you there!

A GIRL'S VOICE [*bright, strong and rough*] Is it me, sir?

ROBERT. Yes, you.

THE VOICE. Be you captain?

ROBERT. Yes, damn your impudence, I be captain. Come up here. [*To the soldiers in the yard*] Shew her the way, you. And shove her along quick. [*He leaves the window, and returns to his place at the table, where he sits magisterially*].

STEWARD [*whispering*] She wants to go and be a soldier herself. She wants you to give her soldier's clothes. Armor, sir! And a sword! Actually! [*He steals behind Robert*].

Joan appears in the turret doorway. She is an ablebodied country girl of 17 or 18, respectably dressed in red, with an uncommon face: eyes very wide apart and bulging as they often do in very imaginative people, a long well-shaped nose with wide nostrils, a short upper lip, resolute but full-lipped mouth, and handsome fighting chin. She comes eagerly to the table, delighted at having penetrated to Baudricourt's presence at last, and full of hope as to the result. His scowl does not check or frighten her in the least. Her voice is normally a hearty coaxing voice, very confident, very appealing, very hard to resist.

JOAN [*bobbing a curtsey*] Good morning, captain squire. Captain: you are to give me a horse and armor and some soldiers, and send me to the Dauphin. Those are your orders from my Lord.

ROBERT [*outraged*] Orders from your lord! And who the devil may your lord be? Go back to him, and tell him that I am neither duke nor peer at his orders: I am squire of Baudricourt; and I take no orders except from the king.

JOAN [*reassuringly*] Yes, squire: that is all right. My Lord is the King of Heaven.

ROBERT. Why, the girl's mad. [*To the steward*] Why didnt you tell me so, you blockhead?

STEWARD. Sir: do not anger her: give her what she wants.

JOAN [*impatient, but friendly*] They all say I am mad until I talk to them, squire. But you see that it is the will of God that you are to do what He has put into my mind.

ROBERT. It is the will of God that I shall send you back to your father with orders to put you under lock and key and thrash the madness out of you. What have you to say to that?

JOAN. You think you will, squire; but you will find it all coming quite different. You said you would not see me; but here I am.

STEWARD [appealing] Yes, sir. You see, sir.

ROBERT. Hold your tongue, you.

STEWARD [abjectly] Yes, sir.

ROBERT [to Joan, with a sour loss of confidence] So you are presuming on my seeing you, are you?

JOAN [sweetly] Yes, squire.

ROBERT [feeling that he has lost ground, brings down his two fists squarely on the table, and inflates his chest imposingly to cure the unwelcome and only too familiar sensation] Now listen to me. I am going to assert myself.

JOAN [busily] Please do, squire. The horse will cost sixteen francs. It is a good deal of money; but I can save it on the armor. I can find a soldier's armor that will fit me well enough: I am very hardy; and I do not need beautiful armor made to my measure like you wear. I shall not want many soldiers: the Dauphin will give me all I need to raise the siege of Orleans.

ROBERT [flabbergasted] To raise the siege of Orleans!

JOAN [simply] Yes, squire: that is what God is sending me to do. Three men will be enough for you to send with me if they are good men and gentle to me. They have promised to come with me. Polly and Jack and—

ROBERT. Polly!! You impudent baggage, do you dare call squire Bertrand de Poulengey Polly to my face?

JOAN. His friends call him so, squire: I did not know he had any other name. Jack—

ROBERT. That is Monsieur John of Metz, I suppose?

JOAN. Yes, squire. Jack will come willingly: he is a very kind gentleman, and gives me money to give to the poor. I think John Godsave will come, and Dick the Archer, and their servants John

61

of Honecourt and Julian. There will be no trouble for you, squire: I have arranged it all: you have only to give the order.

ROBERT [*contemplating her in a stupor of amazement*] Well, I am damned!

JOAN [*with unruffled sweetness*] No, squire: God is very merciful; and the blessed saints Catherine and Margaret, who speak to me every day [*he gapes*], will intercede for you. You will go to paradise; and your name will be remembered for ever as my first helper.

ROBERT [*to the steward, still much bothered, but changing his tone as he pursues a new clue*] Is this true about Monsieur de Poulengey?

STEWARD [*eagerly*] Yes, sir, and about Monsieur de Metz too. They both want to go with her.

ROBERT [*thoughtful*] Mf! [*He goes to the window, and shouts into the courtyard*] Hallo! You there: send Monsieur de Poulengey to me, will you? [*He turns to Joan*] Get out; and wait in the yard.

JOAN [*smiling brightly at him*] Right, squire. [*She goes out*].

ROBERT [*to the steward*] Go with her, you, you dithering imbecile. Stay within call; and keep your eye on her. I shall have her up here again.

STEWARD. Do so in God's name, sir. Think of those hens, the best layers in Champagne; and—

ROBERT. Think of my boot; and take your backside out of reach of it.

The steward retreats hastily and finds himself confronted in the doorway by Bertrand de Poulengey, a lymphatic French gentleman-at-arms, aged 36 or thereabout, employed in the department of the provost-marshal, dreamily absent-minded, seldom speaking unless spoken to, and then slow and obstinate in reply: altogether in contrast to the self-assertive, loud-mouthed, superficially energetic, fundamentally will-less Robert. The steward makes way for him, and vanishes.

Poulengey salutes, and stands awaiting orders.

ROBERT [*genially*] It isnt service, Polly. A friendly talk. Sit down. [*He hooks the stool from under the table with his instep*].

Poulengey, relaxing, comes into the room; places the stool between the table and the window; and sits down ruminatively. Robert, half sitting on the end of the table, begins the friendly talk.

ROBERT. Now listen to me, Polly. I must talk to you like a father.

Poulengey looks up at him gravely for a moment, but says nothing.

ROBERT. It's about this girl you are interested in. Now, I have seen her. I have talked to her. First, she's mad. That doesnt matter. Second, she's not a farm wench. She's a bourgeoise. That matters a good deal. I know her class exactly. Her father came here last year to represent his village in a lawsuit: he is one of their notables. A farmer. Not a gentleman farmer: he makes money by it, and lives by it. Still, not a laborer. Not a mechanic. He might have a cousin a lawyer, or in the Church. People of this sort may be of no account socially; but they can give a lot of bother to the authorities. That is to say, to me. Now no doubt it seems to you a very simple thing to take this girl away, humbugging her into the belief that you are taking her to the Dauphin. But if you get her into trouble, you may get me into no end of a mess, as I am her father's lord, and responsible for her protection. So friends or no friends, Polly, hands off her.

POULENGEY [*with deliberate impressiveness*] I should as soon think of the Blessed Virgin herself in that way, as of this girl.

ROBERT [*coming off the table*] But she says you and Jack and Dick have offered to go with her. What for? You are not going to tell me that you take her crazy notion of going to the Dauphin seriously, are you?

POULENGEY [*slowly*] There is something about her. They are pretty foulmouthed and foulminded down there in the guard-room, some of them. But there hasnt been a word that has anything to do with her being a woman. They have stopped swearing before her. There is something. Something. It may be worth trying.

ROBERT. Oh, come, Polly! pull yourself together. Common-sense was never your strong point; but this is a little too much. [*He retreats disgustedly*].

POULENGEY [*unmoved*] What is the good of commonsense? If

we had any commonsense we should join the Duke of Burgundy and the English king. They hold half the country, right down to the Loire. They have Paris. They have this castle: you know very well that we had to surrender it to the Duke of Bedford, and that you are only holding it on parole. The Dauphin is in Chinon, like a rat in a corner, except that he wont fight. We dont even know that he is the Dauphin: his mother says he isnt; and she ought to know. Think of that! the queen denying the legitimacy of her own son!

ROBERT. Well, she married her daughter to the English king. Can you blame the woman?

POULENGEY. I blame nobody. But thanks to her, the Dauphin is down and out; and we may as well face it. The English will take Orleans: the Bastard will not be able to stop them.

ROBERT. He beat the English the year before last at Montargis. I was with him.

POULENGEY. No matter: his men are cowed now; and he cant work miracles. And I tell you that nothing can save our side now but a miracle.

ROBERT. Miracles are all right, Polly. The only difficulty about them is that they dont happen nowadays.

POULENGEY. I used to think so. I am not so sure now. [*Rising, and moving ruminatively towards the window*] At all events this is not a time to leave any stone unturned. There is something about the girl.

ROBERT. Oh! You think the girl can work miracles, do you?

POULENGEY. I think the girl herself is a bit of a miracle. Anyhow, she is the last card left in our hand. Better play her than throw up the game. [*He wanders to the turret*].

ROBERT [*wavering*] You really think that?

POULENGEY [*turning*] Is there anything else left for us to think?

ROBERT [*going to him*] Look here, Polly. If you were in my place would you let a girl like that do you out of sixteen francs for a horse?

POULENGEY. I will pay for the horse.

ROBERT. You will!

POULENGEY. Yes: I will back my opinion.

ROBERT. You will really gamble on a forlorn hope to the tune of sixteen francs?

POULENGEY. It is not a gamble.

ROBERT. What else is it?

POULENGEY. It is a certainty. Her words and her ardent faith in God have put fire into me.

ROBERT [*giving him up*] Whew! You are as mad as she is.

POULENGEY [*obstinately*] We want a few mad people now. See where the sane ones have landed us!

ROBERT [*his irresoluteness now openly swamping his affected decisiveness*] I shall feel like a precious fool. Still, if you feel sure—?

POULENGEY. I feel sure enough to take her to Chinon—unless you stop me.

ROBERT. This is not fair. You are putting the responsibility on me.

POULENGEY. It is on you whichever way you decide.

ROBERT. Yes: thats just it. Which way am I to decide? You dont see how awkward this is for me. [*Snatching at a dilatory step with an unconscious hope that Joan will make up his mind for him*] Do you think I ought to have another talk to her?

POULENGEY [*rising*] Yes. [*He goes to the window and calls*] Joan!

JOAN'S VOICE. Will he let us go, Polly?

POULENGEY. Come up. Come in. [*Turning to Robert*] Shall I leave you with her?

ROBERT. No: stay here; and back me up.

Poulengey sits down on the chest. Robert goes back to his magisterial chair, but remains standing to inflate himself more imposingly. Joan comes in, full of good news.

JOAN. Jack will go halves for the horse.

ROBERT. Well!! [*He sits, deflated*].

POULENGEY [*gravely*] Sit down, Joan.

JOAN [*checked a little, and looking to Robert*] May I?

ROBERT. Do what you are told.

Joan curtsies and sits down on the stool between them. Robert outfaces his perplexity with his most peremptory air.

ROBERT. What is your name?

JOAN [*chattily*] They always call me Jenny in Lorraine. Here in France I am Joan. The soldiers call me The Maid.

ROBERT. What is your surname?

JOAN. Surname? What is that? My father sometimes calls himself d'Arc; but I know nothing about it. You met my father. He—

ROBERT. Yes, yes: I remember. You come from Domrémy in Lorraine, I think.

JOAN. Yes; but what does it matter? we all speak French.

ROBERT. Dont ask questions: answer them. How old are you?

JOAN. Seventeen: so they tell me. It might be nineteen. I dont remember.

ROBERT. What did you mean when you said that St Catherine and St Margaret talked to you every day?

JOAN. They do.

ROBERT. What are they like?

JOAN [*suddenly obstinate*] I will tell you nothing about that: they have not given me leave.

ROBERT. But you actually see them; and they talk to you just as I am talking to you?

JOAN. No: it is quite different. I cannot tell you: you must not talk to me about my voices.

ROBERT. How do you mean? voices?

JOAN. I hear voices telling me what to do. They come from God.

ROBERT. They come from your imagination.

JOAN. Of course. That is how the messages of God come to us.

POULENGEY. Checkmate.

ROBERT. No fear! [*To Joan*] So God says you are to raise the siege of Orleans?

JOAN. And to crown the Dauphin in Rheims Cathedral.

ROBERT [*gasping*] Crown the D——! Gosh!

JOAN. And to make the English leave France.

ROBERT [*sarcastic*] Anything else?

JOAN [*charming*] Not just at present, thank you, squire.

ROBERT. I suppose you think raising a siege is as easy as chasing a cow out of a meadow. You think soldiering is anybody's job?

JOAN. I do not think it can be very difficult if God is on your side, and you are willing to put your life in His hand. But many soldiers are very simple.

ROBERT [*grimly*] Simple! Did you ever see English soldiers fighting?

JOAN. They are only men. God made them just like us; but He gave them their own country and their own language; and it is not His will that they should come into our country and try to speak our language.

ROBERT. Who has been putting such nonsense into your head? Dont you know that soldiers are subject to their feudal lord, and that it is nothing to them or to you whether he is the duke of Burgundy or the king of England or the king of France? What has their language to do with it?

JOAN. I do not understand that a bit. We are all subject to the King of Heaven; and He gave us our countries and our languages, and meant us to keep to them. If it were not so it would be murder to kill an Englishman in battle; and you, squire, would be in great danger of hell fire. You must not think about your duty to your feudal lord, but about your duty to God.

POULENGEY. It's no use, Robert: she can choke you like that every time.

ROBERT. Can she, by Saint Dennis! We shall see. [*To Joan*] We are not talking about God: we are talking about practical affairs. I ask you again, girl, have you ever seen English soldiers fighting? Have you ever seen them plundering, burning, turning the countryside into a desert? Have you heard no tales of their Black Prince who was blacker than the devil himself, or of the English king's father?

JOAN. You must not be afraid, Robert—

ROBERT. Damn you, I am not afraid. And who gave you leave to call me Robert?

JOAN. You were called so in church in the name of our Lord.

All the other names are your father's or your brother's or any-body's.

ROBERT. Tcha!

JOAN. Listen to me, squire. At Domrémy we had to fly to the next village to escape from the English soldiers. Three of them were left behind, wounded. I came to know these three poor god-dams quite well. They had not half my strength.

ROBERT. Do you know why they are called goddams?

JOAN. No. Everyone calls them goddams.

ROBERT. It is because they are always calling on their God to condemn their souls to perdition. That is what goddam means in their language. How do you like it?

JOAN. God will be merciful to them; and they will act like His good children when they go back to the country He made for them, and made them for. I have heard the tales of the Black Prince. The moment he touched the soil of our country the devil entered into him and made him a black fiend. But at home, in the place made for him by God, he was good. It is always so. If I went into England against the will of God to conquer England, and tried to live there and speak its language, the devil would enter into me; and when I was old I should shudder to remember the wickednesses I did.

ROBERT. Perhaps. But the more devil you were the better you might fight. That is why the goddams will take Orleans. And you cannot stop them, nor ten thousand like you.

JOAN. One thousand like me can stop them. Ten like me can stop them with God on our side. [*She rises impetuously, and goes at him, unable to sit quiet any longer*]. You do not understand, squire. Our soldiers are always beaten because they are fighting only to save their skins; and the shortest way to save your skin is to run away. Our knights are thinking only of the money they will make in ransoms: it is not kill or be killed with them, but pay or be paid. But I will teach them all to fight that the will of God may be done in France; and then they will drive the poor god-dams before them like sheep. You and Polly will live to see the day when there will not be an English soldier on the soil of

France; and there will be but one king there: not the feudal English king, but God's French one.

ROBERT [*to Poulengey*] This may be all rot, Polly; but the troops might swallow it, though nothing that we can say seems able to put any fight into them. Even the Dauphin might swallow it. And if she can put fight into him, she can put it into anybody.

POULENGEY. I can see no harm in trying. Can you? And there is something about the girl—

ROBERT [*turning to Joan*] Now listen you to me; and [*desperately*] dont cut in before I have time to think.

JOAN [*plumping down on the stool again, like an obedient schoolgirl*] Yes, squire.

ROBERT. Your orders are, that you are to go to Chinon under the escort of this gentleman and three of his friends.

JOAN [*radiant, clasping her hands*] Oh, squire! Your head is all circled with light, like a saint's.

POULENGEY. How is she to get into the royal presence?

ROBERT [*who has looked up for his halo rather apprehensively*] I dont know: how did she get into my presence? If the Dauphin can keep her out he is a better man than I take him for. [*Rising*] I will send her to Chinon; and she can say I sent her. Then let come what may: I can do no more.

JOAN. And the dress? I may have a soldier's dress, maynt I, squire?

ROBERT. Have what you please. I wash my hands of it.

JOAN [*wildly excited by her success*] Come, Polly. [*She dashes out*].

ROBERT [*shaking Poulengey's hand*] Goodbye, old man, I am taking a big chance. Few other men would have done it. But as you say, there is something about her.

POULENGEY. Yes: there is something about her. Goodbye. [*He goes out*].

Robert, still very doubtful whether he has not been made a fool of by a crazy female, and a social inferior to boot, scratches his head and slowly comes back from the door.

The steward runs in with a basket.

STEWARD. Sir, sir—

ROBERT. What now?

STEWARD. The hens are laying like mad, sir. Five dozen eggs!

ROBERT [*stiffens convulsively; crosses himself; and forms with his pale lips the words*] Christ in heaven! [*Aloud but breathless*] She did come from God.

SCENE II

Chinon, in Touraine. An end of the throne room in the castle, curtained off to make an antechamber. The Archbishop of Rheims, close on 50, a full-fed political prelate with nothing of the ecclesiastic about him except his imposing bearing, and the Lord Chamberlain, Monseigneur de la Trémouille, a monstrous arrogant wineskin of a man, are waiting for the Dauphin. There is a door in the wall to the right of the two men. It is late in the afternoon on the 8th of March, 1429. The Archbishop stands with dignity whilst the Chamberlain, on his left, fumes about in the worst of tempers.

LA TRÉMOUILLE. What the devil does the Dauphin mean by keeping us waiting like this? I dont know how you have the patience to stand there like a stone idol.

THE ARCHBISHOP. You see, I am an archbishop; and an archbishop is a sort of idol. At any rate he has to learn to keep still and suffer fools patiently. Besides, my dear Lord Chamberlain, it is the Dauphin's royal privilege to keep you waiting, is it not?

LA TRÉMOUILLE. Dauphin be damned! saving your reverence. Do you know how much money he owes me?

THE ARCHBISHOP. Much more than he owes me, I have no doubt, because you are a much richer man. But I take it he owes you all you could afford to lend him. That is what he owes me.

LA TRÉMOUILLE. Twenty-seven thousand: that was his last haul. A cool twenty-seven thousand!

THE ARCHBISHOP. What becomes of it all? He never has a suit of clothes that I would throw to a curate.

LA TRÉMOUILLE. He dines on a chicken or a scrap of mutton. He borrows my last penny; and there is nothing to shew for it. [*A page appears in the doorway*]. At last!

THE PAGE. No, my lord: it is not His Majesty. Monsieur de Rais is approaching.

LA TRÉMOUILLE. Young Bluebeard! Why announce him?

THE PAGE. Captain La Hire is with him. Something has happened, I think.

Gilles de Rais, a young man of 25, very smart and self-possessed, and sporting the extravagance of a little curled beard dyed blue at a clean-shaven court, comes in. He is determined to make himself agreeable, but lacks natural joyousness, and is not really pleasant. In fact when he defies the Church some eleven years later he is accused of trying to extract pleasure from horrible cruelties, and hanged. So far, however, there is no shadow of the gallows on him. He advances gaily to the Archbishop. The page withdraws.

BLUEBEARD. Your faithful lamb, Archbishop. Good day, my lord. Do you know what has happened to La Hire?

LA TRÉMOUILLE. He has sworn himself into a fit, perhaps.

BLUEBEARD. No: just the opposite. Foul Mouthed Frank, the only man in Touraine who could beat him at swearing, was told by a soldier that he shouldnt use such language when he was at the point of death.

THE ARCHBISHOP. Nor at any other point. But was Foul Mouthed Frank on the point of death?

BLUEBEARD. Yes: he has just fallen into a well and been drowned. La Hire is frightened out of his wits.

Captain La Hire comes in: a war dog with no court manners and pronounced camp ones.

BLUEBEARD. I have just been telling the Chamberlain and the Archbishop. The Archbishop says you are a lost man.

LA HIRE [*striding past Bluebeard, and planting himself between the Archbishop and La Trémouille*] This is nothing to joke about. It is worse than we thought. It was not a soldier, but an angel dressed as a soldier.

THE ARCHBISHOP ⎫
THE CHAMBERLAIN ⎬ [*exclaiming all together*] An angel!
BLUEBEARD ⎭

LA HIRE. Yes, an angel. She has made her way from Champagne with half a dozen men through the thick of everything: Burgundians, Goddams, deserters, robbers, and Lord knows who; and they never met a soul except the country folk. I know one of them: de Poulengey. He says she's an angel. If ever I utter an oath again may my soul be blasted to eternal damnation!

THE ARCHBISHOP. A very pious beginning, Captain.

Bluebeard and La Trémouille laugh at him. The page returns.

THE PAGE. His Majesty.

They stand perfunctorily at court attention. The Dauphin, aged 26, really King Charles the Seventh since the death of his father, but as yet uncrowned, comes in through the curtains with a paper in his hands. He is a poor creature physically; and the current fashion of shaving closely, and hiding every scrap of hair under the head-covering or headdress, both by women and men, makes the worst of his appearance. He has little narrow eyes, near together, a long pendulous nose that droops over his thick short upper lip, and the expression of a young dog accustomed to be kicked, yet incorrigible and irrepressible. But he is neither vulgar nor stupid; and he has a cheeky humor which enables him to hold his own in conversation. Just at present he is excited, like a child with a new toy. He comes to the Archbishop's left hand. Bluebeard and La Hire retire towards the curtains.

CHARLES. Oh, Archbishop, do you know what Robert de Baudricourt is sending me from Vaucouleurs?

THE ARCHBISHOP [*contemptuously*] I am not interested in the newest toys.

CHARLES [*indignantly*] It isnt a toy. [*Sulkily*] However, I can get on very well without your interest.

THE ARCHBISHOP. Your Highness is taking offence very unnecessarily.

CHARLES. Thank you. You are always ready with a lecture, arnt you?

LA TRÉMOUILLE [*roughly*] Enough grumbling. What have you got there?

CHARLES. What is that to you?

LA TRÉMOUILLE. It is my business to know what is passing between you and the garrison at Vaucouleurs. [*He snatches the paper from the Dauphin's hand, and begins reading it with some difficulty, following the words with his finger and spelling them out syllable by syllable.*]

CHARLES [*mortified*] You all think you can treat me as you

please because I owe you money, and because I am no good at fighting. But I have the blood royal in my veins.

THE ARCHBISHOP. Even that has been questioned, your Highness. One hardly recognizes in you the grandson of Charles the Wise.

CHARLES. I want to hear no more of my grandfather. He was so wise that he used up the whole family stock of wisdom for five generations, and left me the poor fool I am, bullied and insulted by all of you.

THE ARCHBISHOP. Control yourself, sir. These outbursts of petulance are not seemly.

CHARLES. Another lecture! Thank you. What a pity it is that though you are an archbishop saints and angels dont come to see you!

THE ARCHBISHOP. What do you mean?

CHARLES. Aha! Ask that bully there [*pointing to La Trémouille*].

LA TRÉMOUILLE [*furious*] Hold your tongue. Do you hear?

CHARLES. Oh, I hear. You neednt shout. The whole castle can hear. Why dont you go and shout at the English, and beat them for me?

LA TRÉMOUILLE [*raising his fist*] You young—

CHARLES [*running behind the Archbishop*] Dont you raise your hand to me. It's high treason.

LA HIRE. Steady, Duke! Steady!

THE ARCHBISHOP [*resolutely*] Come, come! this will not do. My Lord Chamberlain: please! please! we must keep some sort of order. [*To the Dauphin*] And you, sir: if you cannot rule your kingdom, at least try to rule yourself.

CHARLES. Another lecture! Thank you.

LA TRÉMOUILLE [*handing the paper to the Archbishop*] Here: read the accursed thing for me. He has sent the blood boiling into my head: I cant distinguish the letters.

CHARLES [*coming back and peering round La Trémouille's left shoulder*] I will read it for you if you like. I can read, you know.

LA TRÉMOUILLE [*with intense contempt, not at all stung by the taunt*] Yes: reading is about all you are fit for. Can you make it out, Archbishop?

THE ARCHBISHOP. I should have expected more commonsense from De Baudricourt. He is sending some cracked country lass here—

CHARLES [*interrupting*] No: he is sending a saint: an angel. And she is coming to me: to me, the king, and not to you, Archbishop, holy as you are. She knows the blood royal if you dont. [*He struts up to the curtains between Bluebeard and La Hire*].

THE ARCHBISHOP. You cannot be allowed to see this crazy wench.

CHARLES [*turning*] But I am the king; and I will.

LA TRÉMOUILLE [*brutally*] Then she cannot be allowed to see you. Now!

CHARLES. I tell you I will. I am going to put my foot down—

BLUEBEARD [*laughing at him*] Naughty! What would your wise grandfather say?

CHARLES. That just shews your ignorance, Bluebeard. My grandfather had a saint who used to float in the air when she was praying, and told him everything he wanted to know. My poor father had two saints, Marie de Maillé and the Gasque of Avignon. It is in our family; and I dont care what you say: I will have my saint too.

THE ARCHBISHOP. This creature is not a saint. She is not even a respectable woman. She does not wear women's clothes. She is dressed like a soldier, and rides round the country with soldiers. Do you suppose such a person can be admitted to your Highness's court?

LA HIRE. Stop. [*Going to the Archbishop*] Did you say a girl in armor, like a soldier?

THE ARCHBISHOP. So De Baudricourt describes her.

LA HIRE. But by all the devils in hell—Oh, God forgive me, what am I saying?—by Our Lady and all the saints, this must be the angel that struck Foul Mouthed Frank dead for swearing.

CHARLES [*triumphant*] You see! A miracle!

LA HIRE. She may strike the lot of us dead if we cross her. For Heaven's sake, Archbishop, be careful what you are doing.

THE ARCHBISHOP [*severely*] Rubbish! Nobody has been struck dead. A drunken blackguard who has been rebuked a hundred times for swearing has fallen into a well, and been drowned. A mere coincidence.

LA HIRE. I do not know what a coincidence is. I do know that the man is dead, and that she told him he was going to die.

THE ARCHBISHOP. We are all going to die, Captain.

LA HIRE [*crossing himself*] I hope not. [*He backs out of the conversation*].

BLUEBEARD. We can easily find out whether she is an angel or not. Let us arrange when she comes that I shall be the Dauphin, and see whether she will find me out.

CHARLES. Yes: I agree to that. If she cannot find the blood royal I will have nothing to do with her.

THE ARCHBISHOP. It is for the Church to make saints: let De Baudricourt mind his own business, and not dare usurp the function of his priest. I say the girl shall not be admitted.

BLUEBEARD. But, Archbishop—

THE ARCHBISHOP [*sternly*] I speak in the Church's name. [*To the Dauphin*] Do you dare say she shall?

CHARLES [*intimidated but sulky*] Oh, if you make it an excommunication matter, I have nothing more to say, of course. But you havnt read the end of the letter. De Baudricourt says she will raise the siege of Orleans, and beat the English for us.

LA TRÉMOUILLE. Rot!

CHARLES. Well, will you save Orleans for us, with all your bullying?

LA TRÉMOUILLE [*savagely*] Do not throw that in my face again: do you hear? I have done more fighting than you ever did or ever will. But I cannot be everywhere.

THE DAUPHIN. Well, thats something.

BLUEBEARD [*coming between the Archbishop and Charles*] You have Jack Dunois at the head of your troops in Orleans: the brave Dunois, the handsome Dunois, the wonderful invincible Dunois, the darling of all the ladies, the beautiful bastard. Is it likely that the country lass can do what he cannot do?

CHARLES. Why doesnt he raise the siege, then?

LA HIRE. The wind is against him.

BLUEBEARD. How can the wind hurt him at Orleans? It is not on the Channel.

LA HIRE. It is on the river Loire; and the English hold the bridgehead. He must ship his men across the river and upstream, if he is to take them in the rear. Well, he cannot, because there is a devil of a wind blowing the other way. He is tired of paying the priests to pray for a west wind. What he needs is a miracle. You tell me that what the girl did to Foul Mouthed Frank was no miracle. No matter: it finished Frank. If she changes the wind for Dunois, that may not be a miracle either; but it may finish the English. What harm is there in trying?

THE ARCHBISHOP [*who has read the end of the letter and become more thoughtful*] It is true that De Baudricourt seems extraordinarily impressed.

LA HIRE. De Baudricourt is a blazing ass; but he is a soldier; and if he thinks she can beat the English, all the rest of the army will think so too.

LA TRÉMOUILLE [*to the Archbishop, who is hesitating*] Oh, let them have their way. Dunois' men will give up the town in spite of him if somebody does not put some fresh spunk into them.

THE ARCHBISHOP. The Church must examine the girl before anything decisive is done about her. However, since his Highness desires it, let her attend the Court.

LA HIRE. I will find her and tell her. [*He goes out*].

CHARLES. Come with me, Bluebeard; and let us arrange so that she will not know who I am. You will pretend to be me. [*He goes out through the curtains*].

BLUEBEARD. Pretend to be that thing! Holy Michael! [*He follows the Dauphin*].

LA TRÉMOUILLE. I wonder will she pick him out!

THE ARCHBISHOP. Of course she will.

LA TRÉMOUILLE. Why? How is she to know?

THE ARCHBISHOP. She will know what everybody in Chinon knows: that the Dauphin is the meanest-looking and worst-dressed figure in the Court, and that the man with the blue beard is Gilles de Rais.

LA TRÉMOUILLE. I never thought of that.

THE ARCHBISHOP. You are not so accustomed to miracles as I am. It is part of my profession.

LA TRÉMOUILLE [*puzzled and a little scandalized*] But that would not be a miracle at all.

THE ARCHBISHOP [*calmly*] Why not?

LA TRÉMOUILLE. Well, come! what is a miracle?

THE ARCHBISHOP. A miracle, my friend, is an event which creates faith. That is the purpose and nature of miracles. They may seem very wonderful to the people who witness them, and very simple to those who perform them. That does not matter: if they confirm or create faith they are true miracles.

LA TRÉMOUILLE. Even when they are frauds, do you mean?

THE ARCHBISHOP. Frauds deceive. An event which creates faith does not deceive: therefore it is not a fraud, but a miracle.

LA TRÉMOUILLE [*scratching his neck in his perplexity*] Well, I suppose as you are an archbishop you must be right. It seems a bit fishy to me. But I am no churchman, and dont understand these matters.

THE ARCHBISHOP. You are not a churchman; but you are a diplomatist and a soldier. Could you make our citizens pay war taxes, or our soldiers sacrifice their lives, if they knew what is really happening instead of what seems to them to be happening?

LA TRÉMOUILLE. No, by Saint Dennis: the fat would be in the fire before sundown.

THE ARCHBISHOP. Would it not be quite easy to tell them the truth?

LA TRÉMOUILLE. Man alive, they wouldnt believe it.

THE ARCHBISHOP. Just so. Well, the Church has to rule men for the good of their souls as you have to rule them for the good of their bodies. To do that, the Church must do as you do: nourish their faith by poetry.

LA TRÉMOUILLE. Poetry! I should call it humbug.

THE ARCHBISHOP. You would be wrong, my friend. Parables

are not lies because they describe events that have never happened. Miracles are not frauds because they are often—I do not say always—very simple and innocent contrivances by which the priest fortifies the faith of his flock. When this girl picks out the Dauphin among his courtiers, it will not be a miracle for me, because I shall know how it has been done, and my faith will not be increased. But as for the others, if they feel the thrill of the supernatural, and forget their sinful clay in a sudden sense of the glory of God, it will be a miracle and a blessed one. And you will find that the girl herself will be more affected than anyone else. She will forget how she really picked him out. So, perhaps, will you.

LA TRÉMOUILLE. Well, I wish I were clever enough to know how much of you is God's archbishop and how much the most artful fox in Touraine. Come on, or we shall be late for the fun; and I want to see it, miracle or no miracle.

THE ARCHBISHOP [detaining him a moment] Do not think that I am a lover of crooked ways. There is a new spirit rising in men: we are at the dawning of a wider epoch. If I were a simple monk, and had not to rule men, I should seek peace for my spirit with Aristotle and Pythagoras rather than with the saints and their miracles.

LA TRÉMOUILLE. And who the deuce was Pythagoras?

THE ARCHBISHOP. A sage who held that the earth is round, and that it moves round the sun.

LA TRÉMOUILLE. What an utter fool! Couldnt he use his eyes?

They go out together through the curtains, which are presently withdrawn, revealing the full depth of the throne room with the Court assembled. On the right are two Chairs of State on a dais. Bluebeard is standing theatrically on the dais, playing the king, and, like the courtiers, enjoying the joke rather obviously. There is a curtained arch in the wall behind the dais; but the main door, guarded by men-at-arms, is at the other side of the room; and a clear path across is kept and lined by the courtiers. Charles is in this path in the middle of the room. La Hire is on his right. The Archbishop, on his left, has taken his place by the dais: La Trémouille at the other side of it. The Duchess de la Trémouille, pretending to be the Queen, sits in the Consort's chair, with a group of ladies in waiting close by, behind the Archbishop.

The chatter of the courtiers makes such a noise that nobody notices the appearance of the page at the door.

THE PAGE. The Duke of— [*Nobody listens*]. The Duke of— [*The chatter continues. Indignant at his failure to command a hearing, he snatches the halberd of the nearest man-at-arms, and thumps the floor with it. The chatter ceases; and everybody looks at him in silence*]. Attention! [*He restores the halberd to the man-at-arms*]. The Duke of Vendôme presents Joan the Maid to his Majesty.

CHARLES [*putting his finger on his lip*] Ssh! [*He hides behind the nearest courtier, peering out to see what happens*].

BLUEBEARD [*majestically*] Let her approach the throne.

Joan, dressed as a soldier, with her hair bobbed and hanging thickly round her face, is led in by a bashful and speechless nobleman, from whom she detaches herself to stop and look round eagerly for the Dauphin.

THE DUCHESS [*to the nearest lady in waiting*] My dear! Her hair! *All the ladies explode in uncontrollable laughter.*

BLUEBEARD [*trying not to laugh, and waving his hand in deprecation of their merriment*] Ssh—ssh! Ladies! Ladies!!

JOAN [*not at all embarrassed*] I wear it like this because I am a soldier. Where be Dauphin?

A titter runs through the Court as she walks to the dais.

BLUEBEARD [*condescendingly*] You are in the presence of the Dauphin.

Joan looks at him sceptically for a moment, scanning him hard up and down to make sure. Dead silence, all watching her. Fun dawns in her face.

JOAN. Coom, Bluebeard! Thou canst not fool me. Where be Dauphin?

A roar of laughter breaks out as Gilles, with a gesture of surrender, joins in the laugh, and jumps down from the dais beside La Trémouille. Joan, also on the broad grin, turns back, searching along the row of courtiers, and presently makes a dive, and drags out

Charles by the arm.

JOAN [*releasing him and bobbing him a little curtsey*] Gentle little Dauphin, I am sent to you to drive the English away from Orleans and from France, and to crown you king in the cathedral at Rheims, where all true kings of France are crowned.

CHARLES [*triumphant, to the Court*] You see, all of you: she knew the blood royal. Who dare say now that I am not my father's son [*To Joan*] But if you want me to be crowned at Rheims you must talk to the Archbishop, not to me. There he is [*he is standing behind her*]!

JOAN [*turning quickly, overwhelmed with emotion*] Oh, my lord! [*She falls on both knees before him, with bowed head, not daring to look up*] My lord: I am only a poor country girl; and you are filled with the blessedness and glory of God Himself; but you will touch me with your hands, and give me your blessing, wont you?

BLUEBEARD [*whispering to La Trémouille*] The old fox blushes.

LA TRÉMOUILLE. Another miracle!

THE ARCHBISHOP [*touched, putting his hand on her head*] Child: you are in love with religion.

JOAN [*startled: looking up at him*] Am I? I never thought of that. Is there any harm in it?

THE ARCHBISHOP. There is no harm in it, my child. But there is danger.

JOAN [*rising, with a sunflush of reckless happiness irradiating her face*] There is always danger, except in heaven. Oh, my lord, you have given me such strength, such courage. It must be a most wonderful thing to be Archbishop.

The Court smiles broadly: even titters a little.

THE ARCHBISHOP [*drawing himself up sensitively*] Gentlemen: your levity is rebuked by this maid's faith. I am, God help me, all unworthy; but your mirth is a deadly sin.

Their faces fall. Dead silence.

BLUEBEARD. My lord: we were laughing at her, not at you.

THE ARCHBISHOP. What? Not at my unworthiness but at her faith! Gilles de Rais: this maid prophesied that the blasphemer

81   G

should be drowned in his sin—

JOAN [*distressed*] No!

THE ARCHBISHOP [*silencing her by a gesture*] I prophesy now that you will be hanged in yours if you do not learn when to laugh and when to pray.

BLUEBEARD. My lord: I stand rebuked. I am sorry: I can say no more. But if you prophesy that I shall be hanged, I shall never be able to resist temptation, because I shall always be telling myself that I may as well be hanged for a sheep as a lamb.

The courtiers take heart at this. There is more tittering.

JOAN [*scandalized*] You are an idle fellow, Bluebeard; and you have great impudence to answer the Archbishop.

LA HIRE [*with a huge chuckle*] Well said, lass! Well said!

JOAN [*impatiently to the Archbishop*] Oh, my lord, will you send all these silly folks away so that I may speak to the Dauphin alone?

LA HIRE [*goodhumoredly*] I can take a hint. [*He salutes; turns on his heel; and goes out*].

THE ARCHBISHOP. Come, gentlemen. The Maid comes with God's blessing, and must be obeyed.

The courtiers withdraw, some through the arch, others at the opposite side. The Archbishop marches across to the door, followed by the Duchess and La Trémouille. As the Archbishop passes Joan, she falls on her knees, and kisses the hem of his robe fervently. He shakes his head in instinctive remonstrance; gathers the robe from her; and goes out. She is left kneeling directly in the Duchess's way.

THE DUCHESS [*coldly*] Will you allow me to pass, please?

JOAN [*hastily rising, and standing back*] Beg pardon, maam, I am sure.

The Duchess passes on. Joan stares after her; then whispers to the Dauphin.

JOAN. Be that Queen?

CHARLES. No. She thinks she is.

JOAN [*again staring after the Duchess*] Oo-oo-ooh! [*Her awe-struck amazement at the figure cut by the magnificently dressed lady is not wholly complimentary*].

LA TRÉMOUILLE [*very surly*] I'll trouble your Highness not to gibe at my wife. [*He goes out. The others have already gone*].

JOAN [*to the Dauphin*] Who be old Gruff-and-Grum?

CHARLES. He is the Duke de la Trémouille.

JOAN. What be his job?

CHARLES. He pretends to command the army. And whenever I find a friend I can care for, he kills him.

JOAN. Why dost let him?

CHARLES [*petulantly moving to the throne side of the room to escape from her magnetic field*] How can I prevent him? He bullies me. They all bully me.

JOAN. Art afraid?

CHARLES. Yes: I am afraid. It's no use preaching to me about it. It's all very well for these big men with their armor that is too heavy for me, and their swords that I can hardly lift, and their muscle and their shouting and their bad tempers. They like fighting: most of them are making fools of themselves all the time they are not fighting; but I am quiet and sensible; and I dont want to kill people: I only want to be left alone to enjoy myself in my own way. I never asked to be a king: it was pushed on me. So if you are going to say "Son of St Louis: gird on the sword of your ancestors, and lead us to victory" you may spare your breath to cool your porridge; for I cannot do it. I am not built that way; and there is an end of it.

JOAN [*trenchant and masterful*] Blethers! We are all like that to begin with. I shall put courage into thee.

CHARLES. But I dont want to have courage put into me. I want to sleep in a comfortable bed, and not live in continual terror of being killed or wounded. Put courage into the others, and let them have their bellyful of fighting; but let me alone.

JOAN. It's no use, Charlie: thou must face what God puts on thee. If thou fail to make thyself king, thoult be a beggar: what else art fit for? Come! Let me see thee sitting on the throne. I have looked forward to that.

CHARLES. What is the good of sitting on the throne when the

other fellows give all the orders? However! [*he sits enthroned, a piteous figure*] here is the king for you! Look your fill at the poor devil.

JOAN. Thourt not king yet, lad: thourt but Dauphin. Be not led away by them around thee. Dressing up dont fill empty noddle. I know the people: the real people that make thy bread for thee; and I tell thee they count no man king of France until the holy oil has been poured on his hair, and himself consecrated and crowned in Rheims Cathedral. And thou needs new clothes, Charlie. Why does not Queen look after thee properly?

CHARLES. We're too poor. She wants all the money we can spare to put on her own back. Besides, I like to see her beautifully dressed; and I dont care what I wear myself: I should look ugly anyhow.

JOAN. There is some good in thee, Charlie; but it is not yet a king's good.

CHARLES. We shall see. I am not such a fool as I look. I have my eyes open; and I can tell you that one good treaty is worth ten good fights. These fighting fellows lose all on the treaties that they gain on the fights. If we can only have a treaty, the English are sure to have the worst of it, because they are better at fighting than at thinking.

JOAN. If the English win, it is they that will make the treaty; and then God help poor France! Thou must fight, Charlie, whether thou will or no. I will go first to hearten thee. We must take our courage in both hands: aye, and pray for it with both hands too.

CHARLES [*descending from his throne and again crossing the room to escape from her dominating urgency*] Oh do stop talking about God and praying. I cant bear people who are always praying. Isnt it bad enough to have to do it at the proper times?

JOAN [*pitying him*] Thou poor child, thou hast never prayed in thy life. I must teach thee from the beginning.

CHARLES. I am not a child: I am a grown man and a father; and I will not be taught any more.

JOAN. Aye, you have a little son. He that will be Louis the

Eleventh when you die. Would you not fight for him?

CHARLES. No: a horrid boy. He hates me. He hates everybody, selfish little beast! I dont want to be bothered with children. I dont want to be a father; and I dont want to be a son: especially a son of St Louis. I dont want to be any of these fine things you all have your heads full of: I want to be just what I am. Why cant you mind your own business, and let me mind mine?

JOAN [again contemptuous] Minding your own business is like minding your own body: it's the shortest way to make yourself sick. What is my business? Helping mother at home. What is thine? Petting lapdogs and sucking sugar-sticks. I call that muck. I tell thee it is God's business we are here to do: not our own. I have a message to thee from God; and thou must listen to it, though thy heart break with the terror of it.

CHARLES. I dont want a message; but can you tell me any secrets? Can you do any cures? Can you turn lead into gold, or anything of that sort?

JOAN. I can turn thee into a king, in Rheims Cathedral; and that is a miracle that will take some doing, it seems.

CHARLES. If we go to Rheims, and have a coronation, Anne will want new dresses. We cant afford them. I am all right as I am.

JOAN. As you are! And what is that? Less than my father's poorest shepherd. Thourt not lawful owner of thy own land of France till thou be consecrated.

CHARLES. But I shall not be lawful owner of my own land anyhow. Will the consecration pay off my mortgages? I have pledged my last acre to the Archbishop and that fat bully. I owe money even to Bluebeard.

JOAN [earnestly] Charlie: I come from the land, and have gotten my strength working on the land; and I tell thee that the land is thine to rule righteously and keep God's peace in, and not to pledge at the pawnshop as a drunken woman pledges her children's clothes. And I come from God to tell thee to kneel in the cathedral and solemnly give thy kingdom to Him for ever and ever, and become the greatest king in the world as His steward and His bailiff, His soldier and His servant. The very clay of France will become holy: her soldiers will be the soldiers of God: the rebel dukes will be rebels against God: the English will fall on their knees and beg thee let them return to their lawful homes in peace. Wilt be a poor little Judas, and betray me and Him that sent me?

CHARLES [*tempted at last*] Oh, if I only dare!

JOAN. I shall dare, dare, and dare again, in God's name! Art for or against me?

CHARLES [*excited*] I'll risk it, I warn you I shant be able to keep it up; but I'll risk it. You shall see. [*Running to the main door and shouting*] Hallo! Come back, everybody. [*To Joan, as he runs back to the arch opposite*] Mind you stand by and dont let me be bullied. [*Through the arch*] Come along, will you: the whole Court. [*He sits down in the royal chair as they all hurry in to their former places, chattering and wondering*]. Now I'm in for it; but no matter: here goes! [*To the page*] Call for silence, you little beast, will you?

THE PAGE [*snatching a halberd as before and thumping with it repeatedly*] Silence for His Majesty the King. The King speaks. [*Peremptorily*] Will you be silent there? [*Silence*].

CHARLES [*rising*] I have given the command of the army to The Maid. The Maid is to do as she likes with it. [*He descends from the dais*].

General amazement. La Hire, delighted, slaps his steel thigh-piece with his gauntlet.

LA TRÉMOUILLE [*turning threateningly towards Charles*] What is this? *I* command the army.

Joan quickly puts her hand on Charles's shoulder as he instinctively recoils. Charles, with a grotesque effort culminating in an extravagant gesture, snaps his fingers in the Chamberlain's face.

JOAN. Thourt answered, old Gruff-and-Grum. [*Suddenly flashing out her sword as she divines that her moment has come*] Who is for God and His Maid? Who is for Orleans with me?

LA HIRE [*carried away, drawing also*] For God and His Maid! To Orleans!

ALL THE KNIGHTS [*following his lead with enthusiasm*] To Orleans!

Joan, radiant, falls on her knees in thanksgiving to God. They all kneel, except the Archbishop, who gives his benediction with a sign, and La Trémouille, who collapses, cursing.

SCENE III

Orleans, April 29th, 1429. Dunois, aged 26, is pacing up and down a patch of ground on the south bank of the silver Loire, commanding a long view of the river in both directions. He has had his lance stuck up with a pennon, which streams in a strong east wind. His shield with its bend sinister lies beside it. He has his commander's baton in his hand. He is well built, carrying his armor easily. His broad brow and pointed chin give him an equilaterally triangular face, already marked by active service and responsibility, with the expression of a goodnatured and capable man who has no affectations and no foolish illusions. His page is sitting on the ground, elbows on knees, cheeks on fists, idly watching the water. It is evening; and both man and boy are affected by the loveliness of the Loire.

DUNOIS [*halting for a moment to glance up at the streaming pennon and shake his head wearily before he resumes his pacing*] West wind, west wind, west wind. Strumpet: steadfast when you should be wanton, wanton when you should be steadfast. West wind on the silver Loire: what rhymes to Loire? [*He looks again at the pennon, and shakes his fist at it*] Change, curse you, change, English harlot of a wind, change. West, west, I tell you. [*With a growl he resumes his march in silence, but soon begins again*] West wind, wanton wind, wilful wind, womanish wind, false wind from over the water, will you never blow again?

THE PAGE [*bounding to his feet*] See! There! There she goes!

DUNOIS [*startled from his reverie: eagerly*] Where? Who? The Maid?

THE PAGE. No: the kingfisher. Like blue lightning. She went into that bush.

DUNOIS [*furiously disappointed*] Is that all? You infernal young idiot: I have a mind to pitch you into the river.

THE PAGE [*not afraid, knowing his man*] It looked frightfully jolly, that flash of blue. Look! There goes the other!

DUNOIS [*running eagerly to the river brim*] Where? Where?

THE PAGE [*pointing*] Passing the reeds.

DUNOIS [*delighted*] I see.

They follow the flight till the bird takes cover.

THE PAGE. You blew me up because you were not in time to see them yesterday.

DUNOIS. You knew I was expecting The Maid when you set up your yelping. I will give you something to yelp for next time.

THE PAGE. Arnt they lovely? I wish I could catch them.

DUNOIS. Let me catch you trying to trap them, and I will put you in the iron cage for a month to teach you what a cage feels like. You are an abominable boy.

THE PAGE [*laughs, and squats down as before*]!

DUNOIS [*pacing*] Blue bird, blue bird, since I am friend to thee, change thou the wind for me. No: it does not rhyme. He who has sinned for thee: thats better. No sense in it, though. [*He finds himself close to the page*] You abominable boy! [*He turns away from him*] Mary in the blue snood, kingfisher color: will you grudge me a west wind?

A SENTRY'S VOICE WESTWARD. Halt! Who goes there?

JOAN'S VOICE. The Maid.

DUNOIS. Let her pass. Hither, Maid! To me!

Joan, in splendid armor, rushes in in a blazing rage. The wind drops; and the pennon flaps idly down the lance; but Dunois is too much occupied with Joan to notice it.

JOAN [*bluntly*] Be you Bastard of Orleans?

DUNOIS [*cool and stern, pointing to his shield*] You see the bend sinister. Are you Joan the Maid?

JOAN. Sure.

DUNOIS. Where are your troops?

JOAN. Miles behind. They have cheated me. They have brought me to the wrong side of the river.

DUNOIS. I told them to.

JOAN. Why did you? The English are on the other side!

DUNOIS. The English are on both sides.

JOAN. But Orleans is on the other side. We must fight the English there. How can we cross the river?

DUNOIS [*grimly*] There is a bridge.

JOAN. In God's name, then, let us cross the bridge, and fall on them.

DUNOIS. It seems simple; but it cannot be done.

JOAN. Who says so?

DUNOIS. I say so; and older and wiser heads than mine are of the same opinion.

JOAN [*roundly*] Then your older and wiser heads are fat-heads: they have made a fool of you; and now they want to make a fool of me too, bringing me to the wrong side of the river. Do you not know that I bring you better help than ever came to any general or any town?

DUNOIS [*smiling patiently*] Your own?

JOAN. No: the help and counsel of the King of Heaven. Which is the way to the bridge?

DUNOIS. You are impatient, Maid.

JOAN. Is this a time for patience? Our enemy is at our gates; and here we stand doing nothing. Oh, why are you not fighting? Listen to me: I will deliver you from fear. I—

DUNOIS [*laughing heartily, and waving her off*] No, no, my girl: if you delivered me from fear I should be a good knight for a story book, but a very bad commander of the army. Come! let me begin to make a soldier of you. [*He takes her to the water's edge*]. Do you see those two forts at this end of the bridge? the big ones?

JOAN. Yes. Are they ours or the goddams'?

DUNOIS. Be quiet, and listen to me. If I were in either of those forts with only ten men I could hold it against an army. The English have more than ten times ten goddams in those forts to hold them against us.

JOAN. They cannot hold them against God. God did not give them the land under those forts: they stole it from Him. He gave it to us. I will take those forts.

DUNOIS. Single-handed?

JOAN. Our men will take them. I will lead them.

DUNOIS. Not a man will follow you.

JOAN. I will not look back to see whether anyone is following me.

DUNOIS [*recognizing her mettle, and clapping her heartily on the shoulder*] Good. You have the makings of a soldier in you. You are in love with war.

JOAN [*startled*] Oh! And the Archbishop said I was in love with religion.

DUNOIS. I, God forgive me, am a little in love with war myself, the ugly devil! I am like a man with two wives. Do you want to be like a woman with two husbands?

JOAN [*matter-of-fact*] I will never take a husband. A man in Toul took an action against me for breach of promise; but I never promised him. I am a soldier: I do not want to be thought of as a woman. I will not dress as a woman. I do not care for the things women care for. They dream of lovers, and of money. I dream of leading a charge, and of placing the big guns. You soldiers do not know how to use the big guns: you think you can win battles with a great noise and smoke.

DUNOIS [*with a shrug*] True. Half the time the artillery is more trouble than it is worth.

JOAN. Aye, lad; but you cannot fight stone walls with horses: you must have guns, and much bigger guns too.

DUNOIS [*grinning at her familiarity, and echoing it*] Aye, lass; but a good heart and a stout ladder will get over the stoniest wall.

JOAN. I will be first up the ladder when we reach the fort, Bastard. I dare you to follow me.

DUNOIS. You must not dare a staff officer, Joan: only company officers are allowed to indulge in displays of personal courage. Besides, you must know that I welcome you as a saint, not as a soldier. I have daredevils enough at my call, if they could help me.

JOAN. I am not a daredevil: I am a servant of God. My sword is sacred: I found it behind the altar in the church of St Catherine, where God hid it for me; and I may not strike a blow with it. My heart is full of courage, not of anger. I will lead; and your men will follow: that is all I can do. But I must do it: you shall not stop me.

DUNOIS. All in good time. Our men cannot take those forts by a sally across the bridge. They must come by water, and take the English in the rear on this side.

JOAN [*her military sense asserting itself*] Then make rafts and put big guns on them; and let your men cross to us.

DUNOIS. The rafts are ready; and the men are embarked. But they must wait for God.

JOAN. What do you mean? God is waiting for them.

DUNOIS. Let Him send us a wind then. My boats are downstream: they cannot come up against both wind and current. We must wait until God changes the wind. Come: let me take you to the church.

JOAN. No. I love church; but the English will not yield to prayers: they understand nothing but hard knocks and slashes. I will not go to church until we have beaten them.

DUNOIS. You must: I have business for you there.

JOAN. What business?

DUNOIS. To pray for a west wind. I have prayed; and I have given two silver candlesticks; but my prayers are not answered. Yours may be: you are young and innocent.

JOAN. Oh yes: you are right. I will pray: I will tell St Catherine: she will make God give me a west wind. Quick: shew me the way to the church.

THE PAGE [*sneezes violently*] At-cha!!!

JOAN. God bless you, child! Coom, Bastard.

They go out. The page rises to follow. He picks up the shield, and is taking the spear as well when he notices the pennon, which is now streaming eastward.

THE PAGE [*dropping the shield and calling excitedly after them*] Seigneur! Seigneur! Mademoiselle!

DUNOIS [*running back*] What is it? The kingfisher? [*He looks eagerly for it up the river*].

JOAN [*joining them*] Oh, a kingfisher! Where?

THE PAGE. No: the wind, the wind, the wind [*pointing to the pennon*]: that is what made me sneeze.

DUNOIS [*looking at the pennon*] The wind has changed. [*He crosses himself*] God has spoken. [*Kneeling and handing his baton to Joan*] You command the king's army. I am your soldier.

THE PAGE [*looking down the river*] The boats have put off. They are ripping upstream like anything.

DUNOIS [*rising*] Now for the forts. You dared me to follow. Dare you lead?

JOAN [*bursting into tears and flinging her arms round Dunois, kissing him on both cheeks*] Dunois, dear comrade in arms, help me. My eyes are blinded with tears. Set my foot on the ladder, and say "Up, Joan."

DUNOIS [*dragging her out*] Never mind the tears: make for the flash of the guns.

JOAN [*in a blaze of courage*] Ah!

DUNOIS [*dragging her along with him*] For God and Saint Dennis!

THE PAGE [*shrilly*] The Maid! The Maid! God and The Maid! Hurray-ay-ay! [*He snatches up the shield and lance, and capers out after them, mad with excitement*].

SCENE IV

A tent in the English camp. A bullnecked English chaplain of 50 is sitting on a stool at a table, hard at work writing. At the other side of the table an imposing nobleman, aged 46, is seated in a handsome chair turning over the leaves of an illuminated Book of Hours. The nobleman is enjoying himself: the chaplain is struggling with suppressed wrath. There is an unoccupied leather stool on the nobleman's left. The table is on his right.

THE NOBLEMAN. Now this is what I call workmanship. There is nothing on earth more exquisite than a bonny book, with well-placed columns of rich black writing in beautiful borders, and illuminated pictures cunningly inset. But nowadays, instead of looking at books, people read them. A book might as well be one of those orders for bacon and bran that you are scribbling.

THE CHAPLAIN. I must say, my lord, you take our situation very coolly. Very coolly indeed.

THE NOBLEMAN [*supercilious*] What is the matter?

THE CHAPLAIN. The matter, my lord, is that we English have been defeated.

THE NOBLEMAN. That happens, you know. It is only in history books and ballads that the enemy is always defeated.

THE CHAPLAIN. But we are being defeated over and over again. First, Orleans—

THE NOBLEMAN [*poohpoohing*] Oh, Orleans!

THE CHAPLAIN. I know what you are going to say, my lord: that was a clear case of witchcraft and sorcery. But we are still being defeated. Jargeau, Meung, Beaugency, just like Orleans. And now we have been butchered at Patay, and Sir John Talbot taken prisoner. [*He throws down his pen, almost in tears*] I feel it, my lord: I feel it very deeply. I cannot bear to see my countrymen defeated by a parcel of foreigners.

THE NOBLEMAN. Oh! you are an Englishman, are you?

THE CHAPLAIN. Certainly not, my lord: I am a gentleman. Still, like your lordship, I was born in England; and it makes a difference.

THE NOBLEMAN. You are attached to the soil, eh?

THE CHAPLAIN. It pleases your lordship to be satirical at my expense: your greatness privileges you to be so with impunity. But your lordship knows very well that I am not attached to the soil in a vulgar manner, like a serf. Still, I have a feeling about it; [*with growing agitation*] and I am not ashamed of it; and [*rising wildly*] by God, if this goes on any longer I will fling my cassock to the devil, and take arms myself, and strangle the accursed witch with my own hands.

THE NOBLEMAN [*laughing at him goodnaturedly*] So you shall, chaplain: so you shall, if we can do nothing better. But not yet, not quite yet.

The Chaplain resumes his seat very sulkily.

THE NOBLEMAN [*airily*] I should not care very much about the witch—you see, I have made my pilgrimage to the Holy Land; and the Heavenly Powers, for their own credit, can hardly allow me to be worsted by a village sorceress—but the Bastard of Orleans is a harder nut to crack; and as he has been to the Holy Land too, honors are easy between us as far as that goes.

THE CHAPLAIN. He is only a Frenchman, my lord.

THE NOBLEMAN. A Frenchman! Where did you pick up that expression? Are these Burgundians and Bretons and Picards and Gascons beginning to call themselves Frenchmen, just as our fellows are beginning to call themselves Englishmen? They actually talk of France and England as their countries. Theirs, if you please! What is to become of me and you if that way of thinking comes into fashion?

THE CHAPLAIN. Why, my lord? Can it hurt us?

THE NOBLEMAN. Men cannot serve two masters. If this cant of serving their country once takes hold of them, goodbye to the authority of their feudal lords, and goodbye to the authority of the Church. That is, goodbye to you and me.

THE CHAPLAIN. I hope I am a faithful servant of the Church; and there are only six cousins between me and the barony of Stogumber, which was created by the Conqueror. But is that any reason why I should stand by and see Englishmen beaten by a French bastard and a witch from Lousy Champagne?

THE NOBLEMAN. Easy, man, easy: we shall burn the witch and beat the bastard all in good time. Indeed I am waiting at present for the Bishop of Beauvais, to arrange the burning with him. He has been turned out of his diocese by her faction.

THE CHAPLAIN. You have first to catch her, my lord.

THE NOBLEMAN. Or buy her. I will offer a king's ransom.

THE CHAPLAIN. A king's ransom! For that slut!

THE NOBLEMAN. One has to leave a margin. Some of Charles's people will sell her to the Burgundians; the Burgundians will sell her to us; and there will probably be three or four middlemen who will expect their little commissions.

THE CHAPLAIN. Monstrous. It is all those scoundrels of Jews: they get in every time money changes hands. I would not leave a Jew alive in Christendom if I had my way.

THE NOBLEMAN. Why not? The Jews generally give value. They make you pay; but they deliver the goods. In my experience the men who want something for nothing are invariably Christians.

A page appears.

THE PAGE. The Right Reverend the Bishop of Beauvais: Monseigneur Cauchon.

Cauchon, aged about 60, comes in. The page withdraws. The two Englishmen rise.

THE NOBLEMAN [*with effusive courtesy*] My dear Bishop, how good of you to come! Allow me to introduce myself: Richard de Beauchamp, Earl of Warwick, at your service.

CAUCHON. Your lordship's fame is well known to me.

WARWICK. This reverend cleric is Master John de Stogumber.

THE CHAPLAIN [*glibly*] John Bowyer Spenser Neville de Stogumber, at your service, my lord: Bachelor of Theology, and Keeper of the Private Seal to His Eminence the Cardinal of Winchester.

WARWICK [*to Cauchon*] You call him the Cardinal of England, I believe. Our king's uncle.

CAUCHON. Messire John de Stogumber: I am always the very good friend of His Eminence. [*He extends his hand to the chaplain, who kisses his ring*].

WARWICK. Do me the honor to be seated. [*He gives Cauchon his chair, placing it at the head of the table*].

Cauchon accepts the place of honor with a grave inclination. Warwick fetches the leather stool carelessly, and sits in his former place. The chaplain goes back to his chair.

Though Warwick has taken second place in calculated deference to the Bishop, he assumes the lead in opening the proceedings as a matter of course. He is still cordial and expansive; but there is a new note in his voice which means that he is coming to business.

WARWICK. Well, my Lord Bishop, you find us in one of our unlucky moments. Charles is to be crowned at Rheims, practically by the young woman from Lorraine; and—I must not deceive you, nor flatter your hopes—we cannot prevent it. I suppose it will make a great difference to Charles's position.

CAUCHON. Undoubtedly. It is a masterstroke of The Maid's.

THE CHAPLAIN [*again agitated*] We were not fairly beaten, my lord. No Englishman is ever fairly beaten.

Cauchon raises his eyebrow slightly, then quickly composes his face.

WARWICK. Our friend here takes the view that the young woman is a sorceress. It would, I presume, be the duty of your reverend lordship to denounce her to the Inquisition, and have her burnt for that offence.

CAUCHON. If she were captured in my diocese: yes.

WARWICK [*feeling that they are getting on capitally*] Just so. Now I suppose there can be no reasonable doubt that she is a sorceress.

THE CHAPLAIN. Not the least. An arrant witch.

WARWICK [*gently reproving the interruption*] We are asking for the Bishop's opinion, Messire John.

CAUCHON. We shall have to consider not merely our own opinions here, but the opinions—the prejudices, if you like—of a French court.

WARWICK [*correcting*] A Catholic court, my lord.

　　　　　　　　H

CAUCHON. Catholic courts are composed of mortal men, like other courts, however sacred their function and inspiration may be. And if the men are Frenchmen, as the modern fashion calls them, I am afraid the bare fact that an English army has been defeated by a French one will not convince them that there is any sorcery in the matter.

THE CHAPLAIN. What! Not when the famous Sir John Talbot himself has been defeated and actually taken prisoner by a drab from the ditches of Lorraine!

CAUCHON. Sir John Talbot, we all know, is a fierce and formidable soldier, Messire; but I have yet to learn that he is an able general. And though it pleases you to say that he has been defeated by this girl, some of us may be disposed to give a little of the credit to Dunois.

THE CHAPLAIN [contemptuously] The Bastard of Orleans!

CAUCHON. Let me remind—

WARWICK [interposing] I know what you are going to say, my lord. Dunois defeated me at Montargis.

CAUCHON [bowing] I take that as evidence that the Seigneur Dunois is a very able commander indeed.

WARWICK. Your lordship is the flower of courtesy. I admit, on our side, that Talbot is a mere fighting animal, and that it probably served him right to be taken at Patay.

THE CHAPLAIN [chafing] My lord: at Orleans this woman had her throat pierced by an English arrow, and was seen to cry like a child from the pain of it. It was a death wound; yet she fought all day; and when our men had repulsed all her attacks like true Englishmen, she walked alone to the wall of our fort with a white banner in her hand; and our men were paralyzed, and could neither shoot nor strike whilst the French fell on them and drove them on to the bridge, which immediately burst into flames and crumbled under them, letting them down into the river, where they were drowned in heaps. Was this your bastard's generalship? or were those flames the flames of hell, conjured up by witchcraft?

WARWICK. You will forgive Messire John's vehemence, my

lord; but he has put our case. Dunois is a great captain, we admit; but why could he do nothing until the witch came?

CAUCHON. I do not say that there were no supernatural powers on her side. But the names on that white banner were not the names of Satan and Beelzebub, but the blessed names of our Lord and His holy mother. And your commander who was drowned—Clahz-da I think you call him—

WARWICK. Glasdale. Sir William Glasdale.

CAUCHON. Glass-dell, thank you. He was no saint; and many of our people think that he was drowned for his blasphemies against The Maid.

WARWICK [*beginning to look very dubious*] Well, what are we to infer from all this, my lord? Has The Maid converted you?

CAUCHON. If she had, my lord, I should have known better than to have trusted myself here within your grasp.

WARWICK [*blandly deprecating*] Oh! oh! My lord!

CAUCHON. If the devil is making use of this girl—and I believe he is—

WARWICK [*reassured*] Ah! You hear, Messire John? I knew your lordship would not fail us. Pardon my interruption. Proceed.

CAUCHON. If it be so, the devil has longer views than you give him credit for.

WARWICK. Indeed? In what way? Listen to this, Messire John.

CAUCHON. If the devil wanted to damn a country girl, do you think so easy a task would cost him the winning of half a dozen battles? No, my lord: any trumpery imp could do that much if the girl could be damned at all. The Prince of Darkness does not condescend to such cheap drudgery. When he strikes, he strikes at the Catholic Church, whose realm is the whole spiritual world. When he damns, he damns the souls of the entire human race. Against that dreadful design The Church stands ever on guard. And it is as one of the instruments of that design that I see this girl. She is inspired, but diabolically inspired.

THE CHAPLAIN. I told you she was a witch.

CAUCHON [*fiercely*] She is not a witch. She is a heretic.

THE CHAPLAIN. What difference does that make?

CAUCHON. You, a priest, ask me that! You English are strangely blunt in the mind. All these things that you call witchcraft are capable of a natural explanation. The woman's miracles would not impose on a rabbit: she does not claim them as miracles herself. What do her victories prove but that she has a better head on her shoulders than your swearing Glass-dells and mad bull Talbots, and that the courage of faith, even though it be a false faith, will always outstay the courage of wrath?

THE CHAPLAIN [*hardly able to believe his ears*] Does your lordship compare Sir John Talbot, three times Governor of Ireland, to a mad bull?!!!

WARWICK. It would not be seemly for you to do so, Messire John, as you are still six removes from a barony. But as I am an earl, and Talbot is only a knight, I may make bold to accept the comparison. [*To the Bishop*] My lord: I wipe the slate as far as the witchcraft goes. None the less, we must burn the woman.

CAUCHON. I cannot burn her. The Church cannot take life. And my first duty is to seek this girl's salvation.

WARWICK. No doubt. But you do burn people occasionally.

CAUCHON. No. When The Church cuts off an obstinate heretic as a dead branch from the tree of life, the heretic is handed over to the secular arm. The Church has no part in what the secular arm may see fit to do.

WARWICK. Precisely. And I shall be the secular arm in this case. Well, my lord, hand over your dead branch; and I will see that the fire is ready for it. If you will answer for The Church's part, I will answer for the secular part.

CAUCHON [*with smouldering anger*] I can answer for nothing. You great lords are too prone to treat The Church as a mere political convenience.

WARWICK [*smiling and propitiatory*] Not in England, I assure you.

CAUCHON. In England more than anywhere else. No, my lord: the soul of this village girl is of equal value with yours or your king's before the throne of God; and my first duty is to save it. I will not suffer your lordship to smile at me as if I were repeating

a meaningless form of words, and it were well understood between us that I should betray the girl to you. I am no mere
political bishop: my faith is to me what your honor is to you;
and if there be a loophole through which this baptized child of
God can creep to her salvation, I shall guide her to it.

THE CHAPLAIN [*rising in a fury*] You are a traitor.

CAUCHON [*springing up*] You lie, priest. [*Trembling with rage*]
If you dare do what this woman has done—set your country
above the holy Catholic Church—you shall go to the fire with
her.

THE CHAPLAIN. My lord: I—I went too far. I—[*he sits down
with a submissive gesture*].

WARWICK [*who has risen apprehensively*] My lord: I apologize to
you for the word used by Messire John de Stogumber. It does
not mean in England what it does in France. In your language
traitor means betrayer: one who is perfidious, treacherous, un-
faithful, disloyal. In our country it means simply one who is not
wholly devoted to our English interests.

CAUCHON. I am sorry: I did not understand. [*He subsides into
his chair with dignity*].

WARWICK [*resuming his seat, much relieved*] I must apologize on
my own account if I have seemed to take the burning of this
poor girl too lightly. When one has seen whole countrysides
burnt over and over again as mere items in military routine, one
has to grow a very thick skin. Otherwise one might go mad: at
all events, I should. May I venture to assume that your lordship
also, having to see so many heretics burned from time to time, is
compelled to take—shall I say a professional view of what would
otherwise be a very horrible incident?

CAUCHON. Yes: it is a painful duty: even, as you say, a horrible
one. But in comparison with the horror of heresy it is less than
nothing. I am not thinking of this girl's body, which will suffer
for a few moments only, and which must in any event die in
some more or less painful manner, but of her soul, which may
suffer to all eternity.

WARWICK. Just so; and God grant that her soul may be saved!

But the practical problem would seem to be how to save her soul without saving her body. For we must face it, my lord: if this cult of The Maid goes on, our cause is lost.

THE CHAPLAIN [*his voice broken like that of a man who has been crying*] May I speak, my lord?

WARWICK. Really, Messire John, I had rather you did not, unless you can keep your temper.

THE CHAPLAIN. It is only this. I speak under correction; but The Maid is full of deceit: she pretends to be devout. Her prayers and confessions are endless. How can she be accused of heresy when she neglects no observance of a faithful daughter of The Church?

CAUCHON [*flaming up*] A faithful daughter of The Church! The Pope himself at his proudest dare not presume as this woman presumes. She acts as if she herself were The Church. She brings the message of God to Charles; and The Church must stand aside. She will crown him in the cathedral of Rheims: she, not The Church! She sends letters to the king of England giving him God's command through her to return to his island on pain of God's vengeance, which she will execute. Let me tell you that the writing of such letters was the practice of the accursed Mahomet, the anti-Christ. Has she ever in all her utterances said one word of The Church? Never. It is always God and herself.

WARWICK. What can you expect? A beggar on horseback! Her head is turned.

CAUCHON. Who has turned it? The devil. And for a mighty purpose. He is spreading this heresy everywhere. The man Hus, burnt only thirteen years ago at Constance, infected all Bohemia with it. A man named WcLeef, himself an anointed priest, spread the pestilence in England; and to your shame you let him die in his bed. We have such people here in France too: I know the breed. It is cancerous: if it be not cut out, stamped out, burnt out, it will not stop until it has brought the whole body of human society into sin and corruption, into waste and ruin. By it an Arab camel driver drove Christ and His Church out of Jerusalem, and ravaged his way west like a wild beast until at last there stood only the Pyrenees and God's mercy between France and damnation. Yet what did the camel driver do at the beginning more than this shepherd girl is doing? He had his voices from the angel Gabriel: she has her voices from St Catherine and St Margaret and the Blessed Michael. He declared himself the messenger of God, and wrote in God's name to the kings of the earth. Her letters to them are going forth daily. It is not the Mother of God now to whom we must look for intercession, but to Joan the Maid. What will the world be like when The Church's accumulated wisdom and knowledge and experience, its councils of learned, venerable pious men, are thrust into the kennel by every ignorant laborer or dairymaid whom the devil can puff up with the monstrous self-conceit of being directly inspired from heaven? It will be a world of blood, of fury, of devastation, of each man striving for his own hand: in the end a world wrecked back into barbarism. For now you have only Mahomet and his dupes, and the Maid and her dupes; but what will it be when every girl thinks herself a Joan and every man a Mahomet? I shudder to the very marrow of my bones when I think of it. I have fought it all my life; and I will fight it to the end. Let all this woman's sins be forgiven her except only this sin; for it is the sin against the Holy Ghost; and if she does not recant in the dust before the world, and submit herself to the last inch of her soul to her Church, to the fire she shall go if she once falls into my hand.

WARWICK [*unimpressed*] You feel strongly about it, naturally.

CAUCHON. Do not you?

WARWICK. I am a soldier, not a churchman. As a pilgrim I saw something of the Mahometans. They were not so ill-bred as I had been led to believe. In some respects their conduct compared favorably with ours.

CAUCHON [*displeased*] I have noticed this before. Men go to the East to convert the infidels. And the infidels pervert them. The Crusader comes back more than half a Saracen. Not to mention that all Englishmen are born heretics.

THE CHAPLAIN. Englishmen heretics!!! [*Appealing to Warwick*] My lord: must we endure this? His lordship is beside himself.

How can what an Englishman believes be heresy? It is a contradiction in terms.

CAUCHON. I absolve you, Messire de Stogumber, on the ground of invincible ignorance. The thick air of your country does not breed theologians.

WARWICK. You would not say so if you heard us quarrelling about religion, my lord! I am sorry you think I must be either a heretic or a blockhead because, as a travelled man, I know that the followers of Mahomet profess great respect for our Lord, and are more ready to forgive St Peter for being a fisherman than your lordship is to forgive Mahomet for being a camel driver. But at least we can proceed in this matter without bigotry.

CAUCHON. When men call the zeal of the Christian Church bigotry I know what to think.

WARWICK. They are only east and west views of the same thing.

CAUCHON [*bitterly ironical*] Only east and west! Only!!

WARWICK. Oh, my Lord Bishop, I am not gainsaying you. You will carry The Church with you; but you have to carry the nobles also. To my mind there is a stronger case against The Maid than the one you have so forcibly put. Frankly, I am not afraid of this girl becoming another Mahomet, and superseding The Church by a great heresy. I think you exaggerate that risk. But have you noticed that in these letters of hers, she proposes to all the kings of Europe, as she has already pressed on Charles, a transaction which would wreck the whole social structure of Christendom?

CAUCHON. Wreck The Church. I tell you so.

WARWICK [*whose patience is wearing out*] My lord: pray get The Church out of your head for a moment; and remember that there are temporal institutions in the world as well as spiritual ones. I and my peers represent the feudal aristocracy as you represent The Church. We are the temporal power. Well, do you not see how this girl's idea strikes at us?

CAUCHON. How does her idea strike at you, except as it strikes at all of us, through The Church?

WARWICK. Her idea is that the kings should give their realms to God, and then reign as God's bailiffs.

CAUCHON [*not interested*] Quite sound theologically, my lord. But the king will hardly care, provided he reign. It is an abstract idea: a mere form of words.

WARWICK. By no means. It is a cunning device to supersede the aristocracy, and make the king sole and absolute autocrat. Instead of the king being merely the first among his peers, he becomes their master. That we cannot suffer: we call no man master. Nominally we hold our lands and dignities from the king, because there must be a keystone to the arch of human society; but we hold our lands in our own hands, and defend them with our own swords and those of our own tenants. Now by The Maid's doctrine the king will take our lands—our lands! —and make them a present to God; and God will then vest them wholly in the king.

CAUCHON. Need you fear that? You are the makers of kings after all. York or Lancaster in England, Lancaster or Valois in France: they reign according to your pleasure.

WARWICK. Yes; but only as long as the people follow their feudal lords, and know the king only as a travelling show, owning nothing but the highway that belongs to everybody. If the people's thoughts and hearts were turned to the king, and their lords became only the king's servants in their eyes, the king could break us across his knee one by one; and then what should we be but liveried courtiers in his halls?

CAUCHON. Still you need not fear, my lord. Some men are born kings; and some are born statesmen. The two are seldom the same. Where would the king find counsellors to plan and carry out such a policy for him?

WARWICK [*with a not too friendly smile*] Perhaps in the Church, my lord.

Cauchon, with an equally sour smile, shrugs his shoulders, and does not contradict him.

WARWICK. Strike down the barons; and the cardinals will have it all their own way.

CAUCHON [*conciliatory, dropping his polemical tone*] My lord: we shall not defeat The Maid if we strive against one another. I know well that there is a Will to Power in the world. I know that while it lasts there will be a struggle between the Emperor and the Pope, between the dukes and the political cardinals, between the barons and the kings. The devil divides us and governs. I see you are no friend to The Church: you are an earl first and last, as I am a churchman first and last. But can we not sink our differences in the face of a common enemy? I see now that what is in your mind is not that this girl has never once mentioned The Church, and thinks only of God and herself, but that she has never once mentioned the peerage, and thinks only of the king and herself.

WARWICK. Quite so. These two ideas of hers are the same idea at bottom. It goes deep, my lord. It is the protest of the individual soul against the interference of priest or peer between the private man and his God. I should call it Protestantism if I had to find a name for it.

CAUCHON [*looking hard at him*] You understand it wonderfully well, my lord. Scratch an Englishman, and find a Protestant.

WARWICK [*playing the pink of courtesy*] I think you are not entirely void of sympathy with The Maid's secular heresy, my lord. I leave you to find a name for it.

CAUCHON. You mistake me, my lord. I have no sympathy with her political presumptions. But as a priest I have gained a knowledge of the minds of the common people; and there you will find yet another most dangerous idea. I can express it only by such phrases as France for the French, England for the English, Italy for the Italians, Spain for the Spanish, and so forth. It is sometimes so narrow and bitter in country folk that it surprises me that this country girl can rise above the idea of her village for its villagers. But she can. She does. When she threatens to drive the English from the soil of France she is undoubtedly thinking of the whole extent of country in which French is spoken. To her the French-speaking people are what the Holy Scriptures describe as a nation. Call this side of her heresy Nationalism if you will: I can find you no better name for it. I can only tell you that it is essentially anti-Catholic and anti-Christian; for the Catholic Church knows only one realm, and that is the realm of Christ's kingdom. Divide that kingdom into nations, and you dethrone Christ. Dethrone Christ, and who will stand between our throats and the sword? The world will perish in a welter of war.

WARWICK. Well, if you will burn the Protestant, I will burn the Nationalist, though perhaps I shall not carry Messire John with me there. England for the English will appeal to him.

THE CHAPLAIN. Certainly England for the English goes without saying: it is the simple law of nature. But this woman denies to England her legitimate conquests, given her by God because of her peculiar fitness to rule over less civilized races for their own good. I do not understand what your lordships mean by Protestant and Nationalist: you are too learned and subtle for a poor clerk like myself. But I know as a matter of plain commonsense that the woman is a rebel; and that is enough for me. She rebels against Nature by wearing man's clothes, and fighting. She rebels against The Church by usurping the divine authority of the Pope. She rebels against God by her damnable league with Satan and his evil spirits against our army. And all these rebellions are only excuses for her great rebellion against England. That is not to be endured. Let her perish. Let her burn. Let her not infect the whole flock. It is expedient that one woman die for the people.

WARWICK [*rising*] My lord: we seem to be agreed.

CAUCHON [*rising also, but in protest*] I will not imperil my soul. I will uphold the justice of the Church. I will strive to the utmost for this woman's salvation.

WARWICK. I am sorry for the poor girl. I hate these severities. I will spare her if I can.

THE CHAPLAIN [*implacably*] I would burn her with my own hands.

CAUCHON [*blessing him*] Sancta simplicitas!

SCENE V

The ambulatory in the cathedral of Rheims, near the door of the vestry. A pillar bears one of the stations of the cross. The organ is playing the people out of the nave after the coronation. Joan is kneeling in prayer before the station. She is beautifully dressed, but still in male attire. The organ ceases as Dunois, also splendidly arrayed, comes into the ambulatory from the vestry.

DUNOIS. Come, Joan! you have had enough praying. After that fit of crying you will catch a chill if you stay here any longer. It is all over: the cathedral is empty; and the streets are full. They are calling for The Maid. We have told them you are staying here alone to pray; but they want to see you again.

JOAN. No: let the king have all the glory.

DUNOIS. He only spoils the show, poor devil. No, Joan: you have crowned him; and you must go through with it.

JOAN [*shakes her head reluctantly*].

DUNOIS [*raising her*] Come come! it will be over in a couple of hours. It's better than the bridge at Orleans: eh?

JOAN. Oh, dear Dunois, how I wish it were the bridge at Orleans again! We lived at that bridge.

DUNOIS. Yes, faith, and died too: some of us.

JOAN. Isnt it strange, Jack? I am such a coward: I am frightened beyond words before a battle; but it is so dull afterwards when there is no danger: oh, so dull! dull! dull!

DUNOIS. You must learn to be abstemious in war, just as you are in your food and drink, my little saint.

JOAN. Dear Jack: I think you like me as a soldier likes his comrade.

DUNOIS. You need it, poor innocent child of God. You have not many friends at court.

JOAN. Why do all these courtiers and knights and churchmen hate me? What have I done to them? I have asked nothing for myself except that my village shall not be taxed; for we cannot afford war taxes. I have brought them luck and victory: I have set them right when they were doing all sorts of stupid things: I have crowned Charles and made him a real king; and all the honors he is handing out have gone to them. Then why do they not love me?

DUNOIS [*rallying her*] Sim-ple-ton! Do you expect stupid people to love you for shewing them up? Do blundering old military dug-outs love the successful young captains who supersede them? Do ambitious politicians love the climbers who take the front seats from them? Do archbishops enjoy being played off their own altars, even by saints? Why, I should be jealous of you myself if I were ambitious enough.

JOAN. You are the pick of the basket here, Jack: the only friend I have among all these nobles. I'll wager your mother was from the country. I will go back to the farm when I have taken Paris.

DUNOIS. I am not so sure that they will let you take Paris.

JOAN [*startled*] What!

DUNOIS. I should have taken it myself before this if they had all been sound about it. Some of them would rather Paris took you, I think. So take care.

JOAN. Jack: the world is too wicked for me. If the goddams and the Burgundians do not make an end of me, the French will. Only for my voices I should lose all heart. That is why I had to steal away to pray here alone after the coronation. I'll tell you something, Jack. It is in the bells I hear my voices. Not to-day, when they all rang: that was nothing but jangling. But here in this corner, where the bells come down from heaven, and the echoes linger, or in the fields, where they come from a distance through the quiet of the countryside, my voices are in them. [*The cathedral clock chimes the quarter*] Hark! [*She becomes rapt*] Do you hear? "Dear-child-of-God": just what you said. At the half-hour they will say "Be-brave-go-on." At the three-quarters they will say "I-am-thy-Help." But it is at the hour, when the great bell goes after "God-will-save-France": it is then that St Margaret and St Catherine and sometimes even the blessed Michael will say things that I cannot tell beforehand. Then, oh then—

DUNOIS [*interrupting her kindly but not sympathetically*] Then, Joan, we shall hear whatever we fancy in the booming of the bell. You make me uneasy when you talk about your voices: I should think you were a bit cracked if I hadnt noticed that you give me very sensible reasons for what you do, though I hear you telling others you are only obeying Madame Saint Catherine.

JOAN [*crossly*] Well, I have to find reasons for you, because you do not believe in my voices. But the voices come first; and I find the reasons after: whatever you may choose to believe.

DUNOIS. Are you angry, Joan?

JOAN. Yes. [*Smiling*] No: not with you. I wish you were one of the village babies.

DUNOIS. Why?

JOAN. I could nurse you for awhile.

DUNOIS. You are a bit of a woman after all.

JOAN. No: not a bit: I am a soldier and nothing else. Soldiers always nurse children when they get a chance.

DUNOIS. That is true. [*He laughs*].

King Charles, with Bluebeard on his left and La Hire on his right, comes from the vestry, where he has been disrobing. Joan shrinks away behind the pillar. Dunois is left between Charles and La Hire.

DUNOIS. Well, your Majesty is an anointed king at last. How do you like it?

CHARLES. I would not go through it again to be emperor of the sun and moon. The weight of those robes! I thought I should have dropped when they loaded that crown on to me. And the famous holy oil they talked so much about was rancid: phew! The Archbishop must be nearly dead: his robes must have weighed a ton: they are stripping him still in the vestry.

DUNOIS [*drily*] Your majesty should wear armor oftener. That would accustom you to heavy dressing.

CHARLES. Yes: the old jibe! Well, I am not going to wear armor: fighting is not my job. Where is The Maid?

JOAN [*coming forward between Charles and Bluebeard, and falling on her knee*] Sire: I have made you king: my work is done. I am going back to my father's farm.

CHARLES [*surprised, but relieved*] Oh, are you? Well, that will be very nice.

Joan rises, deeply discouraged.

CHARLES [*continuing heedlessly*] A healthy life, you know.

DUNOIS. But a dull one.

BLUEBEARD. You will find the petticoats tripping you up after leaving them off for so long.

LA HIRE. You will miss the fighting. It's a bad habit, but a grand one, and the hardest of all to break yourself of.

CHARLES [*anxiously*] Still, we dont want you to stay if you would really rather go home.

JOAN [*bitterly*] I know well that none of you will be sorry to see me go. [*She turns her shoulder to Charles and walks past him to the more congenial neighborhood of Dunois and La Hire*].

LA HIRE. Well, I shall be able to swear when I want to. But I shall miss you at times.

JOAN. La Hire: in spite of all your sins and swears we shall meet in heaven; for I love you as I love Pitou, my old sheep dog. Pitou could kill a wolf. You will kill the English wolves until they go back to their country and become good dogs of God, will you not?

LA HIRE. You and I together: yes.

JOAN. No: I shall last only a year from the beginning.

ALL THE OTHERS. What!

JOAN. I know it somehow.

DUNOIS. Nonsense!

JOAN. Jack: do you think you will be able to drive them out?

DUNOIS [*with quiet conviction*] Yes: I shall drive them out. They beat us because we thought battles were tournaments and ransom markets. We played the fool while the goddams took war seriously. But I have learnt my lesson, and taken their measure. They have no roots here. I have beaten them before; and I shall beat them again.

JOAN. You will not be cruel to them, Jack?

DUNOIS. The goddams will not yield to tender handling. We did not begin it.

JOAN [*suddenly*] Jack: before I go home, let us take Paris.

CHARLES [*terrified*] Oh no no. We shall lose everything we have gained. Oh dont let us have any more fighting. We can make a very good treaty with the Duke of Burgundy.

JOAN. Treaty! [*She stamps with impatience*].

CHARLES. Well, why not, now that I am crowned and anointed? Oh, that oil!

The Archbishop comes from the vestry, and joins the group between Charles and Bluebeard.

CHARLES. Archbishop: The Maid wants to start fighting again.

THE ARCHBISHOP. Have we ceased fighting, then? Are we at peace?

CHARLES. No: I suppose not; but let us be content with what we have done. Let us make a treaty. Our luck is too good to last; and now is our chance to stop before it turns.

JOAN. Luck! God has fought for us; and you call it luck! And you would stop while there are still Englishmen on this holy earth of dear France!

THE ARCHBISHOP [*sternly*] Maid: the king addressed himself to me, not to you. You forget yourself. You very often forget yourself.

JOAN [*unabashed, and rather roughly*] Then speak, you; and tell him that it is not God's will that he should take his hand from the plough.

THE ARCHBISHOP. If I am not so glib with the name of God as you are, it is because I interpret His will with the authority of the Church and of my sacred office. When you first came you respected it, and would not have dared to speak as you are now speaking. You came clothed with the virtue of humility; and because God blessed your enterprises accordingly, you have stained yourself with the sin of pride. The old Greek tragedy is rising among us. It is the chastisement of hubris.

CHARLES. Yes: she thinks she knows better than everyone else.

JOAN [*distressed, but naïvely incapable of seeing the effect she is producing*] But I do know better than any of you seem to. And I am not proud: I never speak unless I know I am right.

BLUEBEARD] [*exclaiming* { Ha ha!
CHARLES ∫ *together*]] Just so.

THE ARCHBISHOP. How do you know you are right?

JOAN. I always know. My voices—

CHARLES. Oh, your voices, your voices. Why dont the voices come to me? I am king, not you.

JOAN. They do come to you; but you do not hear them. You have not sat in the field in the evening listening for them. When the angelus rings you cross yourself and have done with it; but if you prayed from your heart, and listened to the thrilling of the bells in the air after they stop ringing, you would hear the voices as well as I do. [*Turning brusquely from him*] But what voices do you need to tell you what the blacksmith can tell you: that you must strike while the iron is hot? I tell you we must make a dash at Compiégne and relieve it as we relieved Orleans. Then Paris will open its gates; or if not, we will break through them. What is your crown worth without your capital?

LA HIRE. That is what I say too. We shall go through them like a red hot shot through a pound of butter. What do you say, Bastard?

DUNOIS. If our cannon balls were all as hot as your head, and we had enough of them, we should conquer the earth, no doubt. Pluck and impetuosity are good servants in war, but bad masters: they have delivered us into the hands of the English every time we have trusted to them. We never know when we are beaten: that is our great fault.

JOAN. You never know when you are victorious: that is a worse fault. I shall have to make you carry looking-glasses in battle to convince you that the English have not cut off all your noses. You would have been besieged in Orleans still, you and your councils of war, if I had not made you attack. You should always attack; and if you only hold on long enough the enemy will stop first. You dont know how to begin a battle; and you dont know how to use your cannons. And I do.

She squats down on the flags with crossed ankles, pouting.

DUNOIS. I know what you think of us, General Joan.

JOAN. Never mind that, Jack. Tell them what you think of me.

DUNOIS. I think that God was on your side; for I have not forgotten how the wind changed, and how our hearts changed when you came; and by my faith I shall never deny that it was in your sign that we conquered. But I tell you as a soldier that God is no man's daily drudge, and no maid's either. If you are worthy of it He will sometimes snatch you out of the jaws of death and set you on your feet again; but that is all: once on your feet you must fight with all your might and all your craft. For He has to be fair to your enemy too: dont forget that. Well, He set us on our feet through you at Orleans; and the glory of it has carried us through a few good battles here to the coronation. But if we presume on it further, and trust to God to do the work we should do ourselves, we shall be defeated; and serve us right!

JOAN. But—

DUNOIS. Sh! I have not finished. Do not think, any of you, that these victories of ours were won without generalship. King Charles: you have said no word in your proclamations of my part in this campaign; and I make no complaint of that; for the people will run after The Maid and her miracles and not after the Bastard's hard work finding troops for her and feeding them. But I know exactly how much God did for us through The Maid, and how much He left me to do by my own wits; and I tell you that your little hour of miracles is over, and that from this time on he who plays the war game best will win—if the luck is on his side.

JOAN. Ah! if, if, if, if! If ifs and ans were pots and pans there'd be no need of tinkers. [*Rising impetuously*] I tell you, Bastard, your art of war is no use, because your knights are no good for real fighting. War is only a game to them, like tennis and all their other games: they make rules as to what is fair and what is not fair, and heap armor on themselves and on their poor horses to keep out the arrows; and when they fall they cant get up, and have to wait for their squires to come and lift them to arrange about the ransom with the man that has poked them off their horse. Cant you see that all the like of that is gone by and done with? What use is armor against gunpowder? And if it was, do you think men that are fighting for France and for God will stop to bargain about ransoms, as half your knights live by doing? No: they will fight to win; and they will give up their lives out of their own hand into the hand of God when they go into battle, as I do. Common folks understand this. They cannot afford armor and cannot pay ransoms; but they followed me half naked into the moat and up the ladder and over the wall. With them it is my life or thine, and God defend the right! You may shake your head, Jack; and Bluebeard may twirl his billygoat's beard and cock his nose at me; but remember the day your knights and captains refused to follow me to attack the English at Orleans! You locked the gates to keep me in; and it was the townsfolk and the common people that followed me, and forced the gate, and shewed you the way to fight in earnest.

BLUEBEARD [*offended*] Not content with being Pope Joan, you must be Caesar and Alexander as well.

THE ARCHBISHOP. Pride will have a fall, Joan.

JOAN. Oh, never mind whether it is pride or not: is it true? is it commonsense?

LA HIRE. It is true. Half of us are afraid of having our handsome noses broken; and the other half are out for paying off their mortgages. Let her have her way, Dunois: she does not know everything; but she has got hold of the right end of the stick. Fighting is not what it was; and those who know least about it often make the best job of it.

DUNOIS. I know all that. I do not fight in the old way: I have learnt the lesson of Agincourt, of Poitiers and Crecy. I know how many lives any move of mine will cost; and if the move is worth the cost I make it and pay the cost. But Joan never counts the cost at all: she goes ahead and trusts to God: she thinks she has God in her pocket. Up to now she has had the numbers on her side; and she has won. But I know Joan; and I see that some day she will go ahead when she has only ten men to do the work of a hundred. And then she will find that God is on the side of the big battalions. She will be taken by the enemy. And the lucky man that makes the capture will receive sixteen thousand pounds from the Earl of Ouareek.

JOAN [*flattered*] Sixteen thousand pounds! Eh, laddie, have they offered that for me? There cannot be so much money in the world.

DUNOIS. There is, in England. And now tell me, all of you, which of you will lift a finger to save Joan once the English have got her? I speak first, for the army. The day after she has been dragged from her horse by a goddam or a Burgundian, and he is not struck dead: the day after she is locked in a dungeon, and the bars and bolts do not fly open at the touch of St Peter's angel: the day when the enemy finds out that she is as vulnerable as I am and not a bit more invincible, she will not be worth the life of a single soldier to us; and I will not risk that life, much as I cherish her as a companion-in-arms.

JOAN. I dont blame you, Jack: you are right. I am not worth one soldier's life if God lets me be beaten; but France may think me worth my ransom after what God has done for her through me.

CHARLES. I tell you I have no money; and this coronation, which is all your fault, has cost me the last farthing I can borrow.

JOAN. The Church is richer than you. I put my trust in the Church.

THE ARCHBISHOP. Woman: they will drag you through the streets, and burn you as a witch.

JOAN [*running to him*] Oh, my lord, do not say that. It is impossible. I a witch!

THE ARCHBISHOP. Peter Cauchon knows his business. The University of Paris has burnt a woman for saying that what you have done was well done, and according to God?

JOAN [*bewildered*] But why? What sense is there in it? What I have done is according to God. They could not burn a woman for speaking the truth.

THE ARCHBISHOP. They did.

JOAN. But you know that she was speaking the truth. You would not let them burn me.

THE ARCHBISHOP. How could I prevent them?

JOAN. You would speak in the name of the Church. You are a great prince of the Church. I would go anywhere with your blessing to protect me.

THE ARCHBISHOP. I have no blessing for you while you are proud and disobedient.

JOAN. Oh, why will you go on saying things like that? I am not proud and disobedient. I am a poor girl, and so ignorant that I do not know A from B. How could I be proud? And how can you say that I am disobedient when I always obey my voices, because they come from God.

THE ARCHBISHOP. The voice of God on earth is the voice of the Church Militant; and all the voices that come to you are the echoes of your own wilfulness.

JOAN. It is not true.

THE ARCHBISHOP [*flushing angrily*] You tell the Archbishop in his cathedral that he lies; and yet you say you are not proud and disobedient.

JOAN. I never said you lied. It was you that as good as said my voices lied. When have they ever lied? If you will not believe in them: even if they are only the echoes of my own common-sense, are they not always right? and are not your earthly counsels always wrong?

THE ARCHBISHOP [*indignantly*] It is waste of time admonishing you.

CHARLES. It always comes back to the same thing. She is right; and everyone else is wrong.

THE ARCHBISHOP. Take this as your last warning. If you perish through setting your private judgment above the instructions of your spiritual directors, the Church disowns you, and leaves you to whatever fate your presumption may bring upon you. The Bastard has told you that if you persist in setting up your military conceit above the counsels of your commanders—

DUNOIS [*interposing*] To put it quite exactly, if you attempt to relieve the garrison in Compiègne without the same superiority in numbers you had at Orleans—

THE ARCHBISHOP. The army will disown you, and will not rescue you. And His Majesty the King has told you that the throne has not the means of ransoming you.

CHARLES. Not a penny.

THE ARCHBISHOP. You stand alone: absolutely alone, trusting to your own conceit, your own ignorance, your own headstrong presumption, your own impiety in hiding all these sins under the cloak of a trust in God. When you pass through these doors into the sunlight, the crowd will cheer you. They will bring you their little children and their invalids to heal: they will kiss your hands and feet, and do what they can, poor simple souls, to turn your head, and madden you with the self-confidence that is leading you to your destruction. But you will be none the less alone: they cannot save you. We and we only can stand between you and the stake at which our enemies have burnt that wretched woman in Paris.

JOAN [*her eyes skyward*] I have better friends and better counsel than yours.

THE ARCHBISHOP. I see that I am speaking in vain to a hardened heart. You reject our protection, and are determined to turn us all against you. In future, then, fend for yourself; and if you fail, God have mercy on your soul.

DUNOIS. That is the truth, Joan. Heed it.

JOAN. Where would you all have been now if I had heeded that sort of truth? There is no help, no counsel, in any of you. Yes: I am alone on earth: I have always been alone. My father told my brothers to drown me if I would not stay to mind his sheep while France was bleeding to death: France might perish if only our lambs were safe. I thought France would have friends at the court of the king of France; and I find only wolves fighting for pieces of her poor torn body. I thought God would have friends everywhere, because He is the friend of everyone; and in my innocence I believed that you who now cast me out would be like strong towers to keep harm from me. But I am wiser now;

and nobody is any the worse for being wiser. Do not think you can frighten me by telling me that I am alone. France is alone; and God is alone; and what is my loneliness before the loneliness of my country and my God? I see now that the loneliness of God is His strength: what would He be if He listened to your jealous little counsels? Well, my loneliness shall be my strength too; it is better to be alone with God: His friendship will not fail me, nor His counsel, nor His love. In His strength I will dare, and dare, and dare, until I die. I will go out now to the common people, and let the love in their eyes comfort me for the hate in yours. You will all be glad to see me burnt; but if I go through the fire I shall go through it to their hearts for ever and ever. And so, God be with me!

She goes from them. They stare after her in glum silence for a moment. Then Gilles de Rais twirls his beard.

BLUEBEARD. You know, the woman is quite impossible. I dont dislike her, really; but what are you to do with such a character?

DUNOIS. As God is my judge, if she fell into the Loire I would jump in in full armor to fish her out. But if she plays the fool at Compiègne, and gets caught, I must leave her to her doom.

LA HIRE. Then you had better chain me up; for I could follow her to hell when the spirit rises in her like that.

THE ARCHBISHOP. She disturbs my judgment too: there is a dangerous power in her outbursts. But the pit is open at her feet; and for good or evil we cannot turn her from it.

CHARLES. If only she would keep quiet, or go home!

They follow her dispiritedly.

Rouen, 30th May 1431. A great stone hall in the castle, arranged for a trial-at-law, but not a trial-by-jury, the court being the Bishop's court with the Inquisition participating: hence there are two raised chairs side by side for the Bishop and the Inquisitor as judges. Rows of chairs radiating from them at an obtuse angle are for the canons, the doctors of law and theology, and the Dominican monks, who act as assessors. In the angle is a table for the scribes, with stools. There is also a heavy rough wooden stool for the prisoner. All these are at the inner end of the hall. The further end is open to the courtyard through a row of arches. The court is shielded from the weather by screens and curtains.

Looking down the great hall from the middle of the inner end, the judicial chairs and scribes' table are to the right. The prisoner's stool is to the left. There are arched doors right and left. It is a fine sunshiny May morning.

Warwick comes in through the arched doorway on the judges' side, followed by his page.

THE PAGE [*pertly*] I suppose your lordship is aware that we have no business here. This is an ecclesiastical court; and we are only the secular arm.

WARWICK. I am aware of that fact. Will it please your impudence to find the Bishop of Beauvais for me, and give him a hint that he can have a word with me here before the trial, if he wishes?

THE PAGE [*going*] Yes, my lord.

WARWICK. And mind you behave yourself. Do not address him as Pious Peter.

THE PAGE. No, my lord. I shall be kind to him, because, when The Maid is brought in, Pious Peter will have to pick a peck of pickled pepper.

Cauchon enters through the same door with a Dominican monk and a canon, the latter carrying a brief.

THE PAGE. The Right Reverend his lordship the Bishop of

Beauvais. And two other reverend gentlemen.

WARWICK. Get out; and see that we are not interrupted.

THE PAGE. Right, my lord [*he vanishes airily*].

CAUCHON. I wish your lordship good-morrow.

WARWICK. Good-morrow to your lordship. Have I had the pleasure of meeting your friends before? I think not.

CAUCHON [*introducing the monk, who is on his right*] This, my lord, is Brother John Lemaître, of the order of St Dominic. He is acting as deputy for the Chief Inquisitor into the evil of heresy in France. Brother John: the Earl of Warwick.

WARWICK. Your Reverence is most welcome. We have no Inquisitor in England, unfortunately; though we miss him greatly, especially on occasions like the present.

The Inquisitor smiles patiently, and bows. He is a mild elderly gentleman, but has evident reserves of authority and firmness.

CAUCHON [*introducing the Canon, who is on his left*] This gentleman is Canon John D'Estivet, of the Chapter of Bayeux. He is acting as Promoter.

WARWICK. Promoter?

CAUCHON. Prosecutor, you would call him in civil law.

WARWICK. Ah! prosecutor. Quite, quite. I am very glad to make your acquaintance, Canon D'Estivet.

D'Estivet bows. [He is on the young side of middle age, well mannered, but vulpine beneath his veneer].

WARWICK. May I ask what stage the proceedings have reached? It is now more than nine months since The Maid was captured at Compiègne by the Burgundians. It is fully four months since I bought her from the Burgundians for a very handsome sum, solely that she might be brought to justice. It is very nearly three months since I delivered her up to you, my Lord Bishop, as a person suspected of heresy. May I suggest that you are taking a rather unconscionable time to make up your minds about a very plain case? Is this trial never going to end?

THE INQUISITOR [*smiling*] It has not yet begun, my lord.

WARWICK. Not yet begun! Why, you have been at it eleven weeks!

CAUCHON. We have not been idle, my lord. We have held fifteen examinations of The Maid: six public and nine private.

THE INQUISITOR [*always patiently smiling*] You see, my lord, I have been present at only two of these examinations. They were proceedings of the Bishop's court solely, and not of the Holy Office. I have only just decided to associate myself—that is, to associate the Holy Inquisition—with the Bishop's court. I did not at first think that this was a case of heresy at all. I regarded it as a political case, and The Maid as a prisoner of war. But having now been present at two of the examinations, I must admit that this seems to be one of the gravest cases of heresy within my experience. Therefore everything is now in order, and we proceed to trial this morning. [*He moves towards the judicial chairs*].

CAUCHON. This moment, if your lordship's convenience allows.

WARWICK [*graciously*] Well, that is good news, gentlemen. I will not attempt to conceal from you that our patience was becoming strained.

CAUCHON. So I gathered from the threats of your soldiers to drown those of our people who favor The Maid.

WARWICK. Dear me! At all events their intentions were friendly to you, my lord.

CAUCHON [*sternly*] I hope not. I am determined that the woman shall have a fair hearing. The justice of the Church is not a mockery, my lord.

THE INQUISITOR [*returning*] Never has there been a fairer examination within my experience, my lord. The Maid needs no lawyers to take her part: she will be tried by her most faithful friends, all ardently desirous to save her soul from perdition.

D'ESTIVET. Sir: I am the Promoter; and it has been my painful duty to present the case against the girl; but believe me, I would throw up my case today and hasten to her defence if I did not know that men far my superiors in learning and piety, in eloquence and persuasiveness, have been sent to reason with her, to explain to her the danger she is running, and the ease with which she may avoid it. [*Suddenly bursting into forensic eloquence, to the disgust of Cauchon and the Inquisitor, who have listened to him so far with patronizing approval*] Men have dared to say that we are acting from hate; but God is our witness that they lie. Have we tortured her? No. Have we ceased to exhort her; to implore her to have pity on herself; to come to the bosom of her Church as an erring but beloved child? Have we—

CAUCHON [*interrupting drily*] Take care, Canon. All that you say is true; but if you make his lordship believe it I will not answer for your life, and hardly for my own.

WARWICK [*deprecating, but by no means denying*] Oh, my lord, you are very hard on us poor English. But we certainly do not share your pious desire to save The Maid: in fact I tell you now plainly that her death is a political necessity which I regret but cannot help. If the Church lets her go—

CAUCHON [*with fierce and menacing pride*] If the Church lets her go, woe to the man, were he the Emperor himself, who dares lay a finger on her! The Church is not subject to political necessity, my lord.

THE INQUISITOR [*interposing smoothly*] You need have no anxiety about the result, my lord. You have an invincible ally in the matter: one who is far more determined than you that she shall burn.

WARWICK. And who is this very convenient partisan, may I ask?

THE INQUISITOR. The Maid herself. Unless you put a gag in her mouth you cannot prevent her from convicting herself ten times over every time she opens it.

D'ESTIVET. That is perfectly true, my lord. My hair bristles on my head when I hear so young a creature utter such blasphemies.

WARWICK. Well, by all means do your best for her if you are quite sure it will be of no avail. [*Looking hard at Cauchon*] I should be sorry to have to act without the blessing of the Church.

CAUCHON [*with a mixture of cynical admiration and contempt*] And yet they say Englishmen are hypocrites! You play for your side, my lord, even at the peril of your soul. I cannot but admire such devotion; but I dare not go so far myself. I fear damnation.

WARWICK. If we feared anything we could never govern England, my lord. Shall I send your people in to you?

CAUCHON. Yes: it will be very good of your lordship to withdraw and allow the court to assemble.

Warwick turns on his heel, and goes out through the courtyard. Cauchon takes one of the judicial seats; and D'Estivet sits at the scribes' table, studying his brief.

CAUCHON [*casually, as he makes himself comfortable*] What scoundrels these English nobles are!

THE INQUISITOR [*taking the other judicial chair on Cauchon's left*] All secular power makes men scoundrels. They are not trained for the work; and they have not the Apostolic Succession. Our own nobles are just as bad.

The Bishop's assessors hurry into the hall, headed by Chaplain de Stogumber and Canon de Courcelles, a young priest of 30. The scribes sit at the table, leaving a chair vacant opposite D'Estivet. Some of the assessors take their seats: others stand chatting, waiting for the proceedings to begin formally. De Stogumber, aggrieved and obstinate, will not take his seat: neither will the Canon, who stands on his right.

CAUCHON. Good morning, Master de Stogumber. [*To the Inquisitor*] Chaplain to the Cardinal of England.

THE CHAPLAIN [*correcting him*] Of Winchester, my lord. I have to make a protest, my lord.

CAUCHON. You make a great many.

THE CHAPLAIN. I am not without support, my lord. Here is Master de Courcelles, Canon of Paris, who associates himself with me in my protest.

CAUCHON. Well, what is the matter?

THE CHAPLAIN [*sulkily*] Speak you, Master de Courcelles, since I do not seem to enjoy his lordship's confidence. [*He sits down in dudgeon next to Cauchon, on his right*].

COURCELLES. My lord: we have been at great pains to draw up an indictment of The Maid on sixty-four counts. We are now told that they have been reduced, without consulting us.

THE INQUISITOR. Master de Courcelles: I am the culprit. I am overwhelmed with admiration for the zeal displayed in your sixty-four counts; but in accusing a heretic, as in other things, enough is enough. Also you must remember that all the members of the court are not so subtle and profound as you, and that some of your very great learning might appear to them to be very great nonsense. Therefore I have thought it well to have your sixty-four articles cut down to twelve—

COURCELLES [*thunderstruck*] Twelve!!!

THE INQUISITOR. Twelve will, believe me, be quite enough for your purpose.

THE CHAPLAIN. But some of the most important points have been reduced almost to nothing. For instance, The Maid has actually declared that the blessed saints Margaret and Catherine, and the holy Archangel Michael, spoke to her in French. That is a vital point.

THE INQUISITOR. You think, doubtless, that they should have spoken in Latin?

CAUCHON. No: he thinks they should have spoken in English.

THE CHAPLAIN. Naturally, my lord.

THE INQUISITOR. Well, as we are all here agreed, I think, that these voices of The Maid are the voices of evil spirits tempting her to her damnation, it would not be very courteous to you, Master de Stogumber, or to the King of England, to assume that English is the devil's native language. So let it pass. The matter is not wholly omitted from the twelve articles. Pray take your places, gentlemen; and let us proceed to business.

All who have not taken their seats, do so.

THE CHAPLAIN. Well, I protest. That is all.

COURCELLES. I think it hard that all our work should go for nothing. It is only another example of the diabolical influence which this woman exercises over the court. [*He takes his chair, which is on the Chaplain's right*].

CAUCHON. Do you suggest that I am under diabolical influence?

COURCELLES. I suggest nothing, my lord. But it seems to me that there is a conspiracy here to hush up the fact that The Maid stole the Bishop of Senlis's horse.

CAUCHON [*keeping his temper with difficulty*] This is not a police court. Are we to waste our time on such rubbish?

COURCELLES [*rising, shocked*] My lord: do you call the Bishop's horse rubbish?

THE INQUISITOR [*blandly*] Master de Courcelles: The Maid alleges that she paid handsomely for the Bishop's horse, and that if he did not get the money the fault was not hers. As that may be true, the point is one on which The Maid may well be acquitted.

COURCELLES. Yes, if it were an ordinary horse. But the Bishop's horse! how can she be acquitted for that? [*He sits down again, bewildered and discouraged*].

THE INQUISITOR. I submit to you, with great respect, that if we persist in trying The Maid on trumpery issues on which we may have to declare her innocent, she may escape us on the great main issue of heresy, on which she seems so far to insist on her own guilt. I will ask you, therefore, to say nothing, when The Maid is brought before us, of these stealings of horses, and dancings round fairy trees with the village children, and prayings at haunted wells, and a dozen other things which you were diligently inquiring into until my arrival. There is not a village girl in France against whom you could not prove such things: they all dance round haunted trees, and pray at magic wells. Some of them would steal the Pope's horse if they got the chance. Heresy, gentlemen, heresy is the charge we have to try. The detection and suppression of heresy is my peculiar business: I am here as an inquisitor, not as an ordinary magistrate. Stick to the heresy, gentlemen; and leave the other matters alone.

CAUCHON. I may say that we have sent to the girl's village to make inquiries about her? and there is practically nothing serious against her.

THE CHAPLAIN } [*rising and clamoring together*] { Nothing serious, my lord—
COURCELLES } { What! The fairy tree not—

CAUCHON [*out of patience*] Be silent, gentlemen; or speak one at a time.

Courcelles collapses into his chair, intimidated.

THE CHAPLAIN [*sulkily resuming his seat*] That is what The Maid said to us last Friday.

CAUCHON. I wish you had followed her counsel, sir. When I say nothing serious, I mean nothing that men of sufficiently large mind to conduct an inquiry like this would consider serious. I agree with my colleague the Inquisitor that it is on the count of heresy that we must proceed.

LADVENU [*a young but ascetically fine-drawn Dominican who is sitting next Courcelles, on his right*] But is there any great harm in the girl's heresy? Is it not merely her simplicity? Many saints have said as much as Joan.

THE INQUISITOR [*dropping his blandness and speaking very gravely*] Brother Martin: if you had seen what I have seen of heresy, you would not think it a light thing even in its most apparently harmless and even lovable and pious origins. Heresy begins with people who are to all appearance better than their neighbors. A gentle and pious girl, or a young man who has obeyed the command of our Lord by giving all his riches to the poor, and putting on the garb of poverty, the life of austerity, and the rule of humility and charity, may be the founder of a heresy that will wreck both Church and Empire if not ruthlessly stamped out in time. The records of the holy Inquisition are full of histories we dare not give to the world, because they are beyond the belief of honest men and innocent women; yet they all began with saintly simpletons. I have seen this again and again. Mark what I say: the woman who quarrels with her clothes, and puts on the dress of a man, is like the man who throws off his fur gown and dresses like John the Baptist: they are followed, as surely as the night follows the day, by bands of wild women and men who refuse to wear any clothes at all. When maids will neither marry nor take regular vows, and men reject marriage and exalt their lusts into divine inspirations, then, as surely as the summer follows the spring, they begin with polygamy, and end by incest. Heresy at first seems innocent and even laudable; but it ends in such a monstrous horror of unnatural wickedness that the most tender-hearted among you, if you saw it at work as I have seen it, would clamor against the mercy of the Church in dealing with it. For two hundred years the Holy Office has striven with these diabolical madnesses; and it knows that they begin always by vain and ignorant persons setting up their own judgment against the Church, and taking it upon themselves to be the interpreters of God's will. You must not fall into the common error of mistaking these simpletons for liars and hypocrites. They believe honestly and sincerely that their diabolical inspiration is divine. Therefore you must be on your guard against your natural compassion. You are all, I hope, merciful men: how else could you have devoted your lives to the service of our gentle Savior? You are going to see before you a young girl, pious and chaste; for I must tell you, gentlemen, that the things said of her by our English friends are supported by no evidence, whilst there is abundant testimony that her excesses have been excesses of religion and charity and not of worldliness and wantonness. This girl is not one of those whose hard features are the sign of hard hearts, and whose brazen looks and lewd demeanor condemn them before they are accused. The devilish pride that has led her into her present peril has left no mark on her countenance. Strange as it may seem to you, it has even left no mark on her character outside those special matters in which she is proud; so that you will see a diabolical pride and a natural humility seated side by side in the selfsame soul. Therefore be on your guard. God forbid that I should tell you to harden your hearts; for her punishment if we condemn her will be so cruel that we should forfeit our own hope of divine mercy were there one grain of malice against her in our hearts. But if you hate cruelty—and if any man here does not hate it I command him on his soul's salvation to quit this holy court—I say, if you hate cruelty, remember that nothing is so cruel in its consequences as the toleration of heresy. Remember also that no court of law can be so cruel as the common people are to those whom they suspect of heresy. The heretic in the hands of the Holy Office is safe from violence, is assured of a fair trial, and cannot suffer death, even when guilty, if repentance follows sin. Innumerable lives of heretics have been saved because the Holy Office has taken them out of the hands of the people, and because the people have yielded them up, knowing that the Holy Office would deal with them. Before the Holy Inquisition existed, and even now when its officers are not within reach, the unfortunate wretch suspected of heresy, perhaps quite ignorantly and unjustly, is stoned, torn in pieces, drowned, burned in his house with all his innocent children, without a trial, unshriven, unburied save as a dog is buried: all of them deeds hateful to God and most cruel to man. Gentlemen: I am compassionate by nature as well as by my profession; and though the work I have to do may seem cruel to those who do not know how much more cruel it would be to leave it undone, I would go to the stake myself sooner than do it if I did not know its righteousness, its necessity, its essential mercy. I ask you to address yourself to this trial in that conviction. Anger is a bad counsellor: cast out anger. Pity is sometimes worse: cast out pity. But do not cast out mercy. Remember only that justice comes first. Have you anything to say, my lord, before we proceed to trial?

CAUCHON. You have spoken for me, and spoken better than I could. I do not see how any sane man could disagree with a word that has fallen from you. But this I will add. The crude heresies of which you have told us are horrible; but their horror is like that of the black death: they rage for a while and then die out, because sound and sensible men will not under any incitement be reconciled to nakedness and incest and polygamy and the like. But we are confronted today throughout Europe with a heresy that is spreading among men not weak in mind nor diseased in brain: nay, the stronger the mind, the more obstinate the heretic. It is neither discredited by fantastic extremes nor corrupted by the common lusts of the flesh; but it, too, sets up the private judgment of the single erring mortal against the considered wisdom and experience of the Church. The mighty structure of Catholic Christendom will never be shaken by naked madmen or by the sins of Moab and Ammon. But it may be betrayed from within, and brought to barbarous ruin and desolation, by this arch heresy which the English Commander calls Protestantism.

THE ASSESSORS [*whispering*] Protestantism! What was that? What does the Bishop mean? Is it a new heresy? The English Commander, he said. Did you ever hear of Protestantism? etc., etc.

CAUCHON [*continuing*] And that reminds me. What provision has the Earl of Warwick made for the defence of the secular arm should The Maid prove obdurate, and the people be moved to pity her?

THE CHAPLAIN. Have no fear on that score, my lord. The noble earl has eight hundred men-at-arms at the gates. She will not slip through our English fingers even if the whole city be on her side.

CAUCHON [*revolted*] Will you not add, God grant that she repent and purge her sin?

THE CHAPLAIN. That does not seem to me to be consistent; but of course I agree with your lordship.

CAUCHON [*giving him up with a shrug of contempt*] The court sits.

THE INQUISITOR. Let the accused be brought in.

LADVENU [*calling*] The accused. Let her be brought in.

Joan, chained by the ankles, is brought in through the arched door behind the prisoner's stool by a guard of English soldiers. With them is the Executioner and his assistants. They lead her to the prisoner's stool, and place themselves behind it after taking off her chain. She wears a page's black suit. Her long imprisonment and the strain of the examinations which have preceded the trial have left their mark on her; but her vitality still holds: she confronts the court unabashed, without a trace of the awe which their formal solemnity seems to require for the complete success of its impressiveness.

THE INQUISITOR [*kindly*] Sit down, Joan. [*She sits on the prisoner's stool*]. You look very pale today. Are you not well?

JOAN. Thank you kindly: I am well enough. But the Bishop sent me some carp; and it made me ill.

CAUCHON. I am sorry. I told them to see that it was fresh.

JOAN. You meant to be good to me, I know; but it is a fish that does not agree with me. The English thought you were trying to poison me—

CAUCHON ⎱ [*together*] ⎰ What!
THE CHAPLAIN ⎰   ⎱ No, my lord.

JOAN [*continuing*] They are determined that I shall be burnt as
a witch; and they sent their doctor to cure me; but he was forbidden to bleed me because the silly people believe that a witch's
witchery leaves her if she is bled; so he only called me filthy
names. Why do you leave me in the hands of the English? I
should be in the hands of the Church. And why must I be chained
by the feet to a log of wood? Are you afraid I will fly away?

D'ESTIVET [*harshly*] Woman: it is not for you to question the
court: it is for us to question you.

COURCELLES. When you were left unchained, did you not try to
escape by jumping from a tower sixty feet high? If you cannot fly
like a witch, how is it that you are still alive?

JOAN. I suppose because the tower was not so high then. It has
grown higher every day since you began asking me questions
about it.

D'ESTIVET. Why did you jump from the tower?

JOAN. How do you know that I jumped?

D'ESTIVET. You were found lying in the moat. Why did you
leave the tower?

JOAN. Why would anybody leave a prison if they could get
out?

D'ESTIVET. You tried to escape?

JOAN. Of course I did; and not for the first time either. If you
leave the door of the cage open the bird will fly out.

D'ESTIVET [*rising*] That is a confession of heresy. I call the
attention of the court to it.

JOAN. Heresy, he calls it! Am I a heretic because I try to escape
from prison?

D'ESTIVET. Assuredly, if you are in the hands of the Church,
and you wilfully take yourself out of its hands, you are deserting
the Church; and that is heresy.

JOAN. It is great nonsense. Nobody could be such a fool as to
think that.

D'ESTIVET. You hear, my lord, how I am reviled in the execution of my duty by this woman. [*He sits down indignantly*].

CAUCHON. I have warned you before, Joan, that you are doing yourself no good by these pert answers.

JOAN. But you will not talk sense to me. I am reasonable if you will be reasonable.

THE INQUISITOR [*interposing*] This is not yet in order. You forget, Master Promoter, that the proceedings have not been formally opened. The time for questions is after she has sworn on the Gospels to tell us the whole truth.

JOAN. You say this to me every time. I have said again and again that I will tell you all that concerns this trial. But I cannot tell you the whole truth: God does not allow the whole truth to be told. You do not understand it when I tell it. It is an old saying that he who tells too much truth is sure to be hanged. I am weary of this argument: we have been over it nine times already. I have sworn as much as I will swear; and I will swear no more.

COURCELLES. My lord: she should be put to the torture.

THE INQUISITOR. You hear, Joan? That is what happens to the obdurate. Think before you answer. Has she been shewn the instruments?

THE EXECUTIONER. They are ready, my lord. She has seen them.

JOAN. If you tear me limb from limb until you separate my soul from my body you will get nothing out of me beyond what I have told you. What more is there to tell that you could understand? Besides, I cannot bear to be hurt; and if you hurt me I will say anything you like to stop the pain. But I will take it all back afterwards; so what is the use of it?

LADVENU. There is much in that. We should proceed mercifully.

COURCELLES. But the torture is customary.

THE INQUISITOR. It must not be applied wantonly. If the accused will confess voluntarily, then its use cannot be justified.

COURCELLES. But this is unusual and irregular. She refuses to take the oath.

LADVENU [*disgusted*] Do you want to torture the girl for the mere pleasure of it?

COURCELLES [*bewildered*] But it is not a pleasure. It is the law. It is customary. It is always done.

THE INQUISITOR. That is not so, Master, except when the inquiries are carried on by people who do not know their legal business.

COURCELLES. But the woman is a heretic. I assure you it is always done.

CAUCHON [*decisively*] It will not be done today if it is not necessary. Let there be an end of this. I will not have it said that we proceeded on forced confessions. We have sent our best preachers and doctors to this woman to exhort and implore her to save her soul and body from the fire: we shall not now send the executioner to thrust her into it.

COURCELLES. Your lordship is merciful, of course. But it is a great responsibility to depart from the usual practice.

JOAN. Thou art a rare noodle, Master. Do what was done last time is thy rule, eh?

COURCELLES [*rising*] Thou wanton: dost thou dare call me noodle?

THE INQUISITOR. Patience, Master, patience: I fear you will soon be only too terribly avenged.

COURCELLES [*mutters*] Noodle indeed! [*He sits down, much discontented*].

THE INQUISITOR. Meanwhile, let us not be moved by the rough side of a shepherd lass's tongue.

JOAN. Nay: I am no shepherd lass, though I have helped with the sheep like anyone else. I will do a lady's work in the house— spin or weave—against any woman in Rouen.

THE INQUISITOR. This is not a time for vanity, Joan. You stand in great peril.

JOAN. I know it: have I not been punished for my vanity? If I had not worn my cloth of gold surcoat in battle like a fool, that Burgundian soldier would never have pulled me backwards off my horse; and I should not have been here.

THE CHAPLAIN. If you are so clever at woman's work why do you not stay at home and do it?

JOAN. There are plenty of other women to do it; but there is nobody to do my work.

CAUCHON. Come! we are wasting time on trifles. Joan: I am going to put a most solemn question to you. Take care how you answer; for your life and salvation are at stake on it. Will you for all you have said and done, be it good or bad, accept the judgment of God's Church on earth? More especially as to the acts and words that are imputed to you in this trial by the Promoter here, will you submit your case to the inspired interpretation of the Church Militant?

JOAN. I am a faithful child of the Church. I will obey the Church—

CAUCHON [*hopefully leaning forward*] You will?

JOAN. —provided it does not command anything impossible.

Cauchon sinks back in his chair with a heavy sigh. The Inquisitor purses his lips and frowns. Ladvenu shakes his head pitifully.

D'ESTIVET. She imputes to the Church the error and folly of commanding the impossible.

JOAN. If you command me to declare that all that I have done and said, and all the visions and revelations I have had, were not from God, then that is impossible: I will not declare it for anything in the world. What God made me do I will never go back on; and what He has commanded or shall command I will not fail to do in spite of any man alive. That is what I mean by impossible. And in case the Church should bid me do anything contrary to the command I have from God, I will not consent to it, no matter what it may be.

THE ASSESSORS [*shocked and indignant*] Oh! The Church contrary to God! What do you say now? Flat heresy. This is beyond everything, etc., etc.

D'ESTIVET [*throwing down his brief*] My lord: do you need anything more than this?

CAUCHON. Woman: you have said enough to burn ten heretics. Will you not be warned? Will you not understand?

THE INQUISITOR. If the Church Militant tells you that your revelations and visions are sent by the devil to tempt you to your damnation, will you not believe that the Church is wiser than you?

JOAN. I believe that God is wiser than I; and it is His commands that I will do. All the things that you call my crimes have come to me by the command of God. I say that I have done them by the order of God: it is impossible for me to say anything else. If any Churchman says the contrary I shall not mind him: I shall mind God alone, whose command I always follow.

LADVENU [*pleading with her urgently*] You do not know what you are saying, child. Do you want to kill yourself? Listen. Do you not believe that you are subject to the Church of God on earth?

JOAN. Yes. When have I ever denied it?

LADVENU. Good. That means, does it not, that you are subject to our Lord the Pope, to the cardinals, the archbishops, and the bishops for whom his lordship stands here today?

JOAN. God must be served first.

D'ESTIVET. Then your voices command you not to submit yourself to the Church Militant?

JOAN. My voices do not tell me to disobey the Church; but God must be served first.

CAUCHON. And you, and not the Church, are to be the judge?

JOAN. What other judgment can I judge by but my own?

THE ASSESSORS [*scandalized*] Oh! [*They cannot find words*].

CAUCHON. Out of your own mouth you have condemned yourself. We have striven for your salvation to the verge of sinning ourselves: we have opened the door to you again and again; and you have shut it in our faces and in the face of God. Dare you pretend, after what you have said, that you are in a state of grace?

JOAN. If I am not, may God bring me to it: if I am, may God keep me in it!

LADVENU. That is a very good reply, my lord.

COURCELLES. Were you in a state of grace when you stole the Bishop's horse?

CAUCHON [*rising in a fury*] Oh, devil take the Bishop's horse and you too! We are here to try a case of heresy; and no sooner do we come to the root of the matter than we are thrown back by idiots who understand nothing but horses. [*Trembling with rage, he forces himself to sit down*].

THE INQUISITOR. Gentlemen, gentlemen: in clinging to these small issues you are The Maid's best advocates. I am not surprised that his lordship has lost patience with you. What does the Promoter say? Does he press these trumpery matters?

D'ESTIVET. I am bound by my office to press everything; but when the woman confesses a heresy that must bring upon her the doom of excommunication, of what consequence is it that she has been guilty also of offences which expose her to minor penances? I share the impatience of his lordship as to these minor charges. Only, with great respect, I must emphasize the gravity of two very horrible and blasphemous crimes which she does not deny. First, she has intercourse with evil spirits, and is therefore a sorceress. Second, she wears men's clothes, which is indecent, unnatural, and abominable; and in spite of our most earnest remonstrances and entreaties, she will not change them even to receive the sacrament.

JOAN. Is the blessed St Catherine an evil spirit? Is St Margaret? Is Michael the Archangel?

COURCELLES. How do you know that the spirit which appears to you is an archangel? Does he not appear to you as a naked man?

JOAN. Do you think God cannot afford clothes for him?

The assessors cannot help smiling, especially as the joke is against Courcelles.

LADVENU. Well answered, Joan.

THE INQUISITOR. It is, in effect, well answered. But no evil spirit would be so simple as to appear to a young girl in a guise that would scandalize her when he meant her to take him for a messenger from the Most High? Joan: the Church instructs you that these apparitions are demons seeking your soul's perdition. Do you accept the instruction of the Church?

JOAN. I accept the messenger of God. How could any faithful believer in the Church refuse him?

CAUCHON. Wretched woman: again I ask you, do you know what you are saying?

THE INQUISITOR. You wrestle in vain with the devil for her soul, my lord: she will not be saved. Now as to this matter of the man's dress. For the last time, will you put off that impudent attire, and dress as becomes your sex?

JOAN. I will not.

D'ESTIVET [*pouncing*] The sin of disobedience, my lord.

JOAN [*distressed*] But my voices tell me I must dress as a soldier.

LADVENU. Joan, Joan: does not that prove to you that the voices are the voices of evil spirits? Can you suggest to us one good reason why an angel of God should give you such shameless advice?

JOAN. Why, yes: what can be plainer commonsense? I was a soldier living among soldiers. I am a prisoner guarded by soldiers. If I were to dress as a woman they would think of me as a woman; and then what would become of me? If I dress as a soldier they think of me as a soldier, and I can live with them as I do at home with my brothers. That is why St Catherine tells me I must not dress as a woman until she gives me leave.

COURCELLES. When will she give you leave?

JOAN. When you take me out of the hands of the English soldiers. I have told you that I should be in the hands of the Church, and not left night and day with four soldiers of the Earl of Warwick. Do you want me to live with them in petticoats?

LADVENU. My lord: what she says is, God knows, very wrong and shocking; but there is a grain of worldly sense in it such as might impose on a simple village maiden.

JOAN. If we were as simple in the village as you are in your courts and palaces, there would soon be no wheat to make bread for you.

CAUCHON. That is the thanks you get for trying to save her, Brother Martin.

LADVENU. Joan: we are all trying to save you. His lordship is trying to save you. The Inquisitor could not be more just to you if you were his own daughter. But you are blinded by a terrible pride and self-sufficiency.

JOAN. Why do you say that? I have said nothing wrong. I cannot understand.

THE INQUISITOR. The blessed St Athanasius has laid it down in his creed that those who cannot understand are damned. It is not enough to be simple. It is not enough even to be what simple people call good. The simplicity of a darkened mind is no better than the simplicity of a beast.

JOAN. There is great wisdom in the simplicity of a beast, let me tell you; and sometimes great foolishness in the wisdom of scholars.

LADVENU. We know that, Joan: we are not so foolish as you think us. Try to resist the temptation to make pert replies to us. Do you see that man who stands behind you [*he indicates the Executioner*]?

JOAN [*turning and looking at the man*] Your torturer? But the Bishop said I was not to be tortured.

LADVENU. You are not to be tortured because you have confessed everything that is necessary to your condemnation. That man is not only the torturer: he is also the Executioner. Executioner: let The Maid hear your answers to my questions. Are you prepared for the burning of a heretic this day?

THE EXECUTIONER. Yes, Master.

LADVENU. Is the stake ready?

THE EXECUTIONER. It is. In the market-place. The English have built it too high for me to get near her and make the death easier. It will be a cruel death.

JOAN [*horrified*] But you are not going to burn me now?

THE INQUISITOR. You realize it at last.

LADVENU. There are eight hundred English soldiers waiting to take you to the market-place the moment the sentence of excommunication has passed the lips of your judges. You are within a few short moments of that doom.

JOAN [*looking round desperately for rescue*] Oh God!

LADVENU. Do not despair, Joan. The Church is merciful. You can save yourself.

JOAN [*hopefully*] Yes: my voices promised me I should not be burnt. St Catherine bade me be bold.

CAUCHON. Woman: are you quite mad? Do you not yet see that your voices have deceived you?

JOAN. Oh no: that is impossible.

CAUCHON. Impossible! They have led you straight to your excommunication, and to the stake which is there waiting for you.

LADVENU [*pressing the point hard*] Have they kept a single promise to you since you were taken at Compiègne? The devil has betrayed you. The Church holds out its arms to you.

JOAN [*despairing*] Oh, it is true: it is true: my voices have deceived me. I have been mocked by devils: my faith is broken. I have dared and dared; but only a fool will walk into a fire: God, who gave me my commonsense, cannot will me to do that.

LADVENU. Now God be praised that He has saved you at the eleventh hour! [*He hurries to the vacant seat at the scribes' table, and snatches a sheet of paper, on which he sets to work writing eagerly*].

CAUCHON. Amen!

JOAN. What must I do?

CAUCHON. You must sign a solemn recantation of your heresy.

JOAN. Sign? That means to write my name. I cannot write.

CAUCHON. You have signed many letters before.

JOAN. Yes; but someone held my hand and guided the pen. I can make my mark.

THE CHAPLAIN [*who has been listening with growing alarm and indignation*] My lord: do you mean that you are going to allow this woman to escape us?

THE INQUISITOR. The law must take its course, Master de Stogumber. And you know the law.

THE CHAPLAIN [*rising, purple with fury*] I know that there is no faith in a Frenchman. [*Tumult, which he shouts down*]. I know what my lord the Cardinal of Winchester will say when he hears of this. I know what the Earl of Warwick will do when he learns that you intend to betray him. There are eight hundred men at the gate who will see that this abominable witch is burnt in spite of your teeth.

THE ASSESSORS [*meanwhile*] What is this? What did he say? He accuses us of treachery! This is past bearing. No faith in a Frenchman! Did you hear that? This is an intolerable fellow. Who is he? Is this what English Churchmen are like? He must be mad or drunk, etc., etc.

THE INQUISITOR [*rising*] Silence, pray! Gentlemen: pray silence! Master Chaplain: bethink you a moment of your holy office: of what you are, and where you are. I direct you to sit down.

THE CHAPLAIN [*folding his arms doggedly, his face working convulsively*] I will NOT sit down.

CAUCHON. Master Inquisitor: this man has called me a traitor to my face before now.

THE CHAPLAIN. So you are a traitor. You are all traitors. You have been doing nothing but begging this damnable witch on your knees to recant all through this trial.

THE INQUISITOR [*placidly resuming his seat*] If you will not sit, you must stand: that is all.

THE CHAPLAIN. I will NOT stand [*he flings himself back into his chair*].

LADVENU [*rising with the paper in his hand*] My lord: here is the form of recantation for The Maid to sign.

CAUCHON. Read it to her.

JOAN. Do not trouble. I will sign it.

THE INQUISITOR. Woman: you must know what you are putting your hand to. Read it to her, Brother Martin. And let all be silent.

LADVENU [*reading quietly*] "I, Joan, commonly called The Maid, a miserable sinner, do confess that I have most grievously sinned in the following articles. I have pretended to have revelations from God and the angels and the blessed saints, and perversely rejected the Church's warnings that these were temptations by demons. I have blasphemed abominably by wearing an immodest dress, contrary to the Holy Scripture and the canons of the Church. Also I have clipped my hair in the style of a man, and, against all the duties which have made my sex specially acceptable in heaven, have taken up the sword, even to the shedding of human blood, inciting men to slay each other, invoking evil spirits to delude them, and stubbornly and most blasphemously imputing these sins to Almighty God. I confess to the sin of sedition, to the sin of idolatry, to the sin of disobedience, to the sin of pride, and to the sin of heresy. All of which sins I now renounce and abjure and depart from, humbly thanking you Doctors and Masters who have brought me back to the truth and into the grace of our Lord. And I will never return to my errors, but will remain in communion with our Holy Church and in obedience to our Holy Father the Pope of Rome. All this I swear by God Almighty and the Holy Gospels, in witness whereto I sign my name to this recantation."

THE INQUISITOR. You understand this, Joan?

JOAN [*listless*] It is plain enough, sir.

THE INQUISITOR. And it is true?

JOAN. It may be true. If it were not true, the fire would not be ready for me in the market-place.

LADVENU [*taking up his pen and a book, and going to her quickly lest she should compromise herself again*] Come, child: let me guide your hand. Take the pen. [*She does so; and they begin to write, using the book as a desk*] J.E.H.A.N.E. So. Now make your mark by yourself.

JOAN [*makes her mark, and gives him back the pen, tormented by the rebellion of her soul against her mind and body*] There!

LADVENU [*replacing the pen on the table, and handing the recantation to Cauchon with a reverence*] Praise be to God, my brothers, the lamb has returned to the flock; and the shepherd rejoices in her more than in ninety and nine just persons. [*He returns to his seat*].

THE INQUISITOR [*taking the paper from Cauchon*] We declare thee by this act set free from the danger of excommunication in which thou stoodest. [*He throws the paper down to the table*].

JOAN. I thank you.

THE INQUISITOR. But because thou hast sinned most presumptuously against God and the Holy Church, and that thou mayst repent thy errors in solitary contemplation, and be shielded from all temptation to return to them, we, for the good of thy soul, and for a penance that may wipe out thy sins and bring thee finally unspotted to the throne of grace, do condemn thee to eat the bread of sorrow and drink the water of affliction to the end of thy earthly days in perpetual imprisonment.

JOAN [*rising in consternation and terrible anger*] Perpetual imprisonment! Am I not then to be set free?

LADVENU [*mildly shocked*] Set free, child, after such wickedness as yours! What are you dreaming of?

JOAN. Give me that writing. [*She rushes to the table; snatches up the paper; and tears it into fragments*] Light your fire: do you think I dread it as much as the life of a rat in a hole? My voices were right.

LADVENU. Joan! Joan!

JOAN. Yes: they told me you were fools [*the word gives great offence*], and that I was not to listen to your fine words nor trust to your charity. You promised me my life; but you lied [*indignant exclamations*]. You think that life is nothing but not being stone dead. It is not the bread and water I fear: I can live on bread: when have I asked for more? It is no hardship to drink water if the water be clean. Bread has no sorrow for me, and water no affliction. But to shut me from the light of the sky and the sight of the fields and flowers; to chain my feet so that I can never again ride with the soldiers nor climb the hills; to make me breathe foul damp darkness, and keep from me everything that brings me back to the love of God when your wickedness and foolishness tempt me to hate Him: all this is worse than the furnace in the Bible that was heated seven times. I could do without my warhorse; I could drag about in a skirt; I could let the banners and the trumpets and the knights and soldiers pass me and leave me behind as they leave the other women, if only I could still hear the wind in the trees, the larks in the sunshine, the young

142

lambs crying through the healthy frost, and the blessed blessed church bells that send my angel voices floating to me on the wind. But without these things I cannot live; and by your wanting to take them away from me, or from any human creature, I know that your counsel is of the devil, and that mine is of God.

THE ASSESSORS [*in great commotion*] Blasphemy! blasphemy! She is possessed. She said our counsel was of the devil. And hers of God. Monstrous! The devil is in our midst, etc., etc.

D'ESTIVET [*shouting above the din*] She is a relapsed heretic, obstinate, incorrigible, and altogether unworthy of the mercy we have shewn her. I call for her excommunication.

THE CHAPLAIN [*to the Executioner*] Light your fire, man. To the stake with her.

The Executioner and his assistants hurry out through the court-yard.

LADVENU. You wicked girl: if your counsel were of God would He not deliver you?

JOAN. His ways are not your ways. He wills that I go through the fire to His bosom; for I am His child, and you are not fit that I should live among you. That is my last word to you.

The soldiers seize her.

CAUCHON [*rising*] Not yet.

They wait. There is a dead silence. Cauchon turns to the Inquisitor with an inquiring look. The Inquisitor nods affirmatively. They rise solemnly, and intone the sentence antiphonally.

CAUCHON. We decree that thou art a relapsed heretic.

THE INQUISITOR. Cast out from the unity of the Church.

CAUCHON. Sundered from her body.

THE INQUISITOR. Infected with the leprosy of heresy.

CAUCHON. A member of Satan.

THE INQUISITOR. We declare that thou must be excommunicate.

CAUCHON. And now we do cast thee out, segregate thee, and abandon thee to the secular power.

THE INQUISITOR. Admonishing the same secular power that it moderate its judgment of thee in respect of death and division of the limbs. [*He resumes his seat*].

CAUCHON. And if any true sign of penitence appear in thee, to permit our Brother Martin to administer to thee the sacrament of penance.

THE CHAPLAIN. Into the fire with the witch [*he rushes at her, and helps the soldiers to push her out*].

Joan is taken away through the courtyard. The assessors rise in disorder, and follow the soldiers, except Ladvenu, who has hidden his face in his hands.

CAUCHON [*rising again in the act of sitting down*] No, no: this is irregular. The representative of the secular arm should be here to receive her from us.

THE INQUISITOR [*also on his feet again*] That man is an incorrigible fool.

CAUCHON. Brother Martin: see that everything is done in order.

LADVENU. My place is at her side, my lord. You must exercise your own authority. [*He hurries out*].

CAUCHON. These English are impossible: they will thrust her straight into the fire. Look!

He points to the courtyard, in which the glow and flicker of fire can now be seen reddening the May daylight. Only the Bishop and the Inquisitor are left in the court.

CAUCHON [*turning to go*] We must stop that.

THE INQUISITOR [*calmly*] Yes; but not too fast, my lord.

CAUCHON [*halting*] But there is not a moment to lose.

THE INQUISITOR. We have proceeded in perfect order. If the English choose to put themselves in the wrong, it is not our business to put them in the right. A flaw in the procedure may be useful later on: one never knows. And the sooner it is over, the better for that poor girl.

CAUCHON [*relaxing*] That is true. But I suppose we must see this dreadful thing through.

THE INQUISITOR. One gets used to it. Habit is everything. I am accustomed to the fire: it is soon over. But it is a terrible thing to see a young and innocent creature crushed between these mighty forces, the Church and the Law.

CAUCHON. You call her innocent!

THE INQUISITOR. Oh, quite innocent. What does she know of the Church and the Law? She did not understand a word we were saying. It is the ignorant who suffer. Come, or we shall be late for the end.

CAUCHON [*going with him*] I shall not be sorry if we are: I am not so accustomed as you.

They are going out when Warwick comes in, meeting them.

WARWICK. Oh, I am intruding. I thought it was all over. [*He makes a feint of retiring*].

CAUCHON. Do not go, my lord. It is all over.

THE INQUISITOR. The execution is not in our hands, my lord; but it is desirable that we should witness the end. So by your leave— [*He bows, and goes out through the courtyard*].

CAUCHON. There is some doubt whether your people have observed the forms of law, my lord.

WARWICK. I am told that there is some doubt whether your authority runs in this city, my lord. It is not in your diocese. However, if you will answer for that I will answer for the rest.

CAUCHON. It is to God that we both must answer. Good morning, my lord.

WARWICK. My lord: good morning.

They look at one another for a moment with unconcealed hostility. Then Cauchon follows the Inquisitor out. Warwick looks round. Finding himself alone, he calls for attendance.

WARWICK. Hallo: some attendance here! [*Silence*]. Hallo, there! [*Silence*]. Hallo! Brian, you young blackguard, where are you? [*Silence*]. Guard! [*Silence*]. They have all gone to see the burning: even that child.

The silence is broken by someone frantically howling and sobbing.

WARWICK. What in the devil's name—?

The Chaplain staggers in from the courtyard like a demented creature, his face streaming with tears, making the piteous sounds that Warwick has heard. He stumbles to the prisoner's stool, and throws himself upon it with heartrending sobs.

WARWICK [*going to him and patting him on the shoulder*] What is it, Master John? What is the matter?

THE CHAPLAIN [*clutching at his hands*] My lord, my lord: for Christ's sake pray for my wretched guilty soul.

WARWICK [*soothing him*] Yes, yes: of course I will. Calmly, gently—

THE CHAPLAIN [*blubbering miserably*] I am not a bad man, my lord.

WARWICK. No, no: not at all.

THE CHAPLAIN. I meant no harm. I did not know what it would be like.

WARWICK [*hardening*] Oh! You saw it, then?

THE CHAPLAIN. I did not know what I was doing. I am a hot-headed fool; and I shall be damned to all eternity for it.

WARWICK. Nonsense! Very distressing, no doubt; but it was not your doing.

THE CHAPLAIN [*lamentably*] I let them do it. If I had known, I would have torn her from their hands. You dont know: you havnt seen: it is so easy to talk when you dont know. You madden yourself with words: you damn yourself because it feels grand to throw oil on the flaming hell of your own temper. But when it is brought home to you; when you see the thing you have done; when it is blinding your eyes, stifling your nostrils, tearing your heart, then—then— [*Falling on his knees*] O God, take away this sight from me! O Christ, deliver me from this fire that is consuming me! She cried to Thee in the midst of it: Jesus! Jesus! Jesus! She is in Thy bosom; and I am in hell for evermore.

WARWICK [*summarily hauling him to his feet*] Come come, man! you must pull yourself together. We shall have the whole town talking of this. [*He throws him not too gently into a chair at the table*] If you have not the nerve to see these things, why do you not do as I do, and stay away?

THE CHAPLAIN [*bewildered and submissive*] She asked for a cross. A soldier gave her two sticks tied together. Thank God he was an Englishman! I might have done it; but I did not: I am a coward, a mad dog, a fool. But he was an Englishman too.

WARWICK. The fool! they will burn him too if the priests get hold of him.

THE CHAPLAIN [*shaken with a convulsion*] Some of the people laughed at her. They would have laughed at Christ. They were French people, my lord: I know they were French.

WARWICK. Hush? someone is coming. Control yourself.

Ladvenu comes back through the courtyard to Warwick's right hand, carrying a bishop's cross which he has taken from a church. He is very grave and composed.

WARWICK. I am informed that it is all over, Brother Martin.

LADVENU [*enigmatically*] We do not know, my lord. It may have only just begun.

WARWICK. What does that mean, exactly?

LADVENU. I took this cross from the church for her that she might see it to the last: she had only two sticks that she put into her bosom. When the fire crept round us, and she saw that if I held the cross before her I should be burnt myself, she warned me to get down and save myself. My lord: a girl who could think of another's danger in such a moment was not inspired by the devil. When I had to snatch the cross from her sight, she looked up to heaven. And I do not believe that the heavens were empty. I firmly believe that her Savior appeared to her then in His tenderest glory. She called to Him and died. This is not the end for her, but the beginning.

WARWICK. I am afraid it will have a bad effect on the people.

LADVENU. It had, my lord, on some of them. I heard laughter. Forgive me for saying that I hope and believe it was English laughter.

THE CHAPLAIN [*rising frantically*] No: it was not. There was only one Englishman there that disgraced his country; and that was the mad dog, de Stogumber. [*He rushes wildly out, shrieking*] Let them torture him. Let them burn him. I will go pray among her ashes. I am no better than Judas: I will hang myself.

WARWICK. Quick, Brother Martin: follow him: he will do himself some mischief. After him, quick.

Ladvenu hurries out, Warwick urging him. The Executioner comes in by the door behind the judges' chairs; and Warwick, returning, finds himself face to face with him.

WARWICK. Well, fellow: who are you?

THE EXECUTIONER [*with dignity*] I am not addressed as fellow, my lord. I am the Master Executioner of Rouen: it is a highly skilled mystery. I am come to tell your lordship that your orders have been obeyed.

WARWICK. I crave your pardon, Master Executioner; and I will see that you lose nothing by having no relics to sell. I have your word, have I, that nothing remains, not a bone, not a nail, not a hair?

THE EXECUTIONER. Her heart would not burn, my lord; but everything that was left is at the bottom of the river. You have heard the last of her.

WARWICK [*with a wry smile, thinking of what Ladvenu said*] The last of her? Hm! I wonder!

EPILOGUE

A restless fitfully windy night in June 1456, full of summer lightning after many days of heat. King Charles the Seventh of France, formerly Joan's Dauphin, now Charles the Victorious, aged 51, is in bed in one of his royal chateaux. The bed, raised on a dais of two steps, is towards the side of the room so as to avoid blocking a tall lancet window in the middle. Its canopy bears the royal arms in embroidery. Except for the canopy and the huge down pillows there is nothing to distinguish it from a broad settee with bed-clothes and a valance. Thus its occupant is in full view from the foot.

Charles is not asleep: he is reading in bed, or rather looking at the pictures in Fouquet's Boccaccio with his knees doubled up to make a reading desk. Beside the bed on his left is a little table with a picture of the Virgin, lighted by candles of painted wax. The walls are hung from ceiling to floor with painted curtains which stir at times in the draughts. At first glance the prevailing yellow and red in these hanging pictures is somewhat flamelike when the folds breathe in the wind.

The door is on Charles's left, but in front of him close to the corner farthest from him. A large watchman's rattle, handsomely designed and gaily painted, is in the bed under his hand.

Charles turns a leaf. A distant clock strikes the half-hour softly. Charles shuts the book with a clap; throws it aside; snatches up the rattle; and whirls it energetically, making a deafening clatter. Ladvenu enters, 25 years older, strange and stark in bearing, and still carrying the cross from Rouen. Charles evidently does not expect him; for he springs out of bed on the farther side from the door.

CHARLES. Who are you? Where is my gentleman of the bed-chamber? What do you want?

LADVENU [*solemnly*] I bring you glad tidings of great joy. Rejoice, O king; for the taint is removed from your blood, and the stain from your crown. Justice, long delayed, is at last triumphant.

CHARLES. What are you talking about? Who are you?

LADVENU. I am brother Martin.

CHARLES. And who, saving your reverence, may Brother Martin be?

LADVENU. I held this cross when The Maid perished in the fire. Twenty-five years have passed since then: nearly ten thousand days. And on every one of those days I have prayed God to justify His daughter on earth as she is justified in heaven.

CHARLES [*reassured, sitting down on the foot of the bed*] Oh, I remember now. I have heard of you. You have a bee in your bonnet about The Maid. Have you been at the inquiry?

LADVENU. I have given my testimony.

CHARLES. Is it over?

LADVENU. It is over.

CHARLES. Satisfactorily?

LADVENU. The ways of God are very strange.

CHARLES. How so?

LADVENU. At the trial which sent a saint to the stake as a heretic and a sorceress, the truth was told; the law was upheld; mercy was shewn beyond all custom; no wrong was done but the final and dreadful wrong of the lying sentence and the pitiless fire. At this inquiry from which I have just come, there was shameless perjury, courtly corruption, calumny of the dead who did their duty according to their lights, cowardly evasion of the issue, testimony made of idle tales that could not impose on a ploughboy. Yet out of this insult to justice, this defamation of the Church, this orgy of lying and foolishness, the truth is set in the noonday sun on the hilltop; the white robe of innocence is cleansed from the smirch of the burning faggots; the holy life is sanctified; the true heart that lived through the flame is consecrated; a great lie is silenced for ever; and a great wrong is set right before all men.

CHARLES. My friend: provided they can no longer say that I was crowned by a witch and a heretic, I shall not fuss about how the trick has been done. Joan would not have fussed about it if it came all right in the end: she was not that sort: I knew her. Is her rehabilitation complete? I made it pretty clear that there was to be no nonsense about it.

LADVENU. It is solemnly declared that her judges were full of corruption, cozenage, fraud, and malice. Four falsehoods.

CHARLES. Never mind the falsehoods: her judges are dead.

LADVENU. The sentence on her is broken, annulled, annihilated, set aside as non-existent, without value or effect.

CHARLES. Good. Nobody can challenge my consecration now, can they?

LADVENU. Not Charlemagne nor King David himself was more sacredly crowned.

CHARLES [*rising*] Excellent. Think of what that means to me!

LADVENU. I think of what it means to her!

CHARLES. You cannot. None of us ever knew what anything meant to her. She was like nobody else; and she must take care of herself wherever she is; for *I* cannot take care of her; and neither can you, whatever you may think: you are not big enough. But I will tell you this about her. If you could bring her back to life, they would burn her again within six months, for all their present adoration of her. And you would hold up the cross, too, just the same. So [*crossing himself*] let her rest; and let you and I mind our own business, and not meddle with hers.

LADVENU. God forbid that I should have no share in her, nor she in me! [*He turns and strides out as he came, saying*] Henceforth my path will not lie through palaces, nor my conversation be with kings.

CHARLES [*following him towards the door, and shouting after him*] Much good may it do you, holy man! [*He returns to the middle of the chamber, where he halts, and says quizzically to himself*] That was a funny chap. How did he get in? Where are my people? [*He goes impatiently to the bed, and swings the rattle. A rush of wind through the open door sets the walls swaying agitatedly. The candles go out. He calls in the darkness*] Hallo! Someone come and shut the windows: everything is being blown all over the place. [*A flash of summer lightning shews up the lancet window. A figure is seen in silhouette against it*] Who is there? Who is that?

Help! Murder! [*Thunder. He jumps into bed, and hides under the clothes*].

JOAN'S VOICE. Easy, Charlie, easy. What art making all that noise for? No one can hear thee. Thourt asleep. [*She is dimly seen in a pallid greenish light by the bedside*].

CHARLES [*peeping out*] Joan! Are you a ghost, Joan?

JOAN. Hardly even that, lad. Can a poor burnt-up lass have a ghost? I am but a dream that thourt dreaming. [*The light increases: they become plainly visible as he sits up*] Thou looks older, lad.

CHARLES. I am older. Am I really asleep?

JOAN. Fallen asleep over thy silly book.

CHARLES. That's funny.

JOAN. Not so funny as that I am dead, is it?

CHARLES. Are you really dead?

JOAN. As dead as anybody ever is, laddie. I am out of the body.

CHARLES. Just fancy! Did it hurt much?

JOAN. Did what hurt much?

CHARLES. Being burnt.

JOAN. Oh, that! I cannot remember very well. I think it did at first; but then it all got mixed up; and I was not in my right mind until I was free of the body. But do not thou go handling fire and thinking it will not hurt thee. How hast been ever since?

CHARLES. Oh, not so bad. Do you know, I actually lead my army out and win battles? Down into the moat up to my waist in mud and blood. Up the ladders with the stones and hot pitch raining down. Like you.

JOAN. No! Did I make a man of thee after all, Charlie?

CHARLES. I am Charles the Victorious now. I had to be brave because you were. Agnes put a little pluck into me too.

JOAN. Agnes! Who was Agnes?

CHARLES. Agnes Sorel. A woman I fell in love with. I dream of her often. I never dreamed of you before.

JOAN. Is she dead, like me?

CHARLES. Yes. But she was not like you. She was very beautiful.

JOAN [*laughing heartily*] Ha ha! I was no beauty: I was always a rough one: a regular soldier. I might almost as well have been a man. Pity I wasnt: I should not have bothered you all so much then. But my head was in the skies; and the glory of God was upon me; and, man or woman, I should have bothered you as long as your noses were in the mud. Now tell me what has happened since you wise men knew no better than to make a heap of cinders of me?

CHARLES. Your mother and brothers have sued the courts to have your case tried over again. And the courts have declared that your judges were full of corruption and cozenage, fraud and malice.

JOAN. Not they. They were as honest a lot of poor fools as ever burned their betters.

CHARLES. The sentence on you is broken, annihilated, annulled: null, non-existent, without value or effect.

JOAN. I was burned, all the same. Can they unburn me?

CHARLES. If they could, they would think twice before they did it. But they have decreed that a beautiful cross be placed where the stake stood, for your perpetual memory and for your salvation.

JOAN. It is the memory and the salvation that sanctify the cross, not the cross that sanctifies the memory and the salvation. [*She turns away, forgetting him*] I shall outlast that cross. I shall be remembered when men will have forgotten where Rouen stood.

CHARLES. There you go with your self-conceit, the same as ever! I think you might say a word of thanks to me for having had justice done at last.

CAUCHON [*appearing at the window between them*] Liar!

CHARLES. Thank you.

JOAN. Why, if it isnt Peter Cauchon! How are you, Peter? What luck have you had since you burned me?

CAUCHON. None. I arraign the justice of Man. It is not the justice of God.

JOAN. Still dreaming of justice, Peter? See what justice came to with me! But what has happened to thee? Art dead or alive?

CAUCHON. Dead. Dishonored. They pursued me beyond the

grave. They excommunicated my dead body: they dug it up and flung it into the common sewer.

JOAN. Your dead body did not feel the spade and the sewer as my live body felt the fire.

CAUCHON. But this thing that they have done against me hurts justice; destroys faith; saps the foundation of the Church. The solid earth sways like the treacherous sea beneath the feet of men and spirits alike when the innocent are slain in the name of law, and their wrongs are undone by slandering the pure of heart.

JOAN. Well, well, Peter, I hope men will be the better for remembering me; and they would not remember me so well if you had not burned me.

CAUCHON. They will be the worse for remembering me: they will see in me evil triumphing over good, falsehood over truth, cruelty over mercy, hell over heaven. Their courage will rise as they think of you, only to faint as they think of me. Yet God is my witness I was just: I was merciful: I was faithful to my light: I could do no other than I did.

CHARLES [*scrambling out of the sheets and enthroning himself on the side of the bed*] Yes: it is always you good men that do the big mischiefs. Look at me! I am not Charles the Good, nor Charles the Wise, nor Charles the Bold. Joan's worshippers may even call me Charles the Coward because I did not pull her out of the fire. But I have done less harm than any of you. You people with your heads in the sky spend all your time trying to turn the world upside down; but I take the world as it is, and say that top-side-up is right-side-up; and I keep my nose pretty close to the ground. And I ask you, what king of France has done better, or been a better fellow in his little way?

JOAN. Art really king of France, Charlie? Be the English gone?

DUNOIS [*coming through the tapestry on Joan's left, the candles relighting themselves at the same moment, and illuminating his armor and surcoat cheerfully*] I have kept my word: the English are gone.

JOAN. Praised be God! now is fair France a province in heaven. Tell me all about the fighting, Jack. Was it thou that led them?

Wert thou God's captain to thy death?

DUNOIS. I am not dead. My body is very comfortably asleep in my bed at Chateaudun; but my spirit is called here by yours.

JOAN. And you fought them my way, Jack: eh? Not the old way, chaffering for ransoms; but The Maid's way: staking life against death, with the heart high and humble and void of malice, and nothing counting under God but France free and French. Was it my way, Jack?

DUNOIS. Faith, it was any way that would win. But the way that won was always your way. I give you best, lassie. I wrote a fine letter to set you right at the new trial. Perhaps I should never have let the priests burn you; but I was busy fighting; and it was the Church's business, not mine. There was no use in both of us being burned, was there?

CAUCHON. Ay! put the blame on the priests. But I, who am beyond praise and blame, tell you that the world is saved neither by its priests nor its soldiers, but by God and His Saints. The Church Militant sent this woman to the fire; but even as she burned, the flames whitened into the radiance of the Church Triumphant.

The clock strikes the third quarter. A rough male voice is heard trolling an improvised tune.

Rum tum trumpledum,
Bacon fat and rumpledum,
Old Saint mumpledum,
Pull his tail and stumpledum
    O my Ma—ry Ann!

A ruffianly English soldier comes through the curtains and marches between Dunois and Joan.

DUNOIS. What villainous troubadour taught you that doggrel?

THE SOLDIER. No troubadour. We made it up ourselves as we

marched. We were not gentlefolks and troubadours. Music straight
out of the heart of the people, as you might say. Rum tum
trumpledum, Bacon fat and rumpledum, Old Saint mumpledum,
Pull his tail and stumpledum: that dont mean anything, you
know; but it keeps you marching. Your servant, ladies and
gentlemen. Who asked for a saint?

JOAN. Be you a saint?

THE SOLDIER. Yes, lady, straight from hell.

DUNOIS. A saint, and from hell!

THE SOLDIER. Yes, noble captain: I have a day off. Every year,
you know. Thats my allowance for my one good action.

CAUCHON. Wretch! In all the years of your life did you do only
one good action?

THE SOLDIER. I never thought about it: it came natural like.
But they scored it up for me.

CHARLES. What was it?

THE SOLDIER. Why, the silliest thing you ever heard of. I—

JOAN [*interrupting him by strolling across to the bed, where she
sits beside Charles*] He tied two sticks together, and gave them to
a poor lass that was going to be burned.

THE SOLDIER. Right. Who told you that?

JOAN. Never mind. Would you know her if you saw her
again?

THE SOLDIER. Not I. There are so many girls! and they all
expect you to remember them as if there was only one in the
world. This one must have been a prime sort; for I have a day
off every year for her; and so, until twelve o'clock punctually,
I am a saint, at your service, noble lords and lovely ladies.

CHARLES. And after twelve?

THE SOLDIER. After twelve, back to the only place fit for the
likes of me.

JOAN [*rising*] Back there! You! that gave the lass the cross!

THE SOLDIER [*excusing his unsoldierly conduct*] Well, she asked
for it; and they were going to burn her. She had as good a right
to a cross as they had; and they had dozens of them. It was her
funeral, not theirs. Where was the harm in it?

JOAN. Man: I am not reproaching you. But I cannot bear to think of you in torment.

THE SOLDIER [*cheerfully*] No great torment, lady. You see I was used to worse.

CHARLES. What! worse than hell?

THE SOLDIER. Fifteen years' service in the French wars. Hell was a treat after that.

Joan throws up her arms, and takes refuge from despair of humanity before the picture of the Virgin.

THE SOLDIER [*continuing*]—Suits me somehow. The day off was dull at first, like a wet Sunday. I dont mind it so much now. They tell me I can have as many as I like as soon as I want them.

CHARLES. What is hell like?

THE SOLDIER. You wont find it so bad, sir. Jolly. Like as if you were always drunk without the trouble and expense of drinking. Tip top company too: emperors and popes and kings and all sorts. They chip me about giving that young judy the cross; but I dont care: I stand up to them proper, and tell them that if she hadnt a better right to it than they, she'd be where they are. That dumbfounds them, that does. All they can do is gnash their teeth, hell fashion; and I just laugh, and go off singing the old chanty: Rum tum trumple— Hullo! Who's that knocking at the door?

They listen. A long gentle knocking is heard.

CHARLES. Come in.

The door opens; and an old priest, white-haired, bent, with a silly but benevolent smile, comes in and trots over to Joan.

THE NEWCOMER. Excuse me, gentle lords and ladies. Do not let me disturb you. Only a poor old harmless English rector. Formerly chaplain to the cardinal: to my lord of Winchester. John de Stogumber, at your service. [*He looks at them inquiringly*] Did you say anything? I am a little deaf, unfortunately. Also a little—well, not always in my right mind, perhaps; but still, it is a small village with a few simple people. I suffice: I suffice: they love me there; and I am able to do a little good. I am well connected, you see; and they indulge me.

JOAN. Poor old John! What brought thee to this state?

DE STOGUMBER. I tell my folks they must be very careful. I say to them, "If you only saw what you think about you would think quite differently about it. It would give you a great shock. Oh, a great shock." And they all say "Yes, parson: we all know you are a kind man, and would not harm a fly." That is a great comfort to me. For I am not cruel by nature, you know.

THE SOLDIER. Who said you were?

DE STOGUMBER. Well, you see, I did a very cruel thing once because I did not know what cruelty was like. I had not seen it, you know. That is the great thing: you must see it. And then you are redeemed and saved.

CAUCHON. Were not the sufferings of our Lord Christ enough for you?

DE STOGUMBER. No. Oh no: not at all. I had seen them in pictures, and read of them in books, and been greatly moved by them, as I thought. But it was no use: it was not our Lord that redeemed me, but a young woman whom I saw actually burned to death. It was dreadful: oh, most dreadful. But it saved me. I have been a different man ever since, though a little astray in my wits sometimes.

CAUCHON. Must then a Christ perish in torment in every age to save those that have no imagination?

JOAN. Well, if I saved all those he would have been cruel to if he had not been cruel to me, I was not burnt for nothing, was I?

DE STOGUMBER. Oh no; it was not you. My sight is bad: I cannot distinguish your features: but you are not she: oh no: she was burned to a cinder: dead and gone, dead and gone.

THE EXECUTIONER [*stepping from behind the bed curtains on Charles's right, the bed being between them*] She is more alive than you, old man. Her heart would not burn; and it would not drown. I was a master at my craft: better than the master of Paris, better than the master of Toulouse; but I could not kill The Maid. She is up and alive everywhere.

THE EARL OF WARWICK [*sallying from the bed curtains on the other side, and coming to Joan's left hand*] Madam: my congratulations on your rehabilitation. I feel that I owe you an apology.

JOAN. Oh, please dont mention it.

WARWICK [*pleasantly*] The burning was purely political. There was no personal feeling against you, I assure you.

JOAN. I bear no malice, my lord.

WARWICK. Just so. Very kind of you to meet me in that way: a touch of true breeding. But I must insist on apologizing very amply. The truth is, these political necessities sometimes turn out to be political mistakes; and this one was a veritable howler; for your spirit conquered us, madam, in spite of our faggots. History will remember me for your sake, though the incidents of the connection were perhaps a little unfortunate.

JOAN. Ay, perhaps just a little, you funny man.

WARWICK. Still, when they make you a saint, you will owe your halo to me, just as this lucky monarch owes his crown to you.

JOAN [*turning from him*] I shall owe nothing to any man: I owe everything to the spirit of God that was within me. But fancy me a saint! What would St Catherine and St Margaret say if the farm girl was cocked up beside them!

A clerical-looking gentleman in black frockcoat and trousers, and tall hat, in the fashion of the year 1920, *suddenly appears before them in the corner on their right. They all stare at him. Then they burst into uncontrollable laughter.*

THE GENTLEMAN. Why this mirth, gentlemen?

WARWICK. I congratulate you on having invented a most extraordinarily comic dress.

THE GENTLEMAN. I do not understand. You are all in fancy dress: I am properly dressed.

DUNOIS. All dress is fancy dress, is it not, except our natural skins?

THE GENTLEMAN. Pardon me: I am here on serious business, and cannot engage in frivolous discussions. [*He takes out a paper, and assumes a dry official manner*]. I am sent to announce to you that Joan of Arc, formerly known as The Maid, having been the subject of an inquiry instituted by the Bishop of Orleans—

JOAN [*interrupting*] Ah! They remember me still in Orleans.

THE GENTLEMAN [*emphatically, to mark his indignation at the interruption*]—by the Bishop of Orleans into the claim of the said Joan of Arc to be canonized as a saint—

JOAN [*again interrupting*] But I never made any such claim.

THE GENTLEMAN [*as before*]—the Church has examined the claim exhaustively in the usual course, and, having admitted the said Joan successively to the ranks of Venerable and Blessed,—

JOAN [*chuckling*] Me venerable!

THE GENTLEMAN. —has finally declared her to have been endowed with heroic virtues and favored with private revelations, and calls the said Venerable and Blessed Joan to the communion of the Church Triumphant as Saint Joan.

JOAN [*rapt*] Saint Joan!

THE GENTLEMAN. On every thirtieth day of May, being the anniversary of the death of the said most blessed daughter of God, there shall in every Catholic church to the end of time be celebrated a special office in commemoration of her; and it shall be lawful to dedicate a special chapel to her, and to place her image on its altar in every such church. And it shall be lawful and laudable for the faithful to kneel and address their prayers through her to the Mercy Seat.

JOAN. Oh no. It is for the saint to kneel. [*She falls on her knees, still rapt*].

THE GENTLEMAN [*putting up his paper, and retiring beside the Executioner*] In Basilica Vaticana, the sixteenth day of May, nineteen hundred and twenty.

DUNOIS [*raising Joan*] Half an hour to burn you, dear Saint: and four centuries to find out the truth about you!

DE STOGUMBER. Sir: I was chaplain to the Cardinal of Winchester once. They always would call him the Cardinal of England. It would be a great comfort to me and to my master to see a fair statue to The Maid in Winchester Cathedral. Will they put one there, do you think?

THE GENTLEMAN. As the building is temporarily in the hands of the Anglican heresy, I cannot answer for that.

A vision of the statue in Winchester Cathedral is seen through the window.

DE STOGUMBER. Oh look! look! that is Winchester.

JOAN. Is that meant to be me? I was stiffer on my feet.

The vision fades.

THE GENTLEMAN. I have been requested by the temporal
authorities of France to mention that the multiplication of public
statues to The Maid threatens to become an obstruction to
traffic. I do so as a matter of courtesy to the said authorities, but
must point out on behalf of the Church that The Maid's horse
is no greater obstruction to traffic than any other horse.

JOAN. Eh! I am glad they have not forgotten my horse.

A vision of the statue before Rheims Cathedral appears.

JOAN. Is that funny little thing me too?

CHARLES. That is Rheims Cathedral where you had me
crowned. It must be you.

JOAN. Who has broken my sword? My sword was never
broken. It is the sword of France.

DUNOIS. Never mind. Swords can be mended. Your soul is
unbroken; and you are the soul of France.

*The vision fades. The Archbishop and the Inquisitor are now seen
on the right and left of Cauchon.*

JOAN. My sword shall conquer yet: the sword that never struck
a blow. Though men destroyed my body, yet in my soul I have
seen God.

CAUCHON [*kneeling to her*] The girls in the field praise thee; for
thou hast raised their eyes; and they see that there is nothing between them and heaven.

DUNOIS [*kneeling to her*] The dying soldiers praise thee, because thou art a shield of glory between them and the judgment.

THE ARCHBISHOP [*kneeling to her*] The princes of the Church
praise thee, because thou hast redeemed the faith their worldli-
nesses have dragged through the mire.

WARWICK [*kneeling to her*] The cunning counsellors praise thee,
because thou hast cut the knots in which they have tied their own
souls.

DE STOGUMBER [*kneeling to her*] The foolish old men on their deathbeds praise thee, because their sins against thee are turned into blessings.

THE INQUISITOR [*kneeling to her*] The judges in the blindness and bondage of the law praise thee, because thou hast vindicated the vision and the freedom of the living soul.

THE SOLDIER [*kneeling to her*] The wicked out of hell praise thee, because thou hast shewn them that the fire that is not quenched is a holy fire.

THE EXECUTIONER [*kneeling to her*] The tormentors and executioners praise thee, because thou hast shewn that their hands are guiltless of the death of the soul.

CHARLES [*kneeling to her*] The unpretending praise thee, because thou hast taken upon thyself the heroic burdens that are too heavy for them.

JOAN. Woe unto me when all men praise me! I bid you remember that I am a saint, and that saints can work miracles. And now tell me: shall I rise from the dead, and come back to you a living woman?

A sudden darkness blots out the walls of the room as they all spring to their feet in consternation. Only the figures and the bed remain visible.

JOAN. What! Must I burn again? Are none of you ready to receive me?

CAUCHON. The heretic is always better dead. And mortal eyes cannot distinguish the saint from the heretic. Spare them. [*He goes out as he came*].

DUNOIS. Forgive us, Joan: we are not yet good enough for you. I shall go back to my bed. [*He also goes*].

WARWICK. We sincerely regret our little mistake; but political necessities, though occasionally erroneous, are still imperative; so if you will be good enough to excuse me— [*He steals discreetly away*].

THE ARCHBISHOP. Your return would not make me the man you once thought me. The utmost I can say is that though I dare not bless you, I hope I may one day enter into your blessedness Meanwhile, however— [*He goes*].

THE INQUISITOR. I who am of the dead, testified that day that you were innocent. But I do not see how The Inquisition could possibly be dispensed with under existing circumstances. Therefore— [*He goes*].

DE STOGUMBER. Oh, do not come back: you must not come back. I must die in peace. Give us peace in our time, O Lord! [*He goes*].

THE GENTLEMAN. The possibility of your resurrection was not contemplated in the recent proceedings for your canonization. I must return to Rome for fresh instructions. [*He bows formally, and withdraws*].

THE EXECUTIONER. As a master in my profession I have to consider its interests. And, after all, my first duty is to my wife and children. I must have time to think over this. [*He goes*].

CHARLES. Poor old Joan! They have all run away from you except this blackguard who has to go back to hell at twelve o'clock. And what can I do but follow Jack Dunois' example, and go back to bed too? [*He does so*].

JOAN [*sadly*] Goodnight, Charlie.

CHARLES [*mumbling in his pillows*] Goo ni. [*He sleeps. The darkness envelops the bed*].

JOAN [*to the soldier*] And you, my one faithful? What comfort have you for Saint Joan?

THE SOLDIER. Well, what do they all amount to, these kings and captains and bishops and lawyers and such like? They just leave you in the ditch to bleed to death; and the next thing is, you meet them down there, for all the airs they give themselves. What I say is, you have as good a right to your notions as they have to theirs, and perhaps better. [*Settling himself for a lecture on the subject*] You see, it's like this. If— [*the first stroke of midnight is heard softly from a distant bell*]. Excuse me: a pressing appointment— [*He goes on tiptoe*].

The last remaining rays of light gather into a white radiance descending on Joan. The hour continues to strike.

JOAN. O God that madest this beautiful earth, when will it be ready to receive Thy saints? How long, O Lord, how long?

THE APPLE CART

A POLITICAL EXTRAVAGANZA

The Apple Cart, first performed in Warsaw in the Polish version by Floryan Sobieniowski, was produced in England by Sir Barry Jackson at the Malvern Festival on the 19th August, 1929, with Wallace Evennett and Scott Sunderland as Pamphilius and Sempronius, Matthew Boulton as Boanerges, Cedric Hardwicke as King Magnus, Eve Turner as the Princess Royal, Charles Carson as the Prime Minister, Clifford Marquand as the Foreign Secretary, Julian d' Albie as the Colonial Secretary, Aubrey Mallalieu as Chancellor of the Exchequer, Frank Moore as the Home Secretary, Dorothy Holmes-Gore as the Postmistress General, Eileen Beldon as the Powermistress General, Edith Evans as Orinthia, Barbara Everest as Queen Jemima, and James Carew as the American Ambassador.

PREFACE

THE first performances of this play at home and abroad provoked several confident anticipations that it would be published with an elaborate prefatory treatise on Democracy to explain why I, formerly a notorious democrat, have apparently veered round to the opposite quarter and become a devoted Royalist. In Dresden the performance was actually prohibited as a blasphemy against Democracy.

What was all this pother about? I had written a comedy in which a King defeats an attempt by his popularly elected Prime Minister to deprive him of the right to influence public opinion through the press and the platform: in short, to reduce him to a cipher. The King's reply is that rather than be a cipher he will abandon his throne and take his obviously very rosy chance of becoming a popularly elected Prime Minister himself. To those who believe that our system of votes for everybody produces parliaments which represent the people it should seem that this solution of the difficulty is completely democratic, and that the Prime Minister must at once accept it joyfully as such. He knows better. The change would rally the anti-democratic royalist vote against him, and impose on him a rival in the person of the only public man whose ability he has to fear. The comedic paradox of the situation is that the King wins, not by exercising his royal authority, but by threatening to resign it and go to the democratic poll.

That so many critics who believe themselves to be ardent democrats should take the entirely personal triumph of the hereditary king over the elected minister to be a triumph of autocracy over democracy, and its dramatization an act of political apostasy on the part of the author, convinces me that our professed devotion to political principles is only a mask for our idolatry of eminent persons. The Apple Cart exposes the unreality of both democracy and royalty as our idealists conceive them. Our Liberal democrats believe in a figment called a constitutional monarch, a sort of Punch puppet who cannot move until his Prime Minister's fingers are in his sleeves. They believe in another figment called a responsible minister, who moves only when similarly actuated by the million fingers of the electorate. But the most superficial inspection of any two such figures shews that they are not puppets but living men, and that the supposed control of one by the other and of both by the electorate amounts to no more than a not very deterrent fear of uncertain and under ordinary circumstances quite remote consequences. The nearest thing to a puppet in our political system is a Cabinet minister at the head of a great public office. Unless he possesses a very exceptional share of dominating ability and relevant knowledge he is helpless in the hands of his officials. He must sign whatever documents they present to him, and repeat whatever words they put into his mouth when answering questions in parliament, with a docility which cannot be imposed on a king who works at his job; for the king works continuously whilst his ministers are in office for spells only, the spells being few and brief, and often occurring for the first time to men of advanced age with little or no training for and experience of supreme responsibility. George the Third and Queen Victoria were not, like Queen Elizabeth, the natural superiors of their ministers in political genius and general capacity; but they were for many purposes of State necessarily superior to them in experience, in cunning, in exact knowledge of the limits of their responsibility and consequently of the limits of their irresponsibility: in short, in the authority and practical power that these superiorities produce. Very clever men who have come into contact with monarchs have been so impressed that they have attributed to them extraordinary natural qualifications which they, as now visible to us in historical perspective, clearly did not possess. In conflicts between monarchs and popularly elected ministers the monarchs win ever time when personal ability and good sense are at all equally divided.

In The Apple Cart this equality is assumed. It is masked by a strong contrast of character and methods which has led my less considerate critics to complain that I have packed the cards by

making the King a wise man and the minister a fool. But that is
not at all the relation between the two. Both play with equal
skill; and the King wins, not by greater astuteness, but because
he has the ace of trumps in his hand and knows when to play it.
As the prettier player of the two he has the sympathy of the
audience. Not being as pampered and powerful as an operatic
prima donna, and depending as he does not on some commercially
valuable talent but on his conformity to the popular ideal of
dignity and perfect breeding, he has to be trained, and to train
himself, to accept good manners as an indispensable condition
of his intercourse with his subjects, and to leave to the less highly
placed such indulgences as tempers, tantrums, bullyings, sneer-
ings, swearings, kickings: in short, the commoner violences and
intemperances of authority.

His ministers have much laxer standards. It is open to them,
if it will save their time, to get their own way by making scenes,
flying into calculated rages, and substituting vulgar abuse for
argument. A clever minister, not having had a royal training,
will, if he finds himself involved in a duel with his king, be
careful not to choose the weapons at which the king can beat
him. Rather will he in cold blood oppose to the king's perfect
behavior an intentional misbehavior and apparently childish
petulance which he can always drop at the right moment for a
demeanor as urbane as that of the king himself, thus employing
two sets of weapons to the king's one. This gives him the advan-
tages of his own training as a successful ambitious man who has
pushed his way from obscurity to celebrity: a process involving
a considerable use of the shorter and more selfish methods of
dominating the feebly recalcitrant, the unreasonable, the timid,
and the stupid, as well as a sharp sense of the danger of these
methods when dealing with persons of strong character in strong
positions.

In this light the style of fighting adopted by the antagonists
in the scrap between King Magnus and Mr Joseph Proteus is
seen to be a plain deduction from their relative positions and
antecedents, and not a manufactured contrast between demo-

cracy and royalty to the disadvantage of the former. Those who so mistook it are out of date. They still regard democracy as the under dog in the conflict. But to me it is the king who is doomed to be tragically in that position in the future into which the play is projected: in fact, he is visibly at least half in it already; and the theory of constitutional monarchy assumes that he is wholly in it, and has been so since the end of the seventeenth century.

Besides, the conflict is not really between royalty and democracy. It is between both and plutocracy, which, having destroyed the royal power by frank force under democratic pretexts, has bought and swallowed democracy. Money talks: money prints: money broadcasts: money reigns; and kings and labor leaders alike have to register its decrees, and even, by a staggering paradox, to finance its enterprises and guarantee its profits. Democracy is no longer bought: it is bilked. Ministers who are Socialists to the backbone are as helpless in the grip of Breakages Limited as its acknowledged henchmen: from the moment when they attain to what is with unintentional irony called power (meaning the drudgery of carrying on for the plutocrats) they no longer dare even to talk of nationalizing any industry, however socially vital, that has a farthing of profit for plutocracy still left in it, or that can be made to yield a farthing for it by subsidies.

King Magnus's little tactical victory, which bulks so largely in the playhouse, leaves him in a worse plight than his defeated opponent, who can always plead that he is only the instrument of the people's will, whereas the unfortunate monarch, making a desperate bid for dictatorship on the perfectly true plea that democracy has destroyed all other responsibility (has not Mussolini said that there is a vacant throne in every country in Europe waiting for a capable man to fill it?), is compelled to assume full responsibility himself, and face all the reproaches that Mr Proteus can shirk. In his Cabinet there is only one friendly man who has courage, principle, and genuine good manners when he is courteously treated; and that man is an uncompromising republican, his rival for the dictatorship. The splendidly honest and devoted Die-hard lady is too scornfully tactless to help much; but with a little more experience in the art of handling effective men and women as distinguished from the art of handling mass meetings Mr Bill Boanerges might surprise those who, because he makes them laugh, see nothing in him but a caricature.

In short, those critics of mine who have taken The Apple Cart for a story of a struggle between a hero and a roomful of guys have been grossly taken in. It is never safe to take my plays at their suburban face value: it ends in your finding in them only what you bring to them, and so getting nothing for your money.

On the subject of Democracy generally I have nothing to say that can take the problem farther than I have already carried it in my Intelligent Woman's Guide to Socialism and Capitalism. We have to solve two inseparable main problems: the economic problem of how to produce and distribute our subsistence, and the political problem of how to select our rulers and prevent them from abusing their authority in their own interests or those of their class or religion. Our solution of the economic problem is the Capitalist system, which achieves miracles in production, but fails so ludicrously and disastrously to distribute its products rationally, or to produce in the order of social need, that it is always complaining of being paralysed by its "overproduction" of things of which millions of us stand in desperate want. Our solution of the political problem is Votes for Everybody and Every Authority Elected by Vote, an expedient originally devised to prevent rulers from tyrannizing by the very effectual method of preventing them from doing anything, and thus leaving everything to irresponsible private enterprise. But as private enterprise will do nothing that is not profitable to its little self, and the very existence of civilization now depends on the swift and unhampered public execution of enterprises that supersede private enterprise and are not merely profitable but vitally necessary to the whole community, this purely inhibitive check on tyranny has become a stranglehold on genuine democracy. Its painfully evolved machinery of parliament and Party System and Cabinet is so effective in obstruction that we take thirty years by constitutional methods to do thirty minutes work, and shall presently be forced to clear up thirty years arrears in thirty minutes by unconstitutional ones unless we pass a Reform Bill that will make a complete revolution in our political machinery and procedure. When we see parliaments like ours kicked into the gutter by dictators, both in kingdoms and republics, it is foolish to wait until the dictator dies or collapses, and then do nothing but pick the poor old things up and try to scrape the mud off them: the only sane course is to take the step by which the dictatorship could have been anticipated and averted, and construct a political system for rapid positive work instead of slow nugatory work, made to fit into the twentieth century instead of into the sixteenth.

Until we face this task and accomplish it we shall not be able to produce electorates capable of doing anything by their votes except pave the way to their own destruction. An election at present, considered as a means of selecting the best qualified rulers, is so absurd that if the last dozen parliaments had consisted of the candidates who were at the foot of the poll instead of those who were at the head of it there is no reason to suppose that we should have been a step more or less advanced than we are today. In neither case would the electorate have had any real choice of representatives. If it had, we might have had to struggle with parliaments of Titus Oateses and Lord George Gordons dominating a few generals and artists, with Cabinets made up of the sort of orator who is said to carry away his hearers by his eloquence because, having first ascertained by a few cautious feelers what they are ready to applaud, he gives it to them a dozen times over in an overwhelming crescendo, and is in effect carried away by them. As it is, the voters have no real choice of candidates: they have to take what they can get and make the best of it according to their lights, which is often the worst of it by the light of heaven. By chance rather than by judgment they find themselves represented in parliament by a fortunate proportion of reasonably honest and public spirited persons who happen to be also successful public speakers. The rest are in parliament because they can afford it and have a fancy for it or an interest in it.

Last October (1929) I was asked to address the enormous audience created by the new invention of Wireless Broadcast on a range of political and cultural topics introduced by a previous speaker under the general heading of Points of View. Among the topics was Democracy, presented, as usual, in a completely abstract guise as an infinitely beneficent principle in which we must trust though it slay us. I was determined that this time Votes for Everybody and Every Authority Elected by Vote should not escape by wearing its imposing mask. I delivered myself as follows:

Your Majesties, your Royal Highnesses, your Excellencies, your Graces and Reverences, my Lords, Ladies and Gentlemen, fellow-citizens of all degrees: I am going to talk to you about Democracy objectively: that is, as it exists and as we must all reckon with it equally, no matter what our points of view may be. Suppose I were to talk to you not about Democracy, but about the sea, which is in some respects rather like Democracy! We all have our own views of the sea. Some of us hate it and are never well when we are at it or on it. Others love it, and are never so happy as when they are in it or on it or looking at it. Some of us regard it as Britain's natural realm and surest bulwark: others want a Channel Tunnel. But certain facts about the sea are quite independent of our feelings towards it. If I take it for granted that the sea exists, none of you will contradict me. If I say that the sea is sometimes furiously violent and always un-certain, and that those who are most familiar with it trust it least, you will not immediately shriek out that I do not believe in the sea; that I am an enemy of the sea; that I want to abolish the sea; that I am going to make bathing illegal; that I am out to ruin our carrying trade and lay waste all our seaside resorts and scrap the British Navy. If I tell you that you cannot breathe in the sea, you will not take that as a personal insult and ask me indignantly if I consider you inferior to a fish. Well, you must please be equally sensible when I tell you some hard facts about Democracy. When I tell you that it is sometimes furiously violent and always dangerous and treacherous, and that those who are familiar with it as practical statesmen trust it least, you must not at once denounce me as a paid agent of Benito Mussolini, or declare that I have become a Tory Die-hard in my old age, and accuse me of wanting to take away your votes and make an end of parliament, and the franchise, and free speech, and public meeting, and trial by jury. Still less must you rise in your places and give me three rousing cheers as a champion of medieval monarchy and feudalism. I am quite innocent of any such extravagances. All I mean is that whether we are Democrats or Tories, Catholics or Protestants, Communists or Fascists, we are all face to face with a certain force in the world called Democracy; and we must understand the nature of that force whether we want to fight it or to forward it. Our business is not to deny the perils of Democracy, but to provide against them as far as we can, and then consider whether the risks we cannot provide against are worth taking.

Democracy, as you know it, is seldom more than a long word beginning with a capital letter, which we accept reverently or disparage contemptuously without asking any questions. Now we should never accept anything reverently until we have asked it a great many very searching questions, the first two being What are you? and Where do you live? When I put these questions to Democracy the answer I get is "My name is Demos; and I live in the British Empire, the United States of America, and wherever the love of liberty burns in the heart of man. You, my friend Shaw, are a unit of Democracy: your name is also Demos: you are a citizen of a great democratic community: you are a potential constituent of the Parliament of Man, the Federation of the World." At this I usually burst into loud cheers, which do credit to my enthusiastic nature. To-night, however, I shall do nothing of the sort: I shall say "Dont talk nonsense. My name is not Demos: it is Bernard Shaw. My address is not the British Empire, nor the United States of America, nor wherever the love of liberty burns in the heart of man: it is at such and such a

number in such and such a street in London; and it will be
time enough to discuss my seat in the Parliament of Man when
that celebrated institution comes into existence. I dont believe
your name is Demos: nobody's name is Demos; and all I can
make of your address is that you have no address, and are just
a tramp—if indeed you exist at all."

You will notice that I am too polite to call Demos a windbag
or a hot air merchant; but I am going to ask you to begin our
study of Democracy by considering it first as a big balloon,
filled with gas or hot air, and sent up so that you shall be kept
looking up at the sky whilst other people are picking your pockets.
When the balloon comes down to earth every five years or so
you are invited to get into the basket if you can throw out one
of the people who are sitting tightly in it; but as you can afford
neither the time nor the money, and there are forty millions of
you and hardly room for six hundred in the basket, the balloon
goes up again with much the same lot in it and leaves you where
you were before. I think you will admit that the balloon as an
image of Democracy corresponds to the parliamentary facts.

Now let us examine a more poetic conception of Democracy.
Abraham Lincoln is represented as standing amid the carnage
of the battlefield of Gettysburg, and declaring that all that
slaughter of Americans by Americans occurred in order that
Democracy, defined as government *of* the people *for* the people
by the people, should not perish from the earth. Let us pick this
famous peroration to pieces and see what there really is inside
it. (By the way, Lincoln did not really declaim it on the field of
Gettysburg; and the American Civil War was not fought in
defence of any such principle, but, on the contrary, to enable
one half of the United States to force the other half to be governed
as they did not wish to be governed. But never mind that. I
mentioned it only to remind you that it seems impossible for
statesmen to make speeches about Democracy, or journalists to
report them, without obscuring it in a cloud of humbug).

Now for the three articles of the definition. Number One:
Government *of* the people: that, evidently, is necessary: a human

community can no more exist without a government than a human being can exist without a co-ordinated control of its breathing and blood circulation. Number Two: Government *for* the people, is most important. Dean Inge put it perfectly for us when he called Democracy a form of society which means equal consideration for all. He added that it is a Christian principle, and that, as a Christian, he believes in it. So do I. That is why I insist on equality of income. Equal consideration for a person with a hundred a year and one with a hundred thousand is impossible. But Number Three: Government *by* the people, is quite a different matter. All the monarchs, all the tyrants, all the dictators, all the Die-hard Tories are agreed that we must be governed. Democrats like the Dean and myself are agreed that we must be governed with equal consideration for everybody. But we repudiate Number Three on the ground that the people cannot govern. The thing is a physical impossibility. Every citizen cannot be a ruler any more than every boy can be an engine driver or a pirate king. A nation of prime ministers or dictators is as absurd as an army of field marshals. Government by the people is not and never can be a reality: it is only a cry by which demagogues humbug us into voting for them. If you doubt this—if you ask me "Why should not the people make their own laws?" I need only ask you "Why should not the people write their own plays?" They cannot. It is much easier to write a good play than to make a good law. And there are not a hundred men in the world who can write a play good enough to stand daily wear and tear as long as a law must.

Now comes the question, If we cannot govern ourselves, what can we do to save ourselves from being at the mercy of those who *can* govern, and who may quite possibly be thoroughpaced grafters and scoundrels? The primitive answer is that as we are always in a huge majority we can, if rulers oppress us intolerably, burn their houses and tear them to pieces. This is not satisfactory. Decent people never do it until they have quite lost their heads; and when they have lost their heads they are as likely as not to burn the wrong house and tear the wrong man to pieces. When we have what is called a popular movement very few people who take part in it know what it is all about. I once saw a real popular movement in London. People were running excitedly through the streets. Everyone who saw them doing it immediately joined in the rush. They ran simply because everyone else was doing it. It was most impressive to see thousands of people sweeping along at full speed like that. There could be no doubt that it was literally a popular movement. I ascertained afterwards that it was started by a runaway cow. That cow had an important share in my education as a political philosopher; and I can assure you that if you will study crowds, and lost and terrified animals, and things like that, instead of reading books and newspaper articles, you will learn a great deal about politics from them. Most general elections, for instance, are nothing but stampedes. Our last but one was a conspicuous example of this. The cow was a Russian one.

I think we may take it that neither mob violence nor popular movements can be depended on as checks upon the abuse of power by governments. One might suppose that at least they would act as a last resort when an autocrat goes mad and commits outrageous excesses of tyranny and cruelty. But it is a curious fact that they never do. Take two famous cases: those of Nero and Tsar Paul the First of Russia. If Nero had been an ordinary professional fiddler he would probably have been no worse a man than any member of the wireless orchestra. If Paul had been a lieutenant in a line regiment we should never have heard of him. But when these two poor fellows were invested with absolute powers over their fellow-creatures they went mad, and did such appalling things that they had to be killed like mad dogs. Only, it was not the people that rose up and killed them. They were dispatched quite privately by a very select circle of their own bodyguards. For a genuinely democratic execution of unpopular statesmen we must turn to the brothers De Witt, who were torn to pieces by a Dutch mob in the seventeenth century. They were neither tyrants nor autocrats. On the contrary, one of them had been imprisoned and tortured for his resistance to the despotism of William of Orange; and the other had come to meet him as he came out of prison. The mob was on the side of the autocrat. We may take it that the shortest way for a tyrant to get rid of a troublesome champion of liberty is to raise a hue and cry against him as an unpatriotic person, and leave the mob to do the rest after supplying them with a well tipped ringleader. Nowadays this is called direct action by the revolutionary proletariat. Those who put their faith in it soon find that proletariats are never revolutionary, and that their direct action, when it is controlled at all, is usually controlled by police agents.

Democracy, then, cannot be government by the people: it can only be government by consent of the governed. Unfortunately, when democratic statesmen propose to govern us by our own consent, they find that we dont want to be governed at all, and that we regard rates and taxes and rents and death duties as intolerable burdens. What we want to know is how little government we can get along with without being murdered in our beds. That question cannot be answered until we have explained what we mean by getting along. Savages manage to get along. Unruly Arabs and Tartars get along. The only rule in the matter is that the civilized way of getting along is the way of corporate action, not individual action; and corporate action involves more government than individual action.

Thus government, which used to be a comparatively simple affair, today has to manage an enormous development of Socialism and Communism. Our industrial and social life is set in a huge communistic framework of public roadways, streets, bridges, water supplies, power supplies, lighting, tramways, schools, dockyards, and public aids and conveniences, employing a prodigious army of police, inspectors, teachers, and officials of all grades in hundreds of departments. We have found by bitter experience that it is impossible to trust factories, workshops, and mines to private management. Only by stern laws enforced by constant inspection have we stopped the monstrous waste of human life and welfare it cost when it was left uncontrolled by the Government. During the war our attempt to leave the munitioning of the army to private enterprise led us to the verge of defeat and caused an appalling slaughter of our soldiers. When the Government took the work out of private hands and had it done in national factories it was at once successful. The private firms were still allowed to do what little they could; but they had to be taught to do it economically, and to keep their accounts properly, by Government officials. Our big capitalist enterprises now run to the Government for help as a lamb runs to its mother. They cannot even make an extension of the Tube railway in London without Government aid. Unassisted private capitalism is breaking down or getting left behind in all directions. If all our Socialism and Communism and the drastic taxation of unearned incomes which finances it were to stop, our private enterprises would drop like shot stags, and we should all be dead in a month. When Mr Baldwin tried to win the last election by declaring that Socialism had been a failure whenever and wherever it had been tried, Socialism went over him like a steam roller and handed his office to a Socialist Prime Minister. Nothing could save us in the war but a great extension of Socialism; and now it is clear enough that only still greater extensions of it can repair the ravages of the war and keep pace with the growing requirements of civilization.

What we have to ask ourselves, then, is not whether we will have Socialism and Communism or not, but whether Democracy can keep pace with the developments of both that are being forced on us by the growth of national and international corporate action.

Now corporate action is impossible without a governing body. It may be the central Government: it may be a municipal corporation, a county council, a district council, or a parish council. It may be the board of directors of a joint stock company, or of a trust made by combining several joint stock companies. Such boards, elected by the votes of the shareholders, are little States within the State, and very powerful ones, too, some of them. If they have not laws and kings, they have by-laws and chairmen. And you and I, the consumers of their services, are more at the mercy of the boards that organize them than we are at the mercy of parliament. Several active politicians who began as Liberals and are now Socialists have said to me that they were converted by seeing that the nation had to choose, not between governmental control of industry and control by separate private individuals kept in order by their competition for our custom, but between governmental control and control by gigantic trusts wielding great power without responsibility, and having no object but to make as much money out of us as possible. Our Government is at this moment having much more trouble with the private corporations on whom we are dependent for our coals and cotton goods than with France or the United States of America. We are in the hands of our corporate bodies, public or private, for the satisfaction of our everyday needs. Their powers are life and death powers. I need not labor this point: we all know it.

But what we do not all realize is that we are equally dependent on corporate action for the satisfaction of our religious needs. Dean Inge tells us that our general elections have become public auctions at which the contending parties bid against one another for our votes by each promising us a larger share than the other of the plunder of the minority. Now that is perfectly true. The contending parties do not as yet venture to put it exactly in those words; but that is what it comes to. And the Dean's profession obliges him to urge his congregation, which is much wider than that of St Paul's (it extends across the Atlantic), always to vote for the party which pledges itself to go farthest in enabling those of us who have great possessions to sell them and give the price to the poor. But we cannot do this as private persons. It must be done by the Government or not at all. Take my own case. I am not a young man with great possessions; but I am an old man paying enough in income tax and surtax to provide doles for some hundreds of unemployed and old age pensioners. I have not the smallest objection to this: on the contrary, I advocated it strongly for years before I had any income worth taxing. But I could not do it if the Government did not arrange it for me. If the Government ceased taxing my superfluous money and redistributing it among people who have no incomes at all, I could do nothing by myself. What could I do? Can you suggest anything? I could send my war bonds to the Chancellor of the Exchequer and invite him to cancel the part of the National Debt that they represent; and he would undoubtedly thank me in the most courteous official terms for my patriotism. But the poor would not get any of it. The other payers of surtax and income tax and death duties would save the interest they now have to pay on it: that is all. I should only have made the rich richer and myself poorer. I could burn all my share certificates and inform the secretaries of the companies that they might write off that much of their capital indebtedness. The result would be a bigger dividend for the rest of the shareholders, with the poor out in the cold as before. I might sell my war bonds and share certificates for cash, and throw the money into the street to be scrambled for; but it would be snatched up, not by the poorest, but by the best fed and most able-bodied of the scramblers. Besides, if we all tried to sell our bonds and shares—and this is what you have to consider; for Christ's advice was not addressed to me alone but to all who have great possessions—the result would be that their value would fall to nothing, as the Stock Exchange would immediately become a market in which there were all sellers and no buyers. Accordingly, any spare money that the Government leaves me is invested where I can get the highest interest and the best security, as thereby I can make sure that it goes where it is most wanted and gives immediate employment. This is the best I can do without Government interference: indeed any other way of dealing with my spare money would be foolish and demoralizing; but the result is that I become richer and richer, and the poor become relatively poorer and poorer. So you see I cannot even be a Christian except through Government action; and neither can the Dean.

Now let us get down to our problem. We cannot govern ourselves; yet if we entrust the immense powers and revenues which are necessary in an effective modern Government to an absolute monarch or dictator, he goes more or less mad unless he is a quite extraordinary and therefore very seldom obtainable person. Besides, modern government is not a one-man job: it is too big for that. If we resort to a committee or parliament of superior persons, they will set up an oligarchy and abuse their power for their own benefit. Our dilemma is that men in the lump cannot govern themselves; and yet, as William Morris put it, no man is good enough to be another man's master. We need to be governed, and yet to control our governors. But the best governors will not accept any control except that of their own consciences; and, as we who are governed are also apt to abuse any power of control we have, our ignorance, our passions, our private and immediate interests are constantly in conflict with the knowledge, the wisdom, and the public spirit and regard for the future of our best qualified governors.

Still, if we cannot control our governors, can we not at least choose them and change them if they do not suit?

Let me invent a primitive example of democratic choice. It is always best to take imaginary examples: they offend nobody. Imagine then that we are the inhabitants of a village. We have to elect somebody for the office of postman. There are several candidates; but one stands out conspicuously, because he has frequently treated us at the public-house, has subscribed a shilling to our little flower show, has a kind word for the children when he passes, and is a victim of oppression by the squire because his late father was one of our most successful poachers. We elect him triumphantly; and he is duly installed, uniformed, provided with a red bicycle, and given a batch of letters to deliver. As his motive in seeking the post has been pure ambition, he has not thought much beforehand about his duties; and it now occurs to him for the first time that he cannot read. So he hires a boy to come round with him and read the addresses. The boy conceals himself in the lane whilst the postman delivers the letters at the house, takes the Christmas boxes, and gets the whole credit of the transaction. In course of time he dies with a high reputation for efficiency in the discharge of his duties; and we elect another equally illiterate successor on similar grounds. But by this time the boy has grown up and become an institution. He presents himself to the new postman as an established and indispensable feature of the postal system, and finally becomes recognized and paid by the village as such.

Here you have the perfect image of a popularly elected Cabinet Minister and the Civil Service department over which he presides. It may work very well; for our postman, though illiterate, may be a very capable fellow; and the boy who reads the addresses for him may be quite incapable of doing anything more. But this does not always happen. Whether it happens or not, the system is not a democratic reality: it is a democratic illusion. The boy, when he has ability enough to take advantage of the situation, is the master of the man. The person elected to do the work is not really doing it: he is a popular humbug who is merely doing what a permanent official tells him to do. That is how it comes about that we are now governed by a Civil Service which has such enormous power that its regulations are taking the place of the laws of England, though some of them are made for the convenience of the officials without the slightest regard to the convenience or even the rights of the public. And how are our Civil Servants selected? Mostly by an educational test which nobody but an expensively schooled youth can pass, thus making the most powerful and effective part of our government an irresponsible class government.

Now, what control have you or I over the Services? We have votes. I have used mine a few times to see what it is like. Well, it is like this. When the election approaches, two or three persons of whom I know nothing write to me soliciting my vote and enclosing a list of meetings, an election address, and a polling card. One of the addresses reads like an article in The Morning Post, and has a Union Jack on it. Another is like The Daily News or Manchester Guardian. Both might have been compiled from the editorial waste paper baskets of a hundred years ago. A third address, more up-to-date and much better phrased, convinces me that the sender has had it written for him at the headquarters of the Labor Party. A fourth, the most hopelessly out of date of them all, contains scraps of the early English translations of the Communist Manifesto of 1848. I have no guarantee that any of these documents were written by the candidates. They convey nothing whatever to me as to their character or political capacity. The half-tone photographic portraits which adorn the front pages do not even tell me their ages, having been taken twenty years ago. If I go to one of the meetings I find a schoolroom packed with people who find an election meeting cheaper and funnier than a theatre. On the platform sit one or two poor men who have worked hard to keep party politics alive in the constituency. They ought to be the candidates; but they have no more chance of such eminence than they have of possessing a Rolls-Royce car. They move votes of confidence in the candidate, though as the candidate is a stranger to them and to everybody else present nobody can possibly feel any such confidence. They lead the applause for him; they prompt him when questions are asked; and when he is completely floored they jump up and cry "Let me answer that, Mr Chairman!" and then pretend that he has answered it. The old shibboleths are droned over; and nothing has any sense or reality in it except the vituperation of the opposition party, which is received with shouts of relief by the audience. Yet it is nothing but an exhibition of bad manners. If I vote for one of these candidates, and he or she is elected, I am supposed to be enjoying a democratic control of the government —to be exercising government *of* myself, *for* myself, *by* myself. Do you wonder that the Dean cannot believe such nonsense? If I believed it I should not be fit to vote at all. If this is Democracy, who can blame Signor Mussolini for describing it as a putrefying corpse?

The candidates may ask me what more they can do for me but present themselves and answer any questions I may put to them. I quite admit that they can do nothing; but that does not mend matters. What I should like is a real test of their capacity. Shortly before the war a doctor in San Francisco discovered that if a drop of a candidate's blood can be obtained on a piece of blotting paper it is possible to discover within half an hour what is wrong with him physically. What I am waiting for is the discovery of a process by which on delivery of a drop of his blood or a lock of his hair we can ascertain what is right with him mentally. We could then have a graded series of panels of capable persons for all employments, public or private, and not allow any person, however popular, to undertake the employment of governing us unless he or she were on the appropriate panel. At the lower end of the scale there would be a panel of persons qualified to take part in a parish meeting; at the higher end a panel of persons qualified to act as Secretaries of State for Foreign Affairs or Finance Ministers. At present not more than two per thousand of the population would be available for the highest panel. I should then be in no danger of electing a postman and finding that he could neither read nor write. My choice of candidates would be perhaps more restricted than at present; but I do not desire liberty to choose windbags and nincompoops to represent me in parliament; and my power to choose between one qualified candidate and another would give me as much control as is either possible or desirable. The voting and counting would be done by machinery: I should connect my telephone with the proper office; touch a button; and the machinery would do the rest.

Pending such a completion of the American doctor's discovery, how are we to go on? Well, as best we can, with the sort of government that our present system produces. Several reforms are possible without any new discovery. Our present parliament is obsolete: it can no more do the work of a modern State than Julius Cæsar's galley could do the work of an Atlantic liner. We need in these islands two or three additional federal legislatures, working on our municipal committee system instead of our parliamentary party system. We need a central authority to coordinate the federal work. Our obsolete little internal frontiers must be obliterated, and our units of local government enlarged to dimensions compatible with the recent prodigious advances in facility of communication and co-operation. Commonwealth affairs and supernational activities through the League of Nations or otherwise will have to be provided for, and Cabinet function to be transformed. All the pseudo-democratic obstructive functions of our political machinery must be ruthlessly scrapped, and the general problem of government approached from a positive viewpoint at which mere anarchic national sovereignty as distinguished from self-government will have no meaning.

I must conclude by warning you that when everything has been done that can be done, civilization will still be dependent on the consciences of the governors and the governed. Our natural dispositions may be good; but we have been badly brought up, and are full of anti-social personal ambitions and prejudices and snobberies. Had we not better teach our children to be better citizens than ourselves? We are not doing that at present. The Russians *are*. That is my last word. Think over it.

So much for my broadcast on Democracy! And now a word about Breakages, Limited. Like all Socialists who know their business I have an exasperated sense of the mischief done by our system of private Capitalism in setting up huge vested interests in destruction, waste, and disease. The armament firms thrive on war; the glaziers gain by broken windows; the operating surgeons depend on cancer for their children's bread; the distillers and brewers build cathedrals to sanctify the profits of drunkenness; and the prosperity of Dives costs the privation of a hundred Lazaruses.

The title Breakages, Limited, was suggested to me by the fate of that remarkable genius, the late Alfred Warwick Gattie, with whom I was personally acquainted. I knew him first as the author of a play. He was a disturbing man, afflicted—or, as it turned out, gifted—with chronic hyperæsthesia, feeling everything violently and expressing his feelings vehemently and on occasion volcanically. I concluded that he was not sufficiently cold-blooded to do much as a playwright; so that when, having lost sight of him for some years, I was told that he had made an invention of first-rate importance, I was incredulous, and concluded that the invention was only a Utopian project. Our friend Henry Murray was so provoked by my attitude that to appease him I consented to investigate the alleged great invention in person on Gattie's promising to behave like a reasonable being during the process, a promise which he redeemed with the greatest dignity, remaining silent whilst an engineer explained his miracles to me, and contenting himself with the reading of a brief statement shewing that the adoption of his plan would release from industry enough men to utterly overwhelm the Central Empires with whom we were then at war.

I approached the investigation very sceptically. Our friend spoke of "the works." I could not believe that Gattie had any works, except in his fervid imagination. He mentioned "the company." That was more credible: anyone may form a company; but that it had any resources seemed to me doubtful. However, I suffered myself to be taken to Battersea; and there, sure enough, I found a workshop, duly labelled as the premises of The New Transport Company, Limited, and spacious enough to accommodate a double railway line with a platform. The affair was unquestionably real, so far. The platform was not provided with a station: its sole equipment was a table with a row of buttons on it for making electrical contacts. Each line of railway had on it a truck with a steel lid. The practical part of the proceedings began by placing an armchair on the lid of one of the trucks and seating me in it. A brimming glass of water was then set at my feet. I could not imagine what I was expected to do with the water or what was going to happen; and there was a suggestion of electrocution about the chair which made me nervous. Gattie then sat down majestically at the table on the platform with his hand hovering over the buttons. Intimating that the miracle would take place when my truck passed the other truck, he asked me to choose whether it should occur at the first passage or later, and to dictate the order in which it should be repeated. I was by that time incapable of choosing; so I said the sooner the better; and the two trucks started. When the other truck had passed mine I found myself magically sitting on it, chair and all, with the glass of water unspilled at my feet.

The rest of the story is a tragi-comedy. When I said to Gattie apologetically (I felt deeply guilty of having underrated him) that I had never known that he was an engineer, and had taken him to be the usual amateur inventor with no professional training, he told me that this was exactly what he was: just like Sir Christopher Wren. He had been concerned in an electric lighting business, and had been revolted by the prodigious number of breakages of glass bulbs involved by the handling of the crates in which they were packed for transport by rail and road. What was needed was a method of transferring the crates from truck to truck, and from truck to road lorry, and from road lorry to warehouse lift without shock, friction, or handling. Gattie, being, I suppose, by natural genius an inventor though by mistaken vocation a playwright, solved the mechanical problem without apparent difficulty, and offered his nation the means of effecting an enormous saving of labor and smash. But instead of being received with open arms as a social benefactor he found himself up against Breakages, Limited. The glass blowers whose employment was threatened, the exploiters of the great industry of repairing our railway trucks (every time a goods train is stopped a series of 150 violent collisions is propagated from end to end of the train, as those who live within earshot know to their cost), and the railway porters who dump the crates from truck to platform and then hurl them into other trucks, shattering bulbs, battering cans, and too often rupturing themselves in the process, saw in Gattie an enemy of the human race, a wrecker of homes and a starver of innocent babes. He fought them undauntedly; but they were too strong for him; and in due time his patents expired and he died almost unrecognized, whilst Unknown Soldiers were being canonized throughout the world. So far, The Apple Cart is his only shrine; and as it does not even bear his name, I have written it here pending its tardy appearance in the roll of fame.

I must not leave my readers to assume that Gattie was an easy man to deal with, or that he handled the opposition in a conciliatory manner with due allowance for the inertia of a somewhat unimaginative officialdom which had not, like myself, sat on his trucks, and probably set him down as a Utopian (a species much dreaded in Government departments) and thus missed the real point, which was that he was an inventor. Like many men of genius he could not understand why things obvious to him should not be so at once to other people, and found it easier to believe that they were corrupt than that they could be so stupid. Once, after I had urged him to be more diplomatic, he brought me, with some pride, a letter to the Board of Trade which he considered a masterpiece of tact and good temper. It contained not a word descriptive of his invention; and it began somewhat in this fashion: "Sir: If you are an honest man you cannot deny that among the worst abuses of this corrupt age is the acceptance of city directorships by retired members of the Board of Trade." Clearly it was not easy for the Board of Trade to deal with an inventor who wished to interest them, not in his new machines, but in the desirability of its abolishing itself as infamous.

The last time I saw him he called on me to unfold a new scheme of much greater importance, as he declared, than his trucks. He was very interesting on that occasion. He began by giving me a vivid account of the pirates who used to infest the Thames below London Bridge before the docks were built. He described how the docks had come into existence not as wharves for loading and unloading but as strongholds in which ships and their cargoes could be secure from piracy. They are now, he declared, a waste of fabulously valuable ground; and their work should be done in quite another way. He then produced plans of a pier to be built in the middle of the river, communicating directly by rail and road with the shore and the great main lines. The ships would come alongside the pier; and by a simple system of hoists the contents of their holds would be lifted out and transferred (like myself in the armchair) to railway trucks or motor lorries without being touched by a human hand and therefore without risk of breakage. It was all so masterly, so simple in its complexity, so convincing as to its practicability, and so prodigiously valuable socially, that I, taking it very seriously, proceeded to discuss what could be done to interest the proper people in it.

To my amazement Gattie began to shew unmistakeable signs

of disappointment and indignation. "You do not seem to understand me," he said. "I have shewn you all this mechanical stuff merely by way of illustration. What I have come to consult you about is a great melodrama I am going to write, the scene of which will be the Pool of London in the seventeenth century among the pirates!"

What could I or anyone do with a man like that? He was naïvely surprised when I laughed; and he went away only half persuaded that his scheme for turning the docks into building land; expediting the Thames traffic; saving much dangerous and demoralizingly casual labor; and transfiguring the underpaid stevedore into a fullfed electrician, was stupendously more important than any ridiculous melodrama. He admitted that there was of course all that in it; but I could see that his heart was in the melodrama.

As it was evident that officialdom, writhing under his insults and shocked by his utter lack of veneration for bigwigs, besides being hampered as all our Government departments are by the vested interests of Breakages, Limited, would do nothing for him, I induced some less embarrassed public persons to take a ride in the trucks and be convinced that they really existed and worked. But here again the parallel between Gattie and his fellow-amateur Sir Christopher Wren came in. Wren was not content to redesign and rebuild St Paul's: he wanted to redesign London as well. He was quite right: what we have lost by not letting him do it is incalculable. Similarly, Gattie was not content to improve the luggage arrangements of our railways: he would not listen to you if your mind was not large enough to grasp the immediate necessity for a new central clearing house in Farringdon Market, connected with the existing railways by a system of new tubes. He was of course right; and we have already lost by sticking to our old ways more than the gigantic sum his scheme would have cost. But neither the money nor the enterprise was available just then, with the war on our hands. The Clearing House, like the Thames pier, remains on paper; and Gattie is in his grave. But I still hold that there must have been something great in a man who, having not only imagined them but invented their machinery, could, far from being crushed by their rejection, exclaim "Perish all my mechanical trash if only it provides material for one bad play!"

This little history will explain how it actually did provide material for Breakages, Limited, and for the bitter cry of the Powermistress General. Not until Breakages is itself broken will it cease to have a message for us.

AYOT ST LAWRENCE,
   March 1930.

THE APPLE CART

ACT I

An office in the royal palace. Two writing-tables face each other from opposite sides of the room, leaving plenty of room between them. Each table has a chair by it for visitors. The door is in the middle of the farthest wall. The clock shews that it is a little past 11; and the light is that of a fine summer morning.

Sempronius, smart and still presentably young, shews his right profile as he sits at one of the tables opening the King's letters. Pamphilius, middle aged, shews his left as he leans back in his chair at the other table with a pile of the morning papers at his elbow, reading one of them. This goes on silently for some time. Then Pamphilius, putting down his paper, looks at Sempronius for a moment before speaking.

PAMPHILIUS. What was your father?

SEMPRONIUS [*startled*] Eh?

PAMPHILIUS. What was your father?

SEMPRONIUS. My father?

PAMPHILIUS. Yes. What was he?

SEMPRONIUS. A Ritualist.

PAMPHILIUS. I dont mean his religion. I mean his profession. And his politics.

SEMPRONIUS. He was a Ritualist by profession, a Ritualist in politics, a Ritualist in religion: a raging emotional Die Hard Ritualist right down to his boots.

PAMPHILIUS. Do you mean that he was a parson?

SEMPRONIUS. Not at all. He was a sort of spectacular artist. He got up pageants and Lord Mayors' Shows and military tattoos and big public ceremonies and things like that. He arranged the last two coronations. That was how I got my job here in the palace. All our royal people knew him quite well: he was behind the scenes with them.

PAMPHILIUS. Behind the scenes and yet believed they were all real!

SEMPRONIUS. Yes. Believed in them with all his soul.

PAMPHILIUS. Although he manufactured them himself?

SEMPRONIUS. Certainly. Do you suppose a baker cannot believe sincerely in the sacrifice of the Mass or in holy communion because he has baked the consecrated wafer himself?

PAMPHILIUS. I never thought of that.

SEMPRONIUS. My father might have made millions in the theatres and film studios. But he refused to touch them because the things they represented hadnt really happened. He didnt mind doing the christening of Queen Elizabeth in Shakespear's Henry the Eighth because that had really happened. It was a celebration of royalty. But not anything romantic: not though they offered him thousands.

PAMPHILIUS. Did you ever ask him what he really thought about it all? But of course you didnt: one cant ask one's father anything about himself.

SEMPRONIUS. My dear Pam: my father never thought. He didnt know what thought meant. Very few people do, you know. He had vision: actual bodily vision, I mean; and he had an oddly limited sort of imagination. What I mean is that he couldnt imagine anything he didnt see; but he could imagine that what he did see was divine and holy and omniscient and omnipotent and eternal and everything that is impossible if only it looked splendid enough, and the organ was solemn enough, or the military bands brassy enough.

PAMPHILIUS. You mean that he had to get everything from outside.

SEMPRONIUS. Exactly. He'd never have felt anything if he hadnt had parents to feel about in his childhood, and a wife and babies to feel about when he grew up. He'd never have known anything if he hadnt been taught at school. He couldnt amuse himself: he had to pay oceans of money to other people to amuse him with all sorts of ghastly sports and pleasures that would have driven me into a monastery to escape from them. You see it was all ritual: he went to the Riviera every winter just as he went to church.

PAMPHILIUS. By the way, is he alive? I should like to know him.

SEMPRONIUS. No. He died in 1962, of solitude.

PAMPHILIUS. What do you mean? of solitude?

SEMPRONIUS. He couldnt bear to be alone for a moment: it was death to him. Somebody had to be with him always.

PAMPHILIUS. Oh well, come! That was friendly and kindly. It shews he had something inside him after all.

SEMPRONIUS. Not a bit. He never talked to his friends. He played cards with them. They never exchanged a thought.

PAMPHILIUS. He must have been a rum old bird.

SEMPRONIUS. Not rum enough to be noticed. There are millions like him.

PAMPHILIUS. But what about his dying of solitude? Was he imprisoned?

SEMPRONIUS. No. His yacht struck a reef and sank somewhere off the north of Scotland; and he managed to swim to an uninhabited island. All the rest were drowned; and he was not taken off for three weeks. When they found him he was melancholy mad, poor old boy; and he never got over it. Simply from having no one to play cards with, and no church to go to.

PAMPHILIUS. My dear Sem: one isnt alone on an uninhabited island. My mother used to stand me on the table and make me recite about it.

[*He declaims*]

> To sit on rocks; to muse o'er flood and fell;
> To slowly trace the forest's shady scene
> Where things that own not man's dominion dwell
> And mortal foot hath ne'er or rarely been;
> To climb the trackless mountain all unseen
> With the wild flock that never needs a fold;
> Alone o'er steeps and foaming falls to lean:
> This is not solitude: 'tis but to hold
> Converse with Nature's charms, and view her stores
>   unrolled.

SEMPRONIUS. Now you have hit the really funny thing about my father. All that about the lonely woods and the rest of it—what you call Nature—didnt exist for him. It had to be something artificial to get at him. Nature to him meant nakedness; and nakedness only disgusted him. He wouldnt look at a horse grazing in a field; but put splendid trappings on it and stick it into a procession and he just loved it. The same with men and women: they were nothing to him until they were dressed up in fancy costumes and painted and wigged and titled. To him the sacredness of the priest was the beauty of his vestment, the loveliness of women the dazzle of their jewels and robes, the charm of the countryside not in its hills and trees, nor in the blue smoke from its cottages in the winter evenings, but of its temples, palaces, mansions, park gates, and porticoed country houses. Think of the horror of that island to him! A void! a place where he was deaf and dumb and blind and lonely! If only there had been a peacock with its tail in full bloom it might have saved his reason; but all the birds were gulls; and gulls are not decorative. Our King could have lived there for thirty years with nothing but his own thoughts. You would have been all right with a fishing rod and a golf ball with a bag of clubs. I should have been as happy as a man in a picture gallery looking at the dawns and sunsets, the changing seasons, the continual miracle of life ever renewing itself. Who could be dull with pools in the rocks to watch? Yet my father, with all that under his nose, was driven mad by its nothingness. They say that where there is nothing the king loses his rights. My father found that where there is nothing a man loses his reason and dies.

PAMPHILIUS. Let me add that in this palace, when the king's letters are not ready for him at 12 o'clock, a secretary loses his job.

SEMPRONIUS [*hastily resuming his work*] Yes, devil take you: why did you start me talking before I had finished my work? You have nothing to do but pretend to read the newspapers for him; and when you say "Nothing particular this morning, Sir," all he says is "Thank Heaven!" But if I missed a note from one of his aunts inviting herself to tea, or a little line from Orinthia the Beloved marked "Strictly private and confidential: to be opened by His Majesty alone," I should never hear the end of it. He had six love letters yesterday; and all he said when I told him was "Take them to the Queen." He thinks they amuse her. I believe they make her as sick as they make me.

PAMPHILIUS. Do Orinthia's letters go to the Queen?

SEMPRONIUS. No, by George! Even I dont read Orinthia's letters. My instructions are to read everything; but I take care to forget to open hers. And I notice that I am not rebuked for my negligence.

PAMPHILIUS [*thoughtfully*] I suppose—

SEMPRONIUS. Oh shut up, Pam. I shall never get through if you go on talking.

PAMPHILIUS. I was only going to say that I suppose—

SEMPRONIUS. Something about Orinthia. Dont. If you indulge in supposition on that subject, you will lose your job, old chap. So stow it.

PAMPHILIUS. Dont cry out before Orinthia is hurt, young chap. I was going to say that I suppose you know that that bull-roarer Boanerges has just been taken into the Cabinet as President of the Board of Trade, and that he is coming here today to give the King a piece of his mind, or what he calls his mind, about the crisis.

SEMPRONIUS. What does the King care about the crisis? There has been a crisis every two months since he came to the throne; but he has always been too clever for them. He'll turn Boanerges inside out after letting him roar the palace down.

Boanerges enters, dressed in a Russian blouse and peaked cap, which he keeps on. He is fifty, heavily built and aggressively self-assertive.

BOANERGES. Look here. The King has an appointment with me at a quarter to twelve. How long more am I to be kept waiting?

SEMPRONIUS [*with cheerful politeness*] Good morning. Mr Boanerges, I think.

BOANERGES [*shortly, but a little taken aback*] Oh, good morning to you. They say that politeness is the punctuality of kings—

SEMPRONIUS. The other way about, Mr Boanerges. Punctuality is the politeness of kings; and King Magnus is a model in that respect. Your arrival cannot have been announced to His Majesty. I will see about it. [*He hurries out*].

PAMPHILIUS. Be seated, Mr Boanerges.

BOANERGES [*seating himself by Pamphilius's writing-table*] A nice lot of young upstarts you have in this palace, Mr—?

PAMPHILIUS. Pamphilius is my name.

BOANERGES. Oh yes: Ive heard of you. Youre one of the king's private secretaries.

PAMPHILIUS. I am. And what have our young upstarts been doing to you, Mr Boanerges?

BOANERGES. Well, I told one of them to tell the king I was here, and to look sharp about it. He looked at me as if I was a performing elephant, and took himself off after whispering to another flunkey. Then this other chap comes over to me and pretends he doesnt know who I am! asks me can he have my name! "My lad" I said: "not to know me argues yourself unknown. You know who I am as well as I do myself. Go and tell the king I'm waiting for him, d'ye see?" So he took himself off with a flea in his ear. I waited until I was fed up with it, and then opened the nearest door and came in here.

PAMPHILIUS. Young rascals! However, my friend Mr Sempronius will make it all right for you.

BOANERGES. Oh: that was Sempronius, was it. Ive heard of him too.

PAMPHILIUS. You seem to have heard of all of us. You will be quite at home in the palace now that you are a Cabinet Minister. By the way, may I congratulate you on your appointment—or rather congratulate the Cabinet on your accession?

SEMPRONIUS [*returning*] The King. [*He goes to his table and takes the visitor's chair in his hand, ready for the king's instructions as to where to place it*].

Pamphilius rises. Boanerges turns to the door in his chair without rising. King Magnus, a tallish studious looking gentleman of 45 or thereabouts, enters, and comes quickly down the middle of the room to Boanerges, proffering his hand cordially.

MAGNUS. You are very welcome to my little palace, Mr Boanerges. Wont you sit down?

BOANERGES. I am sitting down.

MAGNUS. True, Mr Boanerges. I had not noticed it. Forgive me: force of habit.

He indicates to Sempronius that he wishes to sit near Boanerges, on his right. Sempronius places the chair accordingly.

MAGNUS. You will allow me to be seated?

BOANERGES. Oh, sit down, man, sit down. Youre in your own house: ceremony cuts no ice with me.

MAGNUS [*gratefully*] Thank you.

The King sits. Pamphilius sits. Sempronius returns to his table and sits.

MAGNUS. It is a great pleasure to meet you at last, Mr Boanerges. I have followed your career with interest ever since you contested Northampton twenty-five years ago.

BOANERGES [*pleased and credulous*] I should just think you have, King Magnus. I have made you sit up once or twice, eh?

MAGNUS [*smiling*] Your voice has shaken the throne oftener than that.

BOANERGES [*indicating the secretaries with a jerk of his head*] What about these two? Are they to overhear everything that passes?

MAGNUS. My private secretaries. Do they incommode you?

BOANERGES. Oh, they dont incommode me. I am ready to have our talk out in Trafalgar Square if you like, or have it broadcast on the wireless.

MAGNUS. That would be a treat for my people, Mr Boanerges. I am sorry we have not arranged for it.

BOANERGES [*gathering himself together formidably*] Yes; but do you realize that I am going to say things to you that have never been said to a king before?

MAGNUS. I am very glad indeed to hear it, Mr Boanerges. I

thought I had already heard everything that could possibly be said to a king. I shall be grateful for the smallest novelty.

BOANERGES. I warn you it wont be agreeable. I am a plain man, Magnus: a very plain man.

MAGNUS. Not at all, I assure you—

BOANERGES [*indignantly*] I was not alluding to my personal appearance.

MAGNUS [*gravely*] Nor was I. Do not deceive yourself, Mr Boanerges. You are very far from being a plain man. To me you have always been an Enigma.

BOANERGES [*surprised and enormously flattered: he cannot help smiling with pleasure*] Well, perhaps I am a bit of an enigma. Perhaps I am.

MAGNUS [*humbly*] I wish I could see through you, Mr Boanerges. But I have not your sort of cleverness. I can only ask you to be frank with me.

BOANERGES [*now convinced that he has the upper hand*] You mean about the crisis. Well, frank is just what I have come here to be. And the first thing I am going to tell you frankly about it is that this country has got to be governed, not by you, but by your ministers.

MAGNUS. I shall be only too grateful to them for taking a very difficult and thankless job off my hands.

BOANERGES. But it's not on your hands. It's on your ministers' hands. You are only a constitutional monarch. Do you know what they call that in Belgium?

MAGNUS. An indiarubber stamp, I think. Am I right?

BOANERGES. You are, King Magnus. An indiarubber stamp. Thats what you have got to be; and dont you forget it.

MAGNUS. Yes: thats what we are most of the time: both of us.

BOANERGES [*outraged*] What do you mean? both of us?

MAGNUS. They bring us papers. We sign. You have no time to read them, luckily for you. But I am expected to read everything. I do not always agree; but I must sign: there is nothing else to be done. For instance, death warrants. Not only have I to sign the death warrants of persons who in my opinion ought not to be

killed; but I may not even issue death warrants for a great many
people who in my opinion ought to be killed.

BOANERGES [*sarcastic*] Youd like to be able to say "Off with
his head!" wouldnt you?

MAGNUS. Many men would hardly miss their heads, there is so
little in them. Still, killing is a serious business: at least the person
who is to be killed is usually conceited enough to think so. I
think that if there were a question of killing me—

BOANERGES [*grimly*] There may be, someday. I have heard it
discussed.

MAGNUS. Oh, quite. I have not forgotten King Charles's head.
Well, I hope it will be settled by a living person and not by an
indiarubber stamp.

BOANERGES. It will be settled by the Home Secretary, your
duly constituted democratic minister.

MAGNUS. Another indiarubber stamp, eh?

BOANERGES. At present, perhaps. But not when I am Home
Secretary, by Jingo! Nobody will make an indiarubber stamp of
Bill Boanerges: take that from me.

MAGNUS. Of course not. Is it not curious how people idealize
their rulers? In the old days the king—poor man!—was a god,
and was actually called God and worshipped as infallible and
omniscient. That was monstrous—

BOANERGES. It was silly: just silly.

MAGNUS. But was it half so silly as our pretence that he is an
indiarubber stamp? The ancient Roman emperor-god had not
infinite wisdom, infinite knowledge, infinite power; but he had
some: perhaps even as much as his ministers. He was alive, not
dead. What man has ever approached either a king or a minister
and been able to pick him up from the table and use him as one
picks up and uses a piece of wood and brass and rubber? Permanent officials of your department will try to pick you up and use
you like that. Nineteen times out of twenty you will have to let
them do it, because you cannot know everything; and even if you
could you cannot do everything and be everywhere. But what
about the twentieth time?

BOANERGES. The twentieth time they will find they are up against Bill Boanerges, eh?

MAGNUS. Precisely. The indiarubber stamp theory will not work, Mr Boanerges.˙The old divine theory worked because there is a divine spark in us all; and the stupidest or worst monarch or minister, if not wholly god, is a bit of a god—an attempt at a god—however little the bit and unsuccessful the attempt. But the indiarubber stamp theory breaks down in every real emergency, because no king or minister is the very least little bit like a stamp: he is a living soul.

BOANERGES. A soul, eh? You kings still believe in that, I suppose.

MAGNUS. I find the word convenient: it is short and familiar. But if you dislike being called a soul, let us say that you are animate matter as distinguished from inanimate.

BOANERGES [*not quite liking this*] I think I'd rather you called me a soul, you know, if you must call me anything at all. I know I have too much matter about me: the doctor says I ought to knock off a stone or two; but there's something more to me than beef. Call it a soul if you like; only not in a superstitious sense, if you understand me.

MAGNUS. Perfectly. So you see, Mr Boanerges, that though we have been dealing with one another for less than ten minutes, you have already led me into an intellectual discussion which shews that we are something more than a pair of indiarubber stamps. You are up against my brains, such as they are.

BOANERGES. And you are up against mine.

MAGNUS [*gallantly*] There can be no doubt of that.

BOANERGES [*grinning*] Such as they are, eh?

MAGNUS. It is not for me to make that qualification, except in my own case. Besides, you have given your proofs. No common man could have risen as you have done. As for me, I am a king because I was the nephew of my uncle, and because my two elder brothers died. If I had been the stupidest man in the country I should still be its king. I have not won my position by my merits. If I had been born as you were in the—in the—

BOANERGES. In the gutter. Out with it. Picked up by a policeman at the foot of Captain Coram's statue. Adopted by the policeman's grandmother, bless her!

MAGNUS. Where should *I* have been if the policeman had
picked me up?

BOANERGES. Ah! Where? Not, mind you, that you mightnt
have done pretty well for yourself. Youre no fool, Magnus: I will
say that for you.

MAGNUS. You flatter me.

BOANERGES. Flatter a king! Never. Not Bill Boanerges.

MAGNUS. Yes, yes: everybody flatters the King. But everybody
has not your tact, and, may I say? your good nature.

BOANERGES [*beaming with self-satisfaction*] Perhaps not. Still, I
am a Republican, you know.

MAGNUS. That is what has always surprised me. Do you really
think that any man should have as much personal power as the
presidents of the republican States have? Ambitious kings envy
them.

BOANERGES. What's that? I dont follow that.

MAGNUS [*smiling*] You cannot humbug me, Mr Boanerges. I
see why you are a Republican. If the English people send me packing and establish a republic, no man has a better chance of being
the first British president than you.

BOANERGES [*almost blushing*] Oh! I dont say that.

MAGNUS. Come come! You know it as well as I do. Well, if it
happens you will have ten times more power than I have ever had.

BOANERGES [*not quite convinced*] How can that be? Youre King.

MAGNUS. And what is the King? An idol set up by a group of
plutocrats so that they can rule the country with the King as their
scapegoat and puppet. Presidents, now, are chosen by the people,
who always want a Strong Man to protect them against the rich.

BOANERGES. Well, speaking as a bit of a Strong Man myself,
there may be something in that. But honestly, Magnus, as man
to man, do you tell me youd rather be a president than what you
are?

MAGNUS. By no means. You wouldnt believe me if I did; and

you would be quite right. You see, my security is very comfortable.

BOANERGES. Security, eh? You admitted just now that even a modest individual like myself had given your throne a shake or two.

MAGNUS. True. You are quite right to remind me of it. I know that the monarchy may come to an end at any moment. But while the monarchy lasts—while it lasts, mark you—I am very secure. I escape the dreadful and demoralizing drudgery of electioneering. I have no voters to please. Ministers come and ministers go; but I go on for ever. The terrible precariousness of your position—

BOANERGES. What's that? How is my position precarious?

MAGNUS. The vote may go against you. Yours is a Trade Union seat, is it not? If the Hydro-Electric Workers Federation throw you over, where would you be?

BOANERGES [*confidently*] They wont throw me over. You dont know the workers, Magnus: you have never been a worker.

MAGNUS [*lifts his eyebrows*]!

BOANERGES [*continuing*] No king on earth is as safe in his job as a Trade Union official. There is only one thing that can get him sacked; and that is drink. Not even that, as long as he doesnt actually fall down. I talk democracy to these men and women. I tell them that they have the vote, and that theirs is the kingdom and the power and the glory. I say to them "You are supreme: exercise your power." They say, "That's right: tell us what to do"; and I tell them. I say "Exercise your vote intelligently by voting for me." And they do. That's democracy; and a splendid thing it is too for putting the right men in the right place.

MAGNUS. Magnificent! I have never heard it better described. You certainly have a head on you, Mr Boanerges. You should write an essay on democracy. But—

BOANERGES. But what?

MAGNUS. Suppose a man with a bigger voice comes along! Some fool! Some windbag! Some upstart with a platform trick of gulling the multitude!

BOANERGES. Youre thinking of Iky Jacobus? He is only a talker. [*Snapping his fingers*] I dont give that for him.

MAGNUS. I never even heard of Mr Jacobus. But why do you say "only a talker." Talkers are very formidable rivals for popular favor. The multitude understands talk: it does not understand work. I mean brain work, like yours and mine.

BOANERGES. That's true. But I can talk Iky's head off.

MAGNUS. Lucky man: you have all the trumps in your hand. But I, who cannot pretend to your gifts, am very glad that Iky cannot upset me as long as I am the nephew of my uncle.

A young lady, dressed for walking, rushes in impetuously.

THE YOUNG LADY. Papa: I cannot find the address—

MAGNUS [*cutting her short*] No, no, no, dear: not now. Go away. Dont you see that I am particularly engaged with the President of the Board of Trade? You must excuse my unruly daughter, Mr Boanerges. May I present her to you? Alice, my eldest girl. Mr Boanerges, dear.

ALICE. Oh! Are you the great Mr Boanerges?

BOANERGES [*rising in a glow of gratification*] Well, I dont call myself that, you know. But I believe the expression is in use, as you might say. I am very pleased indeed to make the acquaintance of the Princess Royal.

They shake hands.

ALICE. Why do you wear such awful clothes, Mr Boanerges?

MAGNUS [*remonstrating*] My dear—!

ALICE [*continuing*] I cant go out walking with you in that [*pointing to his blouse*].

BOANERGES. The uniform of Labor, your Royal Highness. I'm proud of it.

ALICE. Oh yes, I know all that, Mr Boanerges. But you dont look the part, you know. Anyone can see that you belong naturally to the governing class.

BOANERGES [*struck by this view*] In a way, perhaps. But I have earned my bread by my hands. Not as a laborer, though. I am a skilled mechanic, or was until my country called on me to lead it.

MAGNUS [*to Alice*] Well, my dear, you have broken up a most interesting conversation, and to me a most instructive one. It's no use our trying to go on, Mr Boanerges: I must go and find what my daughter wants, though I strongly suspect that what she really came in for was to see my wonderful new minister. We shall meet again presently: you know that the Prime Minister is calling on me today with some of his colleagues—including, I hope, yourself—to discuss the crisis. [*Taking Alice's arm and turning towards the door*] You will excuse us, wont you?

BOANERGES [*graciously*] Oh, thats all right. Thats quite all right.

The King and the Princess go out, apparently much pleased.

BOANERGES [*to Sempronius and Pamphilius comprehensively*] Well, say what you will, the King is no fool. Not when you know how to handle him.

PAMPHILIUS. Of course, that makes all the difference.

BOANERGES. And the girl hasnt been spoilt. I was glad to see that. She doesnt seem to know that she is the Princess Royal, eh?

SEMPRONIUS. Well, she wouldnt dream of giving herself any airs with you.

BOANERGES. What! Isnt she always like that?

SEMPRONIUS. Oh no. It's not everybody who is received as you have been. I hope you have enjoyed your visit.

BOANERGES. Well, I pulled Magnus through it pretty well: eh? Dont you think so?

SEMPRONIUS. He was pleased. You have a way with you, Mr President.

BOANERGES. Well, perhaps I have, perhaps I have.

A bevy of five Cabinet Ministers, resplendent in diplomatic uniforms, enters. Proteus the Prime Minister has on his left, Pliny, Chancellor of the Exchequer, goodhumored and conciliatory, and Nicobar, Foreign Secretary, snaky and censorious. On his right Crassus, Colonial Secretary, elderly and anxious, and Balbus, Home Secretary, rude and thoughtless.

BALBUS. Holy snakes! look at Bill. [*To Boanerges*] Go home and dress yourself properly, man.

NICOBAR. Where do you think you are?

CRASSUS. Who do you think you are?

PLINY [*fingering the blouse*] Where did you buy it, Bill?

BOANERGES [*turning on them like a baited bear*] Well, if you come to that, who do you think you are, the lot of you?

PROTEUS [*conciliatory*] Never mind them, Bill: theyre jealous because they didnt think of it themselves. How did you get on with the King?

BOANERGES. Right as rain, Joe. You leave the King to me. I know how to handle him. If I'd been in the Cabinet these last three months there'd have been no crisis.

NICOBAR. He put you through it, did he?

BOANERGES. What do you mean? put me through it? Is this a police office?

PLINY. The third degree is not unknown in this palace, my boy. [*To Pamphilius*] Did the matron take a hand?

PAMPHILIUS. No. But the Princess Alice happened to drop in. She was greatly impressed by the President.

They all laugh uproariously at Boanerges.

BOANERGES. What in hell are you laughing at?

PROTEUS. Take no notice of them, Bill: they are only having their bit of fun with you as a new comer. Come, lads! enough of fooling: lets get to business. [*He takes the chair vacated by the King*].

Sempronius and Pamphilius at once rise and go out busily, taking some of their papers with them. Pliny takes Boanerges' chair, Balbus that of Sempronius, Boanerges that of Pamphilius, whilst Nicobar and Crassus take chairs from the wall and sit down at the ends of the writing tables, left and right of the Prime Minister respectively.

PROTEUS. Now to start with, do you chaps all fully realize that though we wiped out every other party at the last election, and have been in power for the last three years, this country has been governed during that time by the King?

NICOBAR. I dont see that. We—

PROTEUS [*impatiently*] Well, if you dont, then for Heaven's sake either resign and get out of the way of men who can see facts and look them in the face, or else take my job and lead the party yourself.

NICOBAR. The worst of you is that you wont face the fact that though youre Prime Minister youre not God Almighty. The king cant do anything except what we advise him to do. How can he govern the country if we have all the power and he has none?

BOANERGES. Dont talk silly, Nick. This indiarubber stamp theory doesnt work. What man has ever approached a king or a minister and been able to pick him up from the table and use him as youd use a bit of wood and brass and rubber? The King's a live man; and what more are you, with your blessed advice?

PLINY. Hullo, Bill! You have been having your mind improved by somebody.

BOANERGES. What do you mean? Isnt it what I have always said?

PROTEUS [whose nerves are on edge] Oh, will you stop squabbling. What are we going to say to the King when he comes in? If you will only hold together and say the same thing—or let me say it—he must give way. But he is as artful as the very devil. He'll have a pin to stick into the seat of every man of you. If you all start quarrelling and scolding and bawling, which is just what he wants you to do, it will end in his having his own way as usual, because one man that has a mind and knows it can always beat ten men who havnt and dont.

PLINY. Steady, Prime Minister. Youre overwrought.

PROTEUS. It's enough to drive a man mad. I am sorry.

PLINY [changing the subject] Where's Mandy?

NICOBAR. And Lizzie?

PROTEUS. Late as usual. Come! Business, business, business.

BOANERGES [thunderously] Order order!

PROTEUS. The King is working the Press against us. The King is making speeches. Things have come to a head. He said yesterday on the opening of the new Chamber of Commerce building that the king's veto is the only remaining defence of the people against corrupt legislation.

BOANERGES. So it is, by Jingo. What other defence is there? Democracy? Yah! We know what Democracy is worth. What we need is a Strong Man.

NICOBAR [*sneering*] Yourself, for instance.

BOANERGES. I should stand a better chance than you, my lad, if we were a Republic, and the people could choose. And let me tell you that a republican president has more power than a king because the people know that they need a Strong Man to protect them against the rich.

PROTEUS [*flinging himself back in his chair in desperation*] This is a nice thing. Two Labor papers have leading articles this morning supporting the King; and the latest addition to the Cabinet here is a King's man. I resign.

General consternation except on the part of Nicobar, who displays cheerful unconcern, and of Boanerges, who squares himself with an iron face.

PLINY.   ⎫ No: dont do that, Joe.
BALBUS.   ⎬ What! Now! You cant. You mustnt.
CRASSUS.   ⎭ Of course not. Out of the question.

PROTEUS. No use. [*Rising*] I resign, I tell you. You can all go to the devil. I have lost my health, and almost lost my reason, trying to keep this Cabinet together in the face of the cunningest enemy popular government has ever had to face. I have had enough of it. [*Sitting down again*] I resign.

CRASSUS. But not at such a moment as this. Dont let us swop horses when crossing a stream.

NICOBAR. Why not, if the horse you have got is subject to hysterics?

BOANERGES. Not to mention that you may have more than one horse at your disposal.

PROTEUS. Right you are. Perfectly true. Take my job, Nick. It's vacant for you, Bill. I wish you joy of it.

PLINY. Now boys, boys, boys: be good. We cant make a new Cabinet before Magnus comes in. You have something in your pocket, Joe. Out with it. Read it to them.

PROTEUS [*taking a paper from his pocket*] What I was going to propose—and you can take it or leave it—is an ultimatum.

CRASSUS. Good!

PROTEUS. Either he signs this, or—[*he pauses significantly*]—!

NICOBAR. Or what?

PROTEUS [*disgusted*] Oh, you make me sick.

NICOBAR. Youre sick already, by your own account. I only ask, suppose he refuses to sign your ultimatum?

PROTEUS. You call yourself a Cabinet Minister, and you cant answer that!

NICOBAR. No I cant. I press my question. You said he must sign, OR. I ask, or what?

PROTEUS. Or we resign and tell the country that we cant carry on the King's Government under conditions which destroy our responsibility.

BALBUS. Thatll do it. He couldnt face that.

CRASSUS. Yes: thatll bunker him.

PROTEUS. Is that agreed?

PLINY. ⎫
CRASSUS. ⎬ Yes, yes, yes, 'greed 'greed 'greed.
BALBUS. ⎭

BOANERGES. I retain an open mind. Let us hear the ultimatum.

NICOBAR. Yes: lets hear it.

PROTEUS. Memorandum of understanding arrived at—

The King enters, with Amanda, Postmistress General, a merry lady in uniform like the men, on his left, and Lysistrata, Powermistress General, a grave lady in academic robes, on his right. All rise. The Prime Minister's face darkens.

MAGNUS. Welcome, gentlemen. I hope I am not too early. [*Noting the Prime Minister's scowl*] Am I intruding?

PROTEUS. I protest. It is intolerable. I call a conference of my Cabinet to consider our position in regard to the prerogative; and I find the two lady members, the Postmistress General and the Powermistress General, closeted with your Majesty instead of being in their places to confer with me.

LYSISTRATA. You mind your own business, Joe.

MAGNUS. Oh no: really, really, my dear Lysistrata, you must not take that line. Our business is to meddle in everybody's business. A Prime Minister is a busybody by profession. So is a monarch. So are we all.

LYSISTRATA. Well, they say everybody's business is nobody's business, which is just what Joe is fit for. [*She takes a chair from the wall with a powerful hand, and swings it forward to the inside corner of Sempronius's table, where she stands waiting for the King to sit down.*]

PROTEUS. This is what I have to put up with when I am on the verge of a nervous breakdown [*he sits down distractedly, and buries his face in his hands*].

AMANDA [*going to him and petting him*] Come, Joe! dont make a scene. You asked for it, you know.

NICOBAR. What do you go provoking Lizzie for like that? You know she has a temper.

LYSISTRATA. There is nothing whatever wrong with my temper. But I am not going to stand any of Joe's nonsense; and the sooner he makes up his mind to that the smoother our proceedings are likely to be.

BOANERGES. I protest. I say, let us be dignified. I say, let us respect ourselves and respect the throne. All this Joe and Bill and Nick and Lizzie: we might as well be hobnobbing in a fried fish shop. The Prime Minister is the prime minister: he isnt Joe. The Powermistress isnt Lizzie: she's Lysis Traitor.

LYSISTRATA [*who has evidently been a schoolmistress*] Certainly not, Bill. She is Ly Sistrata. You had better say Lizzie: it is easier to pronounce.

BOANERGES [*scornfully*] Ly Sistrata! A more foolish affectation I never heard: you might as well call me Bo Annerjeeze [*he flings himself into his chair*].

MAGNUS [*sweetly*] Shall we sit, ladies and gentlemen?

Boanerges hastily rises and sits down again. The King sits in Pliny's chair. Lysistrata and the rest of the men resume their seats, leaving Pliny and Amanda standing. Amanda takes an empty chair in each hand and plants them side by side between the King and the table of Pamphilius.

AMANDA. There you are, Plin. [*She sits next the table*].

PLINY. Ta ta, Mandy. Pardon me: I should have said Amanda. [*He sits next the King*].

AMANDA. Dont mention it, darling.

BOANERGES. Order, order!

AMANDA [*waves him a kiss*]!!

MAGNUS. Prime Minister: the word is with you. Why have you all simultaneously given me the great pleasure of exercising your constitutional right of access to the sovereign?

LYSISTRATA. Have I that right, sir; or havnt I?

MAGNUS. Most undoubtedly you have.

LYSISTRATA. You hear that, Joe?

PROTEUS. I——

BALBUS. Oh for Heaven's sake dont contradict her, Joe. We shall never get anywhere at this rate. Come to the crisis.

NICOBAR. ⎫
CRASSUS. ⎬ [*together*] ⎰ Yes yes: the crisis!
PLINY. ⎭ ⎱ Yes yes: come along!
⎰ The crisis: out with it!

BALBUS. The ultimatum. Lets have the ultimatum.

MAGNUS. Oh, there is an ultimatum! I gathered from yesterday's evening papers that there is a crisis—another crisis. But the ultimatum is new to me. [*To Proteus*] Have you an ultimatum?

PROTEUS. Your Majesty's allusion to the royal veto in a speech yesterday has brought matters to a head.

MAGNUS. It was perhaps indelicate. But you all allude so freely to your own powers—to the supremacy of Parliament and the voice of the people and so forth—that I fear I have lost any little delicacy I ever possessed. If you may flourish your thunderbolts why may I not shoulder my little popgun of a veto and strut up and down with it for a moment?

NICOBAR. This is not a subject for jesting—

MAGNUS [*interrupting him quickly*] I am not jesting, Mr Nicobar. But I am certainly trying to discuss our differences in a good-humored manner. Do you wish me to lose my temper and make scenes?

AMANDA. Oh please no, your Majesty. We get enough of that from Joe.

PROTEUS. I pro—

MAGNUS [*his hand persuasively on the Prime Minister's arm*]

Take care, Prime Minister: take care: do not let your wily Post-mistress General provoke you to supply the evidence against yourself.

All the rest laugh.

PROTEUS [*coolly*] I thank your Majesty for the caution. The Postmistress General has never forgiven me for not making her First Lady of the Admiralty. She has three nephews in the navy.

AMANDA. Oh you— [*She swallows the epithet, and contents herself with shaking her fist at the Premier*].

MAGNUS. Tch-tch-tch! Gently, Amanda, gently. Three very promising lads: they do you credit.

AMANDA. I never wanted them to go to sea. I could have found them better jobs in the Post Office.

MAGNUS. Apart from Amanda's family relations, am I face to face with a united Cabinet.

PLINY. No, sir. You are face to face with a squabbling Cabinet; but, on the constitutional question, united we stand: divided we fall.

BALBUS. That is so.

NICOBAR. Hear hear!

MAGNUS. What is the constitutional question? Do you deny the royal veto? or do you object only to my reminding my subjects of its existence?

NICOBAR. What we say is that the king has no right to remind his subjects of anything constitutional except by the advice of the Prime Minister, and in words which he has read and approved.

MAGNUS. Which Prime Minister? There are so many of them in the Cabinet.

BOANERGES. There! Serves you all right! Arnt you ashamed of yourselves? But I am not surprised, Joseph Proteus. I own I like a Prime Minister that knows how to be a Prime Minister. Why do you let them take the word out of your mouth every time?

PROTEUS. If His Majesty wants a Cabinet of dumb dogs he will not get it from my party.

BALBUS. Hear, hear, Joe!

MAGNUS. Heaven forbid! The variety of opinion in the Cabinet is always most instructive and interesting. Who is to be its spokesman today?

PROTEUS. I know your Majesty's opinion of me; but let—

MAGNUS [*before he can proceed*] Let me state it quite frankly. My opinion of you is that no man knows better than you when to speak and when to let others speak for you; when to make scenes and threaten resignation; and when to be as cool as a cucumber.

PROTEUS [*not altogether displeased*] Well, sir, I hope I am not such a fool as some fools think me. I may not always keep my temper. You would not be surprised at that if you knew how much temper I have to keep. [*He straightens up and becomes impressively eloquent*]. At this moment my cue is to shew you, not my own temper, but the temper of my Cabinet. What the Foreign Secretary and the Chancellor of the Exchequer and the Home Secretary have told you is true. If we are to carry on your government we cannot have you making speeches that express your own opinions and not ours. We cannot have you implying that everything that is of any value in our legislation is your doing and not ours. We cannot have you telling people that their only safeguard against the political encroachments of big business whilst we are doing nothing but bungling and squabbling is your power of veto. It has got to stop, once for all.

BALBUS. }
NICOBAR. } Hear hear!

PROTEUS. Is that clear?

MAGNUS. Far clearer than I have ever dared to make it, Mr Proteus. Except, by the way, on one point. When you say that all this of which you complain must cease once for all, do you mean that henceforth I am to agree with you or you with me?

PROTEUS. I mean that when you disagree with us you are to keep your disagreement to yourself.

MAGNUS. That would be a very heavy responsibility for me. If I see you leading the nation over the edge of a precipice may I not warn it?

BALBUS. It is our business to warn it, not yours.

MAGNUS. Suppose you dont do your business! Suppose you dont see the danger! That has happened. It may happen again.

CRASSUS [*insinuating*] As democrats, I think we are bound to proceed on the assumption that such a thing cannot happen.

BOANERGES. Rot! It's happening all the time until somebody has the gumption to put his foot down and stop it.

CRASSUS. Yes: I know. But that is not democracy.

BOANERGES. Democracy be— [*he leaves the word unspoken*]! I have thirty years experience of democracy. So have most of you. I say no more.

BALBUS. Wages are too high, if you ask me. Anybody can earn from five to twenty pounds a week now, and a big dole when there is no job for him. And what Englishman will give his mind to politics as long as he can afford to keep a motor car?

NICOBAR. How many voted at the last election? Not seven per cent of the register.

BALBUS. Yes; and the seven per cent were only a parcel of sillies playing at ins and outs. To make democracy work in Crassus's way we need poverty and hardship.

PROTEUS [*emphatically*] And we have abolished poverty and hardship. That is why the people trust us. [*To the King*] And that is why you will have to give way to us. We have the people of England in comfort—solid middle class comfort—at our backs.

MAGNUS. No: we have not abolished poverty and hardship. Our big business men have abolished them. But how? By sending our capital abroad to places where poverty and hardship still exist: in other words, where labor is cheap. We live in comfort on the imported profits of that capital. We are all ladies and gentlemen now.

NICOBAR. Well, what more do you want?

PLINY. You surely dont grudge us our wonderful prosperity, sir.

MAGNUS. I want it to last.

NICOBAR. Why shouldnt it last? [*Rising*] Own the truth. You had rather have the people poor, and pose as their champion and savior, than have to admit that the people are better off under our government—under our squabbling and bungling, as you call it.

MAGNUS. No: it was the Prime Minister who used those expressions.

NICOBAR. Dont quibble: he was quoting them from your reptile press. What I say is that we stand for high wages, and you are always belittling and opposing the men that pay them. Well, the voters like high wages. They know when they are well off; and they dont know what you are grumbling about; and thats what will beat you every time you try to stir them against us [*he resumes his seat*].

PLINY. There is no need to rub it in like that, Nick. We're all good friends. Nobody objects to prosperity.

MAGNUS. You think this prosperity is safe?

NICOBAR. Safe!

PLINY. Oh come, sir! Really!

BALBUS. Safe! Look at my constituency: Northeast-by-north Birmingham, with its four square miles of confectionery works! Do you know that in the Christmas cracker trade Birmingham is the workshop of the world?

CRASSUS. Take Gateshead and Middlesbrough alone! Do you know that there has not been a day's unemployment there for five years past, and that their daily output of chocolate creams totals up to twenty thousand tons?

MAGNUS. It is certainly a consoling thought that if we were peacefully blockaded by the League of Nations we could live for at least three weeks on our chocolate creams.

NICOBAR. You neednt sneer at the sweets: we turn out plenty of solid stuff. Where will you find the equal of the English golf club?

BALBUS. Look at the potteries: the new crown Derby! the new Chelsea! Look at the tapestries! Why, Greenwich Goblin has chased the French stuff out of the market.

CRASSUS. Dont forget our racing motor boats and cars, sir:

the finest on earth, and all individually designed. No cheap mass production stuff there.

PLINY. And our live stock! Can you beat the English polo pony?

AMANDA. Or the English parlormaid? She wins in all the international beauty shows.

PLINY. Now Mandy, Mandy! None of your triviality.

MAGNUS. I am not sure that the British parlormaid is not the only real asset in your balance sheet.

AMANDA [*triumphant*] Aha! [*To Pliny*] You go home to bed and reflect on that, old man.

PROTEUS. Well, sir? Are you satisfied that we have the best paid proletariat in the world on our side?

MAGNUS [*gravely*] I dread revolution.

All except the two women laugh uproariously at this.

BOANERGES. I must join them there, sir. I am as much against chocolate creams as you are: they never agree with me. But a revolution in England!!! Put that out of your head, sir. Not if you were to tear up Magna Carta in Trafalgar Square, and light the fires of Smithfield to burn every member of the House of Commons.

MAGNUS. I was not thinking of a revolution in England. I was thinking of the countries on whose tribute we are living. Suppose it occurs to them to stop paying it! That has happened before.

PLINY. Oh no, sir: no, no, no. What would become of their foreign trade with us?

MAGNUS. At a pinch, I think they could do without the Christmas crackers.

CRASSUS. Oh, thats childish.

MAGNUS. Children in their innocence are sometimes very practical, Mr Colonial Secretary. The more I see of the sort of prosperity that comes of your leaving our vital industries to big business men as long as they keep your constituents quiet with high wages, the more I feel as if I were sitting on a volcano.

LYSISTRATA [*who has been listening with implacable contempt to the discussion, suddenly breaks in in a sepulchral contralto*] Hear hear! My department was perfectly able and ready to deal with the supply of power from the tides in the north of Scotland, and you gave it away, like the boobs you are, to the Pentland Firth Syndicate: a gang of foreign capitalists who will make billions out of it at the people's expense while we are bungling and squabbling. Crassus worked that. His uncle is chairman.

CRASSUS. A lie. A flat lie. He is not related to me. He is only my stepson's father-in-law.

BALBUS. I demand an explanation of the words bungling and squabbling. We have had quite enough of them here today. Who are you getting at? It was not I who bungled the Factory Bill. I found it on my desk when I took office, with all His Majesty's suggestions in the margin; and you know it.

PROTEUS. Have you all done playing straight into His Majesty's hand, and making my situation here impossible?

Guilty silence.

PROTEUS [*proceeding deliberately and authoritatively*] The question before us is not one of our manners and our abilities. His Majesty will not press that question, because if he did he would oblige us to raise the question of his own morals.

MAGNUS [*starts*] What!

BALBUS. Good, Joe!

CRASSUS [*aside to Amanda*] Thats got him.

MAGNUS. Am I to take that threat seriously, Mr Proteus?

PROTEUS. If you try to prejudice what is a purely constitutional question by personal scandal, it will be easy enough for us to throw your mud back. In this conflict we are the challengers. You have the choice of weapons. If you choose scandal, we'll take you on at that. Personally I shall deplore it if you do. No good will come of washing our dirty linen in public. But dont make any mistake as to what will happen. I will be plain with you: I will dot the Is and cross the Ts. You will say that Crassus is a jobber.

CRASSUS [*springing up*] I—

PROTEUS [*fiercely crushing him*] Sit down. Leave this to me.

CRASSUS [*sits*] I a jobber! Well!

PROTEUS [*continuing*] You will say that I should never have given the Home Office to a bully like Balbus—

BALBUS [*intimidated by the fate of Crassus, but unable to forbear a protest*] Look here, Joe—

PROTEUS. You shut up, Bert. It's true.

BALBUS [*subsides with a shrug*]!

PROTEUS. Well, what will happen? There will be no denials, no excuses, no vindications. We shall not fall into that trap, clever as you are at setting it. Crassus will say just simply that you are a freethinker. And Balbus will say that you are a libertine.

THE MALE CABINET [*below their breaths*] Aha-a-a-a-h!!!

PROTEUS. Now, King Magnus! Our cards are on the table. What have you to say?

MAGNUS. Admirably put! People ask how it is that with all these strong characters around you hold your own as the only possible Prime Minister, in spite of your hysterics and tantrums, your secretiveness and your appalling laziness—

BALBUS [*delighted*] Hear hear! Youre getting it now, Joe.

MAGNUS [*continuing*] But when the decisive moment comes, they find out what a wonderful man you are.

PROTEUS. I am not a wonderful man. There is not a man or woman here whose job I could do as well as they do it. I am Prime Minister for the same reason that all Prime Ministers have been Prime Ministers: because I am good for nothing else. But I can keep to the point—when it suits me. And I can keep you to the point, sir, whether it suits you or not.

MAGNUS. At all events you do not flatter kings. One of them, at least, is grateful to you for that.

PROTEUS. Kings, as you and I very well know, rule their ministers by flattering them; and now that you are the only king left in the civilized half of Europe Nature seems to have concentrated in you all the genius for flattery that she used to have to divide between half a dozen kings, three emperors, and a Sultan.

MAGNUS. But what interest has a king in flattering a subject?

AMANDA. Suppose she's a goodlooking woman, sir!

NICOBAR. Suppose he has a lot of money, and the king's hard up!

PROTEUS. Suppose he is a Prime Minister, and you can do nothing except by his advice.

MAGNUS [smiling with his utmost charm] Ah, there you have hit the nail on the head. Well, I suppose I must surrender. I am beaten. You are all too clever for me.

BOANERGES. Well, nothing can be fairer than that.

PLINY [rubbing his hands] You are a gentleman, sir. We shant rub it in, you know.

BALBUS. Ever the best of friends. I am the last to kick a man when he's down.

CRASSUS. I may be a jobber; but nobody shall say that I am an ungenerous opponent.

BOANERGES [suddenly overwhelmed with emotion, rises and begins singing in stentorian tones]

> Should auld acquaintance be forgot,
> And never brought to mind—

Amanda bursts into uncontrollable laughter. The King looks reproachfully at her, struggling hard to keep his countenance. The others are beginning to join in the chorus when Proteus rises in a fury.

PROTEUS. Are you all drunk?

Dead silence. Boanerges sits down hastily. The other singers pretend that they have disapproved of his minstrelsy.

PROTEUS. You are at present engaged in a tug of war with the King: the tug of your lives. You think you have won. You havnt. All that has happened is that the King has let go the rope. You are sprawling on your backs; and he is laughing at you. Look at him! [He sits down contemptuously].

MAGNUS [making no further attempt to conceal his merriment] Come to my rescue, Amanda. It was you who set me off.

AMANDA [wreathed with smiles] You got me so nicely, sir. [To Boanerges] Bill: you are a great boob.

BOANERGES. I dont understand this. I understood His Majesty

to give way to us in, I must say, the handsomest manner. Cant we take our victory like gentlemen?

MAGNUS. Perhaps I had better explain. I quite appreciate the frank and magnanimous spirit—may I say the English spirit?— in which my little concession has been received, especially by you, Mr Boanerges. But in truth it leaves matters just where they were; for I should never have dreamt of entering on a campaign of recrimination such as the Prime Minister suggested. As he has reminded you, my own character is far too vulnerable. A king is not allowed the luxury of a good character. Our country has produced millions of blameless greengrocers, but not one blameless monarch. I have to rule over more religious sects than I can count. To rule them impartially I must not belong to any of them; and they all regard people who do not belong to them as atheists. My court includes several perfectly respectable wives and mothers whose strange vanity it is to be talked about as abandoned females. To gain the reputation of being the king's mistress they would do almost anything except give the unfortunate monarch the pleasure of substantiating their claim. Side by side with them are the ladies who are really unscrupulous. They are so careful of their reputations that they lose no opportunity of indignantly denying that they have ever yielded to solicitations which have in fact never been made to them. Thus every king is supposed to be a libertine; and as, oddly enough, he owes a great part of his popularity to this belief, he cannot deny it without deeply disappointing his subjects.

There is a rather grim silence, during which the King looks round in vain for some encouraging response.

LYSISTRATA [*severely*] Your Majesty's private affairs do not concern us, in any case.

AMANDA [*splutters into an irrepressible laugh*]!!

MAGNUS [*looks reproachfully at Amanda*]!

AMANDA [*composing her features as best she can*] Excuse me.

CRASSUS. I hope your Majesty recognizes that kings are not the only people to whom certain sorts of mud always stick, no matter what fool throws them. Call a minister a jobber—

BALBUS. Or a bungler.

CRASSUS. Yes, or a bungler, and everybody believes it. Jobbery and incompetence are the two sorts of mud that stick to us, no matter how honest or capable we are; and we havnt the royal advantage that you enjoy, that the more the ladies take away your character the better the people like you.

BOANERGES [*suddenly*] Prime Minister: will you tell me what the Postmistress General is sniggering at?

AMANDA. This is a free country, Bill. A sense of humor is not a crime. And when the King is not setting me off, you are.

BOANERGES. Where is the joke? I dont see it.

AMANDA. If you could see a joke, Bill, you wouldnt be the great popular orator you are.

BOANERGES. Thank Heaven, I am not a silly giggler like some I could mention.

AMANDA. Thanks, dearest Bill. Now, Joe: dont you think you have let us run loose long enough? What about that ultimatum?

MAGNUS [*shaking his head at her*] Traitor!

PROTEUS. I am in no hurry. His Majesty's speeches are very wise and interesting; and your back chat amuses both you and him. But the ultimatum is here all the time; and I shall not leave this room until I have His Majesty's signed pledge that its conditions will be observed.

All become gravely attentive.

MAGNUS. What are its terms?

PROTEUS. First, no more royal speeches.

MAGNUS. What! Not even if you dictate them?

PROTEUS. Not even if we dictate them. Your Majesty has a way of unrolling the manuscript and winking—

MAGNUS. Winking!

PROTEUS. You know what I mean. The best speech in the world can be read in such a way as to set the audience laughing at it. We have had enough of that. So, in future, no speeches.

MAGNUS. A dumb king?

PROTEUS. Of course we cannot object to such speeches as "We declare this foundation stone well and truly laid" and so forth.

But politically, yes: a dumb king.

PLINY [*to soften it*] A constitutional king.

PROTEUS [*implacably*] A dumb king.

MAGNUS. Hm! What next?

PROTEUS. The working of the Press from the palace back stairs must cease.

MAGNUS. You know that I have no control of the Press. The Press is in the hands of men much richer than I, who would not insert a single paragraph against their own interests even if it were signed by my own hand and sent to them with a royal command.

PROTEUS. We know that. But though these men are richer than you, they are not cleverer. They get amusing articles, spiced with exclusive backstairs information, that dont seem to them to have anything to do with politics. The next thing they know is that their pet shares have dropped fifteen points; that capital is frightened off their best prospectuses; and that some of the best measures in our party program are made to look like city jobs.

MAGNUS. Am I supposed to write these articles?

NICOBAR. Your man Sempronius does. I can spot his fist out of fifty columns.

CRASSUS. So can I. When he is getting at me he always begins the sentence with "Singularly enough."

PLINY [*chuckling*] Thats his trademark. "Singularly enough." Ha! ha!

MAGNUS. Is there to be any restriction on the other side? I have noticed, for instance, that in a certain newspaper which loses no opportunity of disparaging the throne, the last sentence of the leading article almost invariably begins with the words "Once for all." Whose trademark is that?

PROTEUS. Mine.

MAGNUS. Frank, Mr Proteus.

PROTEUS. I know when to be frank. I learnt the trick from Your Majesty.

AMANDA [*tries not to laugh*]!

MAGNUS [*gently reproachful*] Amanda: what is the joke now?

I am surprised at you.

AMANDA. Joe frank! When I want to find out what he is up to I have to come and ask your Majesty.

LYSISTRATA. That is perfectly true. In this Cabinet there is no such thing as a policy. Every man plays for his own hand.

NICOBAR. It's like a game of cards.

BALBUS. Only there are no partners.

LYSISTRATA. Except Crassus and Nicobar.

PLINY. Good, Lizzie! He! he! he!

NICOBAR. What do you mean?

LYSISTRATA. You know quite well what I mean. When will you learn, Nicobar, that it is no use trying to browbeat me. I began life as a schoolmistress; and I can browbeat any man in this Cabinet or out of it if he is fool enough to try to compete with me in that department.

BOANERGES. Order! order! Cannot the Prime Minister check these unseemly personalities?

PROTEUS. They give me time to think, Bill. When you have had as much parliamentary experience as I have you will be very glad of an interruption occasionally. May I proceed?

Silence.

PROTEUS. His Majesty asks whether the restriction on press campaigning is to be entirely onesided. That, I take it, sir, is your question.

MAGNUS [*nods assent*]!

PROTEUS. The answer is in the affirmative.

BALBUS. Good!

MAGNUS. Anything more?

PROTEUS. Yes: one thing more. The veto must not be mentioned again. That can apply to both sides, if you like. The veto is dead.

MAGNUS. May we not make a historical reference to the corpse?

PROTEUS. No. I cannot carry on the King's government unless I can give pledges and carry them out. What is my pledge worth if our constituents are reminded every day that the King may veto anything that Parliament does? Do you expect me to say, when I am asked for a pledge, "You must ask the King"?

MAGNUS. I have to say "You must ask the Prime Minister."

PLINY [*consoling him*] Thats the constitution, you know.

MAGNUS. Quite. I only mention it to shew that the Prime Minister does not really wish to kill the veto. He only wishes to move it to next door.

PROTEUS. The people live next door. The name on the brass plate is Public Opinion.

MAGNUS [*gravely*] Admirably turned, Mr Prime Minister; but unreal. I am far more subject to public opinion than you, because, thanks to the general belief in democracy, you can always pretend that what you do is done by the will of the people, who, God knows, never dreamt of it, and would not have understood it if they had; whereas, for what a king does, he, and he alone, is held responsible. A demagogue may steal a horse where a king dare not look over a hedge.

LYSISTRATA. I doubt if that is any longer true, sir. I know that I get blamed for everything that goes wrong in my department.

MAGNUS. Ah! But what a despot you are, Lysistrata! Granted, however, that the people have found out long ago that democracy is humbug, and that instead of establishing responsible government it has abolished it, do you not see what this means?

BOANERGES [*scandalized*] Steady, steady! I cannot sit here and listen to such a word as humbug being applied to democracy. I am sorry, sir; but with all respect for you, I really must draw the line at that.

MAGNUS. You are right, Mr Boanerges, as you always are. Democracy is a very real thing, with much less humbug about it than many older institutions. But it means, not that the people govern, but that the responsibility and the veto now belong neither to kings nor demagogues as such, but to whoever is clever enough to get them.

LYSISTRATA. Yourself, sir, for example?

MAGNUS. I think I am in the running. That is why I do not feel bound to accept this ultimatum. By signing it I put myself out of the running. Why should I?

BALBUS. Because youre the king: thats why.

MAGNUS. Does it follow?

PROTEUS. If two men ride the same horse, one must ride behind.

LYSISTRATA. Which?

PROTEUS [*turning to her sharply*] What was that you said?

LYSISTRATA [*with placid but formidable obstinacy and ironical explicitness*] I said Which? You said that if two men rode the same horse one of them must ride behind. I said Which? [*Explanatorily*] Which man must ride behind?

AMANDA. Got it, Joe?

PROTEUS. That is exactly the question that has to be settled here and now.

AMANDA. "Once for all."

Everybody laughs except Proteus, who rises in a fury.

PROTEUS. I will not stand this perpetual tomfooling. I had rather be a dog than the Prime Minister of a country where the only things the inhabitants can be serious about are football and refreshments. Lick the king's boots: that is all you are fit for. [*He dashes out of the room*].

BALBUS. Youve done it now, Mandy. I hope youre proud of yourself.

MAGNUS. It is you, Amanda, who should go and coax him back. But I suppose I must do it myself, as usual. Excuse me, ladies and gentlemen.

He rises. The rest rise. He goes out.

BOANERGES. I told you. I told you what would come of conducting a conference with His Majesty as if it were a smoking concert. I am disgusted. [*He flings himself back into his chair*].

BALBUS. We'd just cornered the old fox; and then Amanda must have her silly laugh and lets him out of it [*he sits*].

NICOBAR. What are we to do now? thats what I want to know.

AMANDA [*incorrigible*] I suggest a little community singing [*she makes conductorlike gestures*].

NICOBAR. Yah!! [*he sits down very sulkily*].

AMANDA [*sits down with a little splutter of laughter*]!

CRASSUS [*thoughtful*] Take it easy, friends. Joe knows what he is about.

LYSISTRATA. Of course he does. I can excuse you, Bill, because it's your first day in the Cabinet. But if the rest of you havnt found out by this time that Joe's rages are invariably calculated, then nothing will ever teach you anything [*she sits down contemptuously*].

BOANERGES [*in his grandest manner*] Well, madam, I know I am a newcomer: everything must have a beginning. I am open to argument and conviction. The Prime Minister brought this conference, in what I admit was a very able and resolute manner, to the verge of a decision. Then, in a fit of childish temper he breaks up the conference, leaving us looking like fools with nothing done. And you tell me he did it on purpose! Where was the advantage to him in such a display? answer me that.

LYSISTRATA. He is settling the whole business with the King behind our backs. That is what Joe always contrives to do, by hook or crook.

PLINY. You didnt arrange it with him, Mandy: did you?

AMANDA. There wasnt any need to arrange it. Joe can always depend on one or other of us saying something that will give him an excuse for flying out.

CRASSUS. In my opinion, ladies and gentlemen, we have done our bit, and may leave the rest to Joe. Matters had reached a point at which it was yes or no between the Cabinet and the Crown. There is only one sort of committee that is better than a committee of two; and that is a committee of one. Like the family in Wordsworth's poem, we are seven—

LYSISTRATA. Eight.

CRASSUS. Well, seven or eight, we were too many for the final grapple. Two persons sticking to the point are worth eight all over the shop. So my advice is that we just sit here quietly until Joe comes back and tells us whats been settled. Perhaps Amanda will oblige with a song. [*He resumes his seat*].

The King returns with Proteus, who looks glum. All rise. The two resume their seats in silence. The rest sit down.

MAGNUS [*very grave*] The Prime Minister has been good enough to pursue the discussion with me in private to a point at which the issue is now clear. If I do not accept the ultimatum I shall receive your resignations and his; and the country will learn from his explanatory speech in the House of Commons that it is to choose between Cabinet government and monarchical government: an issue on which I frankly say that I should be very sorry to win, as I cannot carry on without the support of a body of ministers whose existence gives the English people a sensation of self-government.

AMANDA [*splutters*]!

CRASSUS [*whispers*] Shut up, will you?

MAGNUS [*continuing*] Naturally I want to avert a conflict in which success would damage me and failure disable me. But you tell me that I can do so only by signing pledges which would make me a mere Lord Chamberlain, without even the despotism which he exercises over the theatre. I should sink below the level of the meanest of my subjects, my sole privilege being that of being shot at when some victim of misgovernment resorts to assassination to avenge himself. How am I to defend myself? You are many: I oppose you single-handed. There was a time when the king could depend on the support of the aristocracy and the cultivated bourgeoisie. Today there is not a single aristocrat left in politics, not a single member of the professions, not a single leading personage in big business or finance. They are richer than ever, more powerful than ever, more able and better educated than ever. But not one of them will touch this drudgery of government, this public work that never ends because we cannot finish one job without creating ten fresh ones. We get no thanks for it because ninety-nine hundredths of it is unknown to the people, and the remaining hundredth is resented by them as an invasion of their liberty or an increase in their taxation. It wears out the strongest man, and even the strongest woman, in five or six years. It slows down to nothing when we are fresh from our holidays and best able to bear it, and rises in an overwhelming wave through some unforeseen catastrophe when we are on the verge of nervous breakdown from overwork and fit for rest and sleep only. And this drudgery, remember, is a sweated trade, the only one now left in this country. My civil list leaves me a poor man among multi-millionaires. Your salaries can be earned ten times over in the city by anyone with outstanding organizing or administrative ability. History tells us that the first Lord Chancellor who abandoned the woolsack for the city boardroom struck the nation with amazement: today the nation would be equally amazed if a man of his ability thought it worth his while to prefer the woolsack even to the stool of an office boy as a jumping-off place for his ambition. Our work is no longer even respected. It is looked down on by our men of genius as dirty work. What great actor would exchange his stage? what great barrister his court? what great preacher his pulpit? for the squalor of the political arena in which we have to struggle with foolish factions in parliament and with ignorant voters in the constituencies? The scientists will have nothing to do with us; for the atmosphere of politics is not the atmosphere of science. Even political science, the science by which civilization must live or die, is busy explaining the past whilst we have to grapple with the present: it leaves the ground before our feet in black darkness whilst it lights up every corner of the landscape behind us. All the talent and genius of the country is bought up by the flood of unearned money. On that poisoned wealth talent and genius live far more luxuriously in the service of the rich than we in the service of our country. Politics, once the centre of attraction for ability, public spirit, and ambition, has now become the refuge of a few fanciers of public speaking and party intrigue who find all the other avenues to distinction closed to them either by their lack of practical ability, their comparative poverty and lack of education, or, let me hasten to add, their hatred of oppression and injustice, and their contempt for the chicaneries and false pretences of commercialized professionalism. History tells us of a gentleman-statesman who declared that such people were not fit to govern. Within a year it was discovered that they could govern at least as

well as anyone else who could be persuaded to take on the job.
Then began that abandonment of politics by the old governing
class which has ended in all Cabinets, conservative no less than
progressive, being what were called in the days of that rash statesman Labor Cabinets. Do not misunderstand me: I do not want
the old governing class back. It governed so selfishly that the
people would have perished if democracy had not swept it out of
politics. But evil as it was in many ways, at least it stood above
the tyranny of popular ignorance and popular poverty. Today
only the king stands above that tyranny. You are dangerously
subject to it. In spite of my urgings and remonstrances you have
not yet dared to take command of our schools and put a stop to
the inculcation upon your unfortunate children of superstitions
and prejudices that stand like stone walls across every forward
path. Are you well advised in trying to reduce me to your own
slavery to them? If I do not stand above them there is no longer
any reason for my existence at all. I stand for the future and the
past, for the posterity that has no vote and the tradition that
never had any. I stand for the great abstractions: for conscience
and virtue; for the eternal against the expedient; for the evolutionary appetite against the day's gluttony; for intellectual in-
tegrity, for humanity, for the rescue of industry from commercial-
ism and of science from professionalism, for everything that you
desire as sincerely as I, but which in you is held in leash by the
Press, which can organize against you the ignorance and superstition, the timidity and credulity, the gullibility and prudery, the
hating and hunting instinct of the voting mob, and cast you down
from power if you utter a word to alarm or displease the adven-
turers who have the Press in their pockets. Between you and that
tyranny stands the throne. I have no elections to fear; and if any
newspaper magnate dares offend me, that magnate's fashionable
wife and marriageable daughters will soon make him understand
that the King's displeasure is still a sentence of social death within
range of St James's Palace. Think of the things you dare not do!
the persons you dare not offend! Well, a king with a little
courage may tackle them for you. Responsibilities which would

break your backs may still be borne on a king's shoulders. But he must be a king, not a puppet. You would be responsible for a puppet: remember that. But whilst you continue to support me as a separate and independent estate of the realm, I am your scape-goat: you get the credit of all our popular legislation whilst you put the odium of all our resistance to ignorant popular clamor on me. I ask you, before you play your last card and destroy me, to consider where you will be without me. Think once: think twice: for your danger is, not that I may defeat you, but that your success is certain if you insist.

LYSISTRATA. Splendid!

AMANDA. You did speak that piece beautifully, sir.

BALBUS [*grumbling*] All very well; but what about my brother-in-law Mike?

LYSISTRATA [*maddened*] Oh, confound your brother-in-law Mike!

BOANERGES. Order! order!

LYSISTRATA [*to the King*] I beg your pardon, sir; but really—at a moment like this—[*words fail her*].

MAGNUS [*to Balbus*] If I had not put my foot down, Mr Balbus, the Prime Minister would have been unable to keep your brother-in-law out of the Cabinet.

BALBUS [*aggressively*] And why should he not be in the Cabinet?

AMANDA. Booze, my Balby: booze. Raising the elbow!

BALBUS [*bullying*] Who says so?

AMANDA. I do, darling.

BALBUS [*subsiding*] Well, perhaps it would surprise you all to know that Mike doesnt drink as much as I do.

AMANDA. You carry it better, Bert.

PLINY. Mike never knows when to stop.

CRASSUS. The time for Mike to stop is before he begins, if you ask me.

LYSISTRATA [*impetuously*] What sort of animals are you—you men? The King puts before us the most serious question of prin-ciple we shall ever have to deal with; and off you start discussing whether this drunken wretch takes honest whisky like Balbus or methylated spirit or petrol or whatever he can lay his hands on when the fit takes him.

BALBUS. I agree with that. What does it matter what Mike drinks? What does it matter whether he drinks or not? Mike would strengthen the Cabinet because he represents Breakages, Limited, the biggest industrial corporation in the country.

LYSISTRATA [*letting herself go*] Just so! Breakages, Limited! just so! Listen to me, sir; and judge whether I have not reason to feel everything you have just said to the very marrow of my bones. Here am I, the Powermistress Royal. I have to organize and administer all the motor power in the country for the good of the country. I have to harness the winds and the tides, the oils and the coal seams. I have to see that every little sewing machine in the Hebrides, every dentist's drill in Shetland, every carpet sweeper in Margate, has its stream of driving power on tap from a switch in the wall as punctually as the great thundering dynamos of our big industrial plants. I do it; but it costs twice as much as it should. Why? Because every new invention is bought up and suppressed by Breakages, Limited. Every breakdown, every accident, every smash and crash, is a job for them. But for them we should have unbreakable glass, unbreakable steel, imperishable materials of all sorts. But for them our goods trains could be started and stopped without battering and tearing the vitals out of every wagon and sending it to their repair shops once a week instead of once a year. Our national repair bill runs up to hundreds of millions. I could name you a dozen inventions within my own term of office which would have effected enormous economies in breakages and breakdowns; but these people can afford to pay an inventor more for his machine or his process or whatever it may be than he could hope to make by a legitimate use of it; and when they have bought it they smother it. When the inventor is poor and not good at defending himself they make bogus trials of his machine and report that it is no use. I have been shot at twice by inventors driven crazy by this sort of thing: they blamed me for it—as if I could stand up against this monster with its millions and its newspapers and its fingers in every pie. It is heartbreaking. I love my department: I dream of nothing but its efficiency: with me it comes before every personal tie, every happiness that common women run after. I would give my right hand to see these people in the bankruptcy court with half their business abolished and the other half done in public workshops where public losses are not private gains. You stand for that, sir; and I would be with you to the last drop of my blood if I dared. But what can I do? If I said one word of this in public, not a week would pass in the next two years without an article on the inefficiency and corruption of all Government departments, especially departments managed, like mine, by females. They would dig up the very machines they have buried, and make out that it is my fault that they have never been brought into use. They would set their private police to watch me day and night to get something against my private character. One of their directors told me to my face that by lifting up his finger he could get my windows broken by the mob; and that Breakages, Limited, would get the job of putting in new glass. And it is true. It is infamous; it is outrageous; but if I attempt to fight them I shall be hounded out of public life, and they will shove Mouldy Mike into the Cabinet to run my department in their interests: that is, to make such a failure of it that Joe will have to sell it to Breakages, Limited, at scrap iron prices. I—I—oh, it is beyond bearing [*she breaks down*].

There is a troubled silence for a moment. Then the voice of the Prime Minister breaks it impressively as he addresses the King.

PROTEUS. You hear that, sir. Your one supporter in the Cabinet admits that the industrial situation is too strong for her. I do not pretend to be able to control the women in my Cabinet; but not one of them dare support you.

AMANDA [*springing up*] Whats that? Not dare! What do you bet that I dont go down to Mouldy Mike's constituency and say everything that Lizzie has said and a lot more too, if I choose? I tell you, Breakages, Limited, never interferes in my department. I'd like to catch them at it.

MAGNUS. I am afraid that that is only because the efficiency of the Post Office is as important to them as to the general public.

AMANDA. Stuff! They could get rid of me without shutting up the Post Office. Theyre afraid of me—of me, Amanda Postlethwaite.

MAGNUS. You coax them, I am afraid.

AMANDA. Coax! What do you think they care for coaxing? They can have all the coaxing they want from younger and prettier women than I by paying for it. No use trying to coax that lot. Intimidate them: thats the way to handle them.

LYSISTRATA [*her voice still broken*] I wish I could intimidate them.

MAGNUS. But what can Amanda do that you cannot do?

AMANDA. I'll tell you. She cant mimic people. And she cant sing funny songs. I can do both; and that—with all respect, sir— makes me the real queen of England.

BOANERGES. Oh, come! Disgraceful! Shame!

AMANDA. If you provoke me, Bill, I'll drive you out of your constituency inside of two months.

BOANERGES. Ho! You will, will you? How?

AMANDA. Just as I drove the Chairman of Breakages out of my own constituency when he came down there and tried to take my seat from me.

MAGNUS. I never quite understood why he turned tail. How did you do it?

AMANDA. I'll tell you. He opened his campaign with a great Saturday night speech against me in the Home Lovers' Hall to five thousand people. In that same hall a week later, I faced a meeting of the very same people. I didnt argue. I mimicked him. I took all the highfalutin passages in his speech, and repeated them in his best manner until I had the whole five thousand laughing at him. Then I asked them would they like me to sing; and their Yes nearly lifted the roof off. I had two songs. They both had choruses. One went "She lets me go out on Saturday night, on Saturday night, on Saturday night"—like that. The other went "Boo! Hoo! I want Amanda's Teddy bear to play with."

They sang it under the windows of his hotel next time he came. He cancelled his meeting and left. And thats how England is governed by yours truly, sir. Lucky for England that Queen Amanda is a good sort, in spite of some surface faults. [*She resumes her seat with triumphant self-satisfaction*].

BALBUS. Lucky for England theres only one of you: thats what *I* say.

AMANDA [*wafts him a kiss*]!

MAGNUS. Should not the Queen support the King, your Majesty?

AMANDA. Sorry, sir; but there isnt room for two monarchs in my realm. I am against you on principle because the talent for mimicry isnt hereditary.

PROTEUS. No, anybody else? We have heard why the two ladies cannot support the King. Is there anybody who can?

Silence.

MAGNUS. I see that my appeal has been in vain. I do not reproach you, ladies and gentlemen, because I perceive that your situation is a difficult one. The question is, how to change it.

NICOBAR. Sign the ultimatum: that is how.

MAGNUS. I am not quite convinced of that. The Home Secretary's brother-in-law was quite willing to sign the pledge of total abstinence if I would admit him to the Cabinet. His offer was not accepted, because, though none of us doubted that he would sign the pledge, we were not equally certain that the infirmities of his nature would allow him to keep it. My nature is also subject to infirmity. Are you satisfied, Mr Proteus, that if I sign this ultimatum, I shall not inevitably relapse into the conduct that my nature dictates?

PROTEUS [*his patience strained*] What is the use of going on like this? You are like a man on the scaffold, spinning out his prayers to put off the inevitable execution as long as possible. Nothing that you can say will make any difference. You know you must sign. Why not sign and have done with it?

NICOBAR. Now youre talking, Joe.

BALBUS. Thats the stuff to give him.

PLINY. Gulp it down, sir. It wont get any sweeter by keeping: what?

LYSISTRATA. Oh, for God's sake, sign, sir. This is torture to me.

MAGNUS. I perceive, gentlemen, that I have come to the end of your patience. I will tax it no further: you have been very forbearing; and I thank you for it. I will say no more by way of discussion; but I must have until five o'clock this evening to consider my decision. At that hour, if I can find no other way out, I will sign without another word. Meanwhile, ladies and gentlemen, au revoir!

He rises. All rise. He marches out.

PROTEUS. His last wriggle. Never mind: we have him safe enough. What about lunch? I am starving. Will you lunch with me, Lizzie.

LYSISTRATA. Dont speak to me. [*She rushes out distractedly*].

AMANDA. Poor darling Lizzie! She's a regular old true blue Diehard. If only I had her brains and education! or if she had my variety talent! what a queen she'd make! Like old Queen Elizabeth, eh? Dont grieve, Joe: I'll lunch with you since youre so pressing.

CRASSUS. Come and lunch with me—all of you.

AMANDA. What opulence! Can you afford it?

CRASSUS. Breakages will pay. They have a standing account at the Ritz. Over five thousand a year, it comes to.

PROTEUS. Right. Let us spoil the Egyptians.

BOANERGES [*with Roman dignity*] My lunch will cost me one and sixpence; and I shall pay for it myself [*he stalks out*].

AMANDA [*calling after him*] Dont make a beast of yourself, Bill. Ta ta!

PROTEUS. Come on, come on: it's ever so late.

They all hurry out. Sempronius and Pamphilius, entering, have to stand aside to let them pass before returning to their desks. Proteus, with Amanda on his arm, stops in the doorway on seeing them.

PROTEUS. Have you two been listening, may I ask?

PAMPHILIUS. Well, it would be rather inconvenient, wouldnt

it, if we had to be told everything that passed?

SEMPRONIUS. Once for all, Mr Proteus, the King's private secretaries must hear everything, see everything, and know everything.

PROTEUS. Singularly enough, Mr Sempronius, I havnt the slightest objection [*he goes*].

AMANDA [*going with him*] Goodbye, Semmy. So long, Pam.

SEMPRONIUS. } [*seating themselves at their writing tables and*
PAMPHILIUS. } *yawning prodigiously*] Ou-ou-ou-ou-ou-fff!!!

AN INTERLUDE

Orinthia's boudoir at half-past fifteen on the same day. She is at her writing-table scribbling notes. She is romantically beautiful, and beautifully dressed. As the table is against the wall near a corner, with the other wall on her left, her back alone is visible from the middle of the room. The door is near the corner diagonally opposite. There is a large settee in the middle of the room.

The King enters and waits on the threshold.

ORINTHIA [*crossly, without looking round*] Who is that?

MAGNUS. His Majesty the King.

ORINTHIA. I dont want to see him.

MAGNUS. How soon will you be disengaged?

ORINTHIA. I didnt say I was engaged. Tell the king I dont want to see him.

MAGNUS. He awaits your pleasure [*he comes in and seats himself on the settee*].

ORINTHIA. Go away. [*A pause*]. I wont speak to you. [*Another pause*]. If my private rooms are to be broken into at any moment because they are in the palace, and the king is not a gentleman, I must take a house outside. I am writing to the agents about one now.

MAGNUS. What is our quarrel today, belovéd?

ORINTHIA. Ask your conscience.

MAGNUS. I have none when you are concerned. You must tell me.

She takes a book from the table and rises; then sweeps superbly forward to the settee and flings the book into his hands.

ORINTHIA. There!

MAGNUS. What is this?

ORINTHIA. Page 16. Look at it.

MAGNUS [*looking at the title on the back of the book*] "Songs of our Great Great Grandparents." What page did you say?

ORINTHIA [*between her teeth*] Six-teen.

MAGNUS [*opening the book and finding the page, his eye lighting up with recognition as he looks at it*] Ah! The Pilgrim of Love!

ORINTHIA. Read the first three words—if you dare.

MAGNUS [*smiling as he caresses the phrase*] "Orinthia, my belovéd".

ORINTHIA. The name you pretended to invent specially for me, the only woman in the world for you. Picked up out of the rubbish basket in a secondhand bookseller's! And I thought you were a poet!

MAGNUS. Well, one poet may consecrate a name for another. Orinthia is a name full of magic for me. It could not be that if I had invented it myself. I heard it at a concert of ancient music when I was a child; and I have treasured it ever since.

ORINTHIA. You always have a pretty excuse. You are the King of liars and humbugs. You cannot understand how a falsehood like that wounds me.

MAGNUS [*remorsefully, stretching out his arms towards her*] Belovéd: I am sorry.

ORINTHIA. Put your hands in your pockets: they shall not touch me ever again.

MAGNUS [*obeying*] Dont pretend to be hurt unless you really are, dearest. It wrings my heart.

ORINTHIA. Since when have you set up a heart? Did you buy that, too, secondhand?

MAGNUS. I have something in me that winces when you are hurt—or pretend to be.

ORINTHIA [*contemptuously*] Yes: I have only to squeal, and you will take me up and pet me as you would a puppy run over by a car. [*Sitting down beside him, but beyond arm's length*] That is what you give me when my heart demands love. I had rather you kicked me.

MAGNUS. I should like to kick you sometimes, when you are specially aggravating. But I shouldnt do it well. I should be afraid of hurting you all the time.

ORINTHIA. I believe you would sign my death warrant without turning a hair.

MAGNUS. That is true, in a way. It is wonderful how subtle

your mind is, as far as it goes.

ORINTHIA. It does not go as far as yours, I suppose.

MAGNUS. I dont know. Our minds go together half way. Whether it is that your mind stops there or else that the road forks, and you take the high road and I take the low road, I cannot say; but somehow after a certain point we lose one another.

ORINTHIA. And then you go back to your Amandas and Lysistratas: creatures whose idea of romance is a minister in love with a department, and whose bedside books are blue books.

MAGNUS. They are not always thinking of some man or other. That is a rather desirable extension of their interests, in my opinion. If Lysistrata had a lover I should not be interested in him in the least; and she would bore me to distraction if she could talk of nothing else. But I am very much interested in her department. Her devotion to it gives us a topic of endless interest.

ORINTHIA. Well, go to her: I am not detaining you. But dont tell her that I have nothing to talk about but men; for that is a lie; and you know it.

MAGNUS. It is, as you say, a lie; and I know it. But I did not say it.

ORINTHIA. You implied it. You meant it. When those ridiculous political women are with us you talk to them all the time, and never say a word to me.

MAGNUS. Nor you to me. We cannot talk to one another in public: we have nothing to say that could be said before other people. Yet we find enough to say to one another when we are alone together. Would you change that if you could?

ORINTHIA. You are as slippery as an eel; but you shall not slip through my fingers. Why do you surround yourself with political bores and frumps and dowdy busybodies who cant talk: they can only debate about their dull departments and their fads and their election chances. [*Rising impatiently*] Who could talk to such people? If it were not for the nonentities of wives and husbands they drag about with them, there would be nobody to talk to at all. And even they can talk of nothing but the servants and the baby. [*Suddenly returning to her seat*] Listen to me, Magnus. Why can you not be a real king?

MAGNUS. In what way, belovédest?

ORINTHIA. Send all these stupid people packing. Make them do their drudgeries in their departments without bothering you about it, as you make your servants here sweep the floors and dust the furniture. Live a really noble and beautiful life—a kingly life—with me. What you need to make you a real king is a real queen.

MAGNUS. But I have got one.

ORINTHIA. Oh, you are blind. You are worse than blind: you have low tastes. Heaven is offering you a rose; and you cling to a cabbage.

MAGNUS [*laughing*] That is a very apt metaphor, belovéd. But what wise man, if you force him to choose between doing without roses and doing without cabbages, would not secure the cabbages? Besides, all these old married cabbages were once roses; and, though young things like you dont remember that, their husbands do. They dont notice the change. Besides, you should know better than anyone else that when a man gets tired of his wife and leaves her it is never because she has lost her good looks. The new love is often older and uglier than the old.

ORINTHIA. Why should I know it better than anyone else?

MAGNUS. Why, because you have been married twice; and both your husbands have run away from you to much plainer and stupider women. When I begged your present husband to come back to court for a while for the sake of appearances he said no man could call his soul his own in the same house with you. And yet that man was utterly infatuated with your beauty when he married you. Your first husband actually forced a good wife to divorce him so that he might marry you; but before two years were out he went back to her and died in her arms, poor chap.

ORINTHIA. Shall I tell you why these men could not live with me? It was because I am a thoroughbred, and they are only hacks. They had nothing against me: I was perfectly faithful to them.

I kept their houses beautifully: I fed them better than they had ever been fed in their lives. But because I was higher than they were, and greater, they could not stand the strain of trying to live up to me. So I let them go their way, poor wretches, back to their cabbages. Look at the old creature Ignatius is living with now! She gives you his real measure.

MAGNUS. An excellent woman. Ignatius is quite happy with her. I never saw a man so changed.

ORINTHIA. Just what he is fit for. Commonplace. Bourgeoise. She trots through the streets shopping. [*Rising*] I tread the plains of Heaven. Common women cannot come where I am; and common men find themselves out and slink away.

MAGNUS. It must be magnificent to have the consciousness of a goddess without ever doing a thing to justify it.

ORINTHIA. Give me a goddess's work to do; and I will do it. I will even stoop to a queen's work if you will share the throne with me. But do not pretend that people become great by doing great things. They do great things because they are great, if the great things come along. But they are great just the same when the great things do not come along. If I never did anything but sit in this room and powder my face and tell you what a clever fool you are, I should still be heavens high above the millions of common women who do their domestic duty, and sacrifice themselves, and run Trade departments and all the rest of the vulgarities. Has all the tedious public work you have done made you any the better? I have seen you before and after your boasted strokes of policy; and you were the same man, and would have been the same man to me and to yourself if you had never done them. Thank God my self-consciousness is something nobler than vulgar conceit in having done something. It is what I am, not what I do, that you must worship in me. If you want deeds, go to your men and women of action, as you call them, who are all in a conspiracy to pretend that the mechanical things they do, the foolhardy way they risk their worthless lives, or their getting up in the morning at four and working sixteen hours a day for thirty years, like coral insects, make them great. What are they for? these dull slaves? To keep the streets swept for me. To enable me to reign over them in beauty like the stars without having anything to do with their slavery except to console it, to dazzle it, to enable them to forget it in adoring dreams of me. Am I not worth it? [*She sits, fascinating him*]. Look into my eyes and tell the truth. Am I worth it or not?

MAGNUS. To me, who love beauty, yes. But you should hear the speeches Balbus makes about your pension.

ORINTHIA. And my debts: do not forget my debts, my mortgages, the bill of sale on my furniture, the thousands I have had from the moneylenders to save me from being sold up because I will not borrow from my friends. Lecture me again about them; but do not dare pretend that the people grudge me my pension. They glory in it, and in my extravagance, as you call it.

MAGNUS [*more gravely*] By the way, Orinthia, when your dressmakers took up that last bill for you, they were speculating, were they not, in your chances of becoming my queen some day?

ORINTHIA. Well, what if they were?

MAGNUS. They would hardly have ventured on that without a hint from somebody. Was it from you?

ORINTHIA. You think me capable of that! You have a very low side to you, Magnus.

MAGNUS. No doubt: like other mortal fabrics I have a wrong side and a right side. But it is no use your giving yourself airs, belovédest. You are capable of anything. Do you deny that there was some suggestion of the kind?

ORINTHIA. How dare you challenge me to deny it? I never deny. Of course there was a suggestion of the kind.

MAGNUS. I thought so.

ORINTHIA. Oh, stupid! stupid! Go keep a grocer's shop: that is what you are fit for. Do you suppose that the suggestion came from me? Why, you great oaf, it is in the air: when my dressmaker hinted at it I told her that if she ever dared to repeat such a thing she should never get another order from me. But can I help people seeing what is as plain as the sun in the heavens? [*Rising again*] Everyone knows that I am the real queen. Everyone treats me as the real queen. They cheer me in the streets. When I open one of the art exhibitions or launch a new ship they crowd the place out. I am one of Nature's queens; and they know it. If you do not, you are not one of Nature's kings.

MAGNUS. Sublime! Nothing but genuine inspiration could give a woman such cheek.

ORINTHIA. Yes: inspiration, not cheek. [*Sitting as before*] Magnus: when are you going to face my destiny, and your own?

MAGNUS. But my wife? the queen? What is to become of my poor dear Jemima?

ORINTHIA. Oh, drown her: shoot her: tell your chauffeur to drive her into the Serpentine and leave her there. The woman makes you ridiculous.

MAGNUS. I dont think I should like that. And the public would think it illnatured.

ORINTHIA. Oh, you know what I mean. Divorce her. Make her divorce you. It is quite easy. That was how Ronny married me. Everybody does it when they need a change.

MAGNUS. But I cant imagine what I should do without Jemima.

ORINTHIA. Nobody else can imagine what you do with her. But you need not do without her. You can see as much of her as you like when we are married. I shall not be jealous and make scenes.

MAGNUS. That is very magnanimous of you. But I am afraid it does not settle the difficulty. Jemima would not think it right to keep up her present intimacy with me if I were married to you.

ORINTHIA. What a woman! Would she be in any worse position then than I am in now?

MAGNUS. No.

ORINTHIA. You mean, then, that you do not mind placing me in a position that you do not think good enough for her?

MAGNUS. Orinthia: I did not place you in your present position. You placed yourself in it. I could not resist you. You gathered me like a daisy.

ORINTHIA. Did you want to resist me?

MAGNUS. Oh no. I never resist temptation, because I have

found that things that are bad for me do not tempt me.

ORINTHIA. Well, then, what are we talking about?

MAGNUS. I forget. I think I was explaining the impossibility of my wife changing places with you.

ORINTHIA. Why impossible, pray?

MAGNUS. I cannot make you understand: you see you have never been really married, though you have led two captives to the altar, and borne children to one of them. Being your husband is only a job for which one man will do as well as another, and which the last man holds subject to six months notice in the divorce court. Being my wife is something quite different. The smallest derogation to Jemima's dignity would hit me like the lash of a whip across the face. About yours, somehow, I do not care a rap.

ORINTHIA. Nothing can derogate from my dignity: it is divine. Hers is only a convention: that is why you tremble when it is challenged.

MAGNUS. Not a bit. It is because she is a part of my real workaday self. You belong to fairyland.

ORINTHIA. Suppose she dies! Will you die too?

MAGNUS. Not immediately. I shall have to carry on as best I can without her, though the prospect terrifies me.

ORINTHIA. Might not carrying on without her include marrying me?

MAGNUS. My dear Orinthia, I had rather marry the devil. Being a wife is not your job.

ORINTHIA. You think so because you have no imagination. And you dont know me because I have never let you really possess me. I should make you more happy than any man has ever yet been on earth.

MAGNUS. I defy you to make me more happy than our strangely innocent relations have already made me.

ORINTHIA [rising restlessly] You talk like a child or a saint. [Turning on him] I can give you a new life: one of which you have no conception. I can give you beautiful, wonderful children: have you ever seen a lovelier boy than my Basil?

MAGNUS. Your children are beautiful; but they are fairy children; and I have several very real ones already. A divorce would not sweep them out of the way of the fairies.

ORINTHIA. In short, when your golden moment comes—when the gates of heaven open before you, you are afraid to come out of your pigsty.

MAGNUS. If I am a pig, a pigsty is the proper place for me.

ORINTHIA. I cannot understand it. All men are fools and moral cowards when you come to know them. But you are less of a fool and less of a moral coward than any man I have ever known. You have almost the makings of a first rate woman in you. When I leave the earth and soar up to the regions which are my real eternal home, you can follow me: I can speak to you as I can speak to no one else; and you can say things to me that would just make your stupid wife cry. There is more of you in me than of any other man within my reach. There is more of me in you than of any other woman within your reach. We are meant for oneanother: it is written across the sky that you and I are queen and king. How can you hesitate? What attraction is there for you in your common healthy jolly lumps of children and your common housekeeper wife and the rabble of dowdies and upstarts and intriguers and clowns that think they are governing the country when they are only squabbling with you? Look again at me, man: again and again. Am I not worth a million such? Is not life with me as high above them as the sun is above the gutter?

MAGNUS. Yes yes yes yes, of course. You are lovely: you are divine [*she cannot restrain a gesture of triumph*]. And you are enormously amusing.

This anti-climax is too much for Orinthia's exaltation; but she is too clever not to appreciate it. With another gesture, this time of deflation, she sits down at his left hand with an air of suffering patience, and listens in silence to the harangue which follows.

MAGNUS. Some day perhaps Nature will graft the roses on the cabbages and make every woman as enchanting as you; and then what a glorious lark life will be! But at present, what I come here for is to enjoy talking to you like this when I need an hour's respite from royalty: when my stupid wife has been worrying me, or my jolly lumps of children bothering me, or my turbulent Cabinet obstructing me: when, as the doctors say, what I need is a change. You see, my dear, there is no wife on earth so precious, no children so jolly, no Cabinet so tactful that it is impossible ever to get tired of them. Jemima has her limitations, as you have observed. And I have mine. Now if our limitations exactly corresponded I should never want to talk to anyone else; and neither would she. But as that never happens, we are like all other married couples: that is, there are subjects which can never be discussed between us because they are sore subjects. There are people we avoid mentioning to oneanother because one of us likes them and the other doesnt. Not only individuals, but whole sorts of people. For instance, your sort. My wife doesnt like your sort, doesnt understand it, mistrusts and dreads it. Not without reason; for women like you are dangerous to wives. But I dont dislike your sort: I understand it, being a little in that line myself. At all events I am not afraid of it; though the least allusion to it brings a cloud over my wife's face. So when I want to talk freely about it I come and talk to you. And I take it she talks to friends of hers about people of whom she never talks to me. She has men friends from whom she can get some things that she cannot get from me. If she didnt do so she would be limited by my limitations, which would end in her hating me. So I always do my best to make her men friends feel at home with us.

ORINTHIA. A model husband in a model household! And when the model household becomes a bore, I am the diversion.

MAGNUS. Well, what more can you ask? Do not let us fall into the common mistake of expecting to become one flesh and one spirit. Every star has its own orbit; and between it and its nearest neighbor there is not only a powerful attraction but an infinite distance. When the attraction becomes stronger than the distance the two do not embrace: they crash together in ruin. We two also have our orbits, and must keep an infinite distance between us to avoid a disastrous collision. Keeping our distance is the whole secret of good manners; and without good manners human society is intolerable and impossible.

ORINTHIA. Would any other woman stand your sermons, and even like them?

MAGNUS. Orinthia: we are only two children at play; and you must be content to be my queen in fairyland. And [*rising*] I must go back to my work.

ORINTHIA. What work have you that is more important than being with me?

MAGNUS. None.

ORINTHIA. Then sit down.

MAGNUS. Unfortunately, this silly business of government must be carried on. And there is a crisis this evening, as usual.

ORINTHIA. But the crisis is not until five: I heard all about it from Sempronius. Why do you encourage that greedy schemer Proteus? He humbugs you. He humbugs everybody. He even humbugs himself; and of course he humbugs that Cabinet which is a disgrace to you: it is like an overcrowded third class carriage. Why do you allow such riffraff to waste your time? After all, what are you paid for? To be a king: that is, to wipe your boots on common people.

MAGNUS. Yes: but this king business, as the Americans call it, has got itself so mixed up with democracy that half the country expects me to wipe my perfectly polished boots on the Cabinet, and the other half expects me to let the Cabinet wipe its muddy boots on me. The Crisis at five o'clock is to decide which of us is to be the doormat.

ORINTHIA. And you will condescend to fight with Proteus for power?

MAGNUS. Oh no: I never fight. But I sometimes win.

ORINTHIA. If you let yourself be beaten by that trickster and poseur, never dare to approach me again.

MAGNUS. Proteus is a clever fellow: even on occasion a fine fellow. It would give me no satisfaction to beat him: I hate beating people. But there would be some innocent fun in out-witting him.

ORINTHIA. Magnus: you are a mollycoddle. If you were a real man you would just delight in beating him to a jelly.

MAGNUS. A real man would never do as a king. I am only an idol, my love; and all I can do is to draw the line at being a cruel idol. [*He looks at his watch*] Now I must really be off. Au revoir.

ORINTHIA [*looking at her wrist watch*] But it is only twenty-five minutes past four. You have heaps of time before five.

MAGNUS. Yes; but tea is at half-past four.

ORINTHIA [*catching him by the arm with a snakelike dart*] Never mind your tea. I will give you your tea.

MAGNUS. Impossible, belovéd. Jemima does not like to be kept waiting.

ORINTHIA. Oh, bother Jemima! You shall not leave me to go to Jemima [*she pulls him back so vigorously that he falls into the seat beside her*].

MAGNUS. My dear, I must.

ORINTHIA. No, not today. Listen, Magnus. I have something very particular to say to you.

MAGNUS. You have not. You are only trying to make me late to annoy my wife. [*He tries to rise, but is pulled back*]. Let me go, please.

ORINTHIA [*holding on*] Why are you so afraid of your wife? You are the laughing stock of London, you poor henpecked darling.

MAGNUS. Henpecked! What do you call this? At least my wife does not restrain me by bodily violence.

ORINTHIA. I will not be deserted for your old Dutch.

MAGNUS. Listen, Orinthia. Dont be absurd. You know I must go. Do be good.

ORINTHIA. Only ten minutes more.

MAGNUS. It is half-past already.

He tries to rise; but she holds him back.

MAGNUS [*pausing for breath*] You are doing this out of sheer devilment. You are so abominably strong that I cannot break loose without hurting you. Must I call the guard?

ORINTHIA. Do, do. It will be in all the papers tomorrow.

MAGNUS. Fiend. [*Summoning all his dignity*] Orinthia: I command you.

ORINTHIA [*laughs wildly*]!!!

MAGNUS [*furious*] Very well, then, you she-devil: you shall let go.

He tackles her in earnest. She flings her arms round him and holds on with mischievous enjoyment. There is a tapping at the door; but they do not hear it. As he is breaking loose she suddenly shifts her grip to his waist and drags him on to the floor, where they roll over one another. Sempronius enters. He stares at the scandalous scene for a moment; then hastily slips out; shuts the door; clears his throat and blows his nose noisily; and knocks loudly and repeatedly. The two combatants cease hostilities and scramble hastily to their feet.

MAGNUS. Come in.

SEMPRONIUS [*entering*] Her Majesty sent me to remind you that tea is waiting, sir.

MAGNUS. Thank you. [*He goes quickly out*].

ORINTHIA [*panting but greatly pleased with herself*] The King forgets everything when he is here. So do I, I am afraid. I am so sorry.

SEMPRONIUS [*stiffly*] No explanations are needed. I saw what happened. [*He goes out*].

ORINTHIA. The beast! He must have looked through the keyhole. [*She throws her hand up with a gesture of laughing defiance, and dances back to her seat at the writing-table*].

ACT II

Later in the afternoon. The Terrace of the Palace. A low balustrade separates it from the lawn. Terrace chairs in abundance, ranged along the balustrade. Some dining room chairs also, not ranged, but standing about as if they had just been occupied. The terrace is accessible from the lawn by a central flight of steps.

The King and Queen are sitting apart near the corners of the steps, the Queen to the King's right. He is reading the evening paper: she is knitting. She has a little work table on her right, with a small gong on it.

THE QUEEN. Why did you tell them to leave the chairs when they took away the tea?

MAGNUS. I shall receive the Cabinet here.

THE QUEEN. Here! Why?

MAGNUS. Well, I think the open air and the evening light will have a quieting effect on them. They cannot make speeches at me so easily as in a room.

THE QUEEN. Are you sure? When Robert asked Boanerges where he learnt to speak so beautifully, he said "In Hyde Park."

MAGNUS. Yes; but with a crowd to stimulate him.

THE QUEEN. Robert says you have tamed Boanerges.

MAGNUS. No: I have not tamed him. I have taught him how to behave. I have to valet all the beginners; but that does not tame them: it teaches them how to use their strength instead of wasting it in making fools of themselves. So much the worse for me when I have to fight them.

THE QUEEN. You get no thanks for it. They think you are only humbugging them.

MAGNUS. Well, so I am, in the elementary lessons. But when it comes to real business humbug is no use: they pick it up themselves too quickly.

Pamphilius enters along the terrace, from the Queen's side.

MAGNUS [*looking at his watch*] Good Heavens! They havnt come, have they? It's not five yet.

PAMPHILIUS. No, sir. It's the American ambassador.

THE QUEEN [*resenting this a little*] Has he an audience?

PAMPHILIUS. No, maam. He is rather excited about something, I think. I cant get anything out of him. He says he must see His Majesty at once.

THE QUEEN. Must!! An American must see the King at once, without an audience! Well!

MAGNUS [*rising*] Send him in, Pam.

Pamphilius goes out.

THE QUEEN. *I* should have told him to write for an audience, and then kept him waiting a week for it.

MAGNUS. What! When we still owe America that old war debt. And with a mad imperialist president like Bossfield! No you wouldnt, my dear: you would be crawlingly civil to him, as I am going to be, confound him!

PAMPHILIUS [*re-appearing*] His Excellency the American Ambassador. Mr Vanhattan.

He retires as Mr Vanhattan enters in an effusive condition, and, like a man assured of an enthusiastic welcome, hurries to the Queen, and salutes her with a handshake so prolonged that she stares in astonishment, first at him, and then appealingly at the King, with her hands being vigorously wrung and waved up and down all the time.

MAGNUS. What on earth is the matter, Mr Vanhattan? You are shaking Her Majesty's rings off.

VANHATTAN [*desisting*] Her Majesty will excuse me when she learns the nature of my errand here. This, King Magnus, is a great historic scene: one of the greatest, perhaps, that history has ever recorded or will ever again record.

MAGNUS. Have you had tea?

VANHATTAN. Tea! Who can think of tea at such a moment as this?

THE QUEEN [*rather coldly*] It is hard for us to share your enthusiasm in complete ignorance of its cause.

VANHATTAN. That is true, maam. I am just behaving like a crazy man. But you shall hear. You shall judge. And then you shall say whether I exaggerate the importance—the immensity—of an occasion that cannot be exaggerated.

MAGNUS. Goodness gracious! Wont you sit down?

VANHATTAN [*taking a chair and placing it between them*] I thank your Majesty. [*He sits*].

MAGNUS. You have some exciting news for us, apparently. Is it private or official?

VANHATTAN. Official, sir. No mistake about it. What I am going to tell you is authentic from the United States of America to the British Empire.

THE QUEEN. Perhaps I had better go.

VANHATTAN. No, maam: you shall not go. Whatever may be the limits of your privileges as the consort of your sovereign, it is your right as an Englishwoman to learn what I have come here to communicate.

MAGNUS. My dear Vanhattan, what the devil is the matter?

VANHATTAN. King Magnus: between your country and mine there is a debt.

MAGNUS. Does that matter, now that our capitalists have invested so heavily in American concerns that after paying yourselves the interest on the debt you have to send us two thousand million dollars a year to balance the account.

VANHATTAN. King Magnus: for the moment, forget figures. Between your country and mine there is not only a debt but a frontier: the frontier that has on it not a single gun nor a single soldier, and across which the American citizen every day shakes the hand of the Canadian subject of your throne.

MAGNUS. There is also the frontier of the ocean, which is somewhat more expensively defended at our joint expense by the League of Nations.

VANHATTAN [*rising to give his words more impressiveness*] Sir: the debt is cancelled. The frontier no longer exists.

THE QUEEN. How can that be?

MAGNUS. Am I to understand, Mr Vanhattan, that by some convulsion of Nature the continent of North America has been submerged in the Atlantic?

VANHATTAN. Something even more wonderful than that has happened. One may say that the Atlantic Ocean has been submerged in the British Empire.

MAGNUS. I think you had better tell us as succinctly as possible what has happened. Pray sit down.

VANHATTAN [*resuming his seat*] You are aware, sir, that the United States of America at one time formed a part of your empire.

MAGNUS. There is a tradition to that effect.

VANHATTAN. No mere tradition, sir. An undoubted historical fact. In the eighteenth century—

MAGNUS. That is a long time ago.

VANHATTAN. Centuries count for but little in the lifetimes of great nations, sir. Let me recall the parable of the prodigal son.

MAGNUS. Oh really, Mr Vanhattan, that was a very very long time ago. I take it that something important has happened since yesterday.

VANHATTAN. It has. It has indeed, King Magnus.

MAGNUS. Then what is it? I have not time to attend to the eighteenth century and the prodigal son at this moment.

THE QUEEN. The King has a Cabinet meeting in ten minutes, Mr Vanhattan.

VANHATTAN. I should like to see the faces of your Cabinet ministers, King Magnus, when they hear what I have to tell you.

MAGNUS. So should I. But I am not in a position to tell it to them, because I dont know what it is.

VANHATTAN. The prodigal, sir, has returned to his father's house. Not poor, not hungry, not ragged, as of old. Oh no. This time he returns bringing with him the riches of the earth to the ancestral home.

MAGNUS [*starting from his chair*] You dont mean to say—

VANHATTAN [*rising also, blandly triumphant*] I do, sir. The Declaration of Independence is cancelled. The treaties which endorsed it are torn up. We have decided to rejoin the British Empire. We shall of course enjoy Dominion Home Rule under the Presidency of Mr Bossfield. I shall revisit you here shortly, not as the Ambassador of a foreign power, but as High Commissioner for the greatest of your dominions, and your very loyal and devoted subject, sir.

MAGNUS [*collapsing into his chair*] The devil you will! [*He stares haggardly into futurity, now for the first time utterly at a loss*].

THE QUEEN. What a splendid thing, Mr Vanhattan!

VANHATTAN. I thought your Majesty would say so. The most splendid thing that has ever happened. [*He resumes his seat*].

THE QUEEN [*looking anxiously at the King*] Dont you think so, Magnus?

MAGNUS [*pulling himself together with a visible effort*] May I ask, Mr Vanhattan, with whom did this—this—this masterstroke of American policy originate? Frankly, I have been accustomed to regard your President as a statesman whose mouth was the most efficient part of his head. He cannot have thought of this himself. Who suggested it to him?

VANHATTAN. I must accept your criticism of Mr Bossfield with all doo reserve, but I may mention that we Americans will probably connect the good news with the recent visit to our shores of the President of the Irish Free State. I cannot pronounce his name in its official Gaelic form; and there is only one typist in our bureau who can spell it; but he is known to his friends as Mick O'Rafferty.

MAGNUS. The rascal! Jemima: we shall have to live in Dublin. This is the end of England.

VANHATTAN. In a sense that may be so. But England will not perish. She will merge—merge, sir—into a bigger and brighter concern. Perhaps I should have mentioned that one of our conditions will be that you shall be Emperor. King may be good enough for this little island; but if we come in we shall require something grander.

MAGNUS. This little island! "This little gem set in a silver sea!" Has it occurred to you, Mr Vanhattan, that rather than be reduced to a mere appendage of a big American concern, we might raise the old warcry of Sinn Fein, and fight for our independence to the last drop of our blood?

VANHATTAN. I should be right sorry to contemplate such a reversion to a barbarous past. Fortunately, it's impossible—immpawsibl. The old warcry would not appeal to the cosmopolitan crews of the fleet of the League of Nations in the Atlantic. That fleet would blockade you, sir. And I fear we should be obliged to boycott you. The two thousand million dollars a year would stop.

MAGNUS. But the continental Powers! Do you suppose they would consent for a moment to such a change in the balance of power?

VANHATTAN. Why not? The change would be only nominal.

MAGNUS. Nominal! You call an amalgamation of the British Commonwealth with the United States a nominal change! What will France and Germany call it?

VANHATTAN [*shaking his head indulgently*] France and Germany? These queer old geographical expressions which you use here from old family habit do not trouble us. I suppose you mean by Germany the chain of more or less Soviet Republics between the Ural Mountains and the North Sea. Well, the clever people at Moscow and Berlin and Geneva are trying to federate them; and it is fully understood between us that if we dont object to their move they will not object to ours. France, by which I take it you mean the Government at New Timgad, is too busy in Africa to fuss about what is happening at the ends of your little Channel Tube. So long as Paris is full of Americans, and Americans are full of money, all's well in the west from the French point of view. One of the great attractions of Paris for Americans is the excursion to Old England. The French want us to feel at home here. And so we do. Why shouldnt we? After all, we are at home here.

MAGNUS. In what sense, may I ask?

VANHATTAN. Well, we find here everything we are accustomed to: our industrial products, our books, our plays, our sports, our Christian Science churches, our osteopaths, our movies and talkies. Put it in a small parcel and say our goods and our ideas. A political union with us will be just the official recognition of an already accomplished fact. A union of hearts, you might call it.

THE QUEEN. You forget, Mr Vanhattan. We have a great national tradition.

VANHATTAN. The United States, maam, have absorbed all the great national traditions, and blended them with their own glorious tradition of Freedom into something that is unique and universal.

THE QUEEN. We have a civilized culture which is peculiar to ourselves. It may not be better than yours; but it is different.

VANHATTAN. Well, is it? We found that culture enshrined in British material works of art: in the stately country homes of your nobility, in the cathedrals our common forefathers built as the country houses of God. What did you do with them? You sold them to us. I was brought up in the shade of Ely cathedral, the removal of which from the county of Cambridge to New Jersey was my dear old father's first big professional job. The building which stands on its former site is a very fine one: in my opinion the best example of reinforced concrete of its period; but it was designed by an American architect, and built by the Synthetic Building Materials Trust, an international affair. Believe me, the English people, the real English people who take things as they come instead of reading books about them, will be more at home with us than they are with the old English notions which our tourists try to keep alive. When you find some country gentleman keeping up the old English customs at Christmas and so forth, who is he? An American who has bought the place. Your people get up the show for him because he pays for it, not because it is natural to them.

THE QUEEN [with a sigh] Our own best families go so much to Ireland nowadays. People should not be allowed to go from England to Ireland. They never come back.

VANHATTAN. Well, can you blame them, maam? Look at the climate!

THE QUEEN. No: it is not the climate. It is the Horse Show.

The King rises very thoughtfully; and Vanhattan follows his example.

MAGNUS. I must think over this. I have known for years past that it was on the cards. When I was young, and under the influence of our family tradition, which of course never recognized the rebellion of the American colonies as valid, I actually dreamt of a reunited English speaking empire at the head of civilization.

VANHATTAN. Fine! Great! And now come true.

MAGNUS. Not yet. Now that I am older and wiser I find the reality less attractive than the dream.

VANHATTAN. And is that all I am to report to the President, sir? He will be disappointed. I am a little taken aback, myself.

MAGNUS. For the present, that is all. This may be a great idea—

VANHATTAN. Surely, surely.

MAGNUS. It may also be a trap in which England will perish.

VANHATTAN [*encouragingly*] Oh, I shouldnt look at it that way. Besides, nothing—not even dear old England—can last for ever. Progress, you know, sir, progress, progress!

MAGNUS. Just so, just so. We may survive only as another star on your flag. Still, we cling to the little scrap of individuality you have left us. If we must merge, as you call it—or did you say submerge?—some of us will swim to the last. [*To the Queen*] My dear.

The Queen strikes her gong.

Pamphilius returns.

MAGNUS. You shall hear from me after the Cabinet meets. Not tonight: you must not sit up waiting for a message. Early tomorrow, I hope. Thank you for bringing me the news before the papers got it: that seldom happens now. Pamphilius: you will reconduct his Excellency. Good evening. [*He shakes hands*].

VANHATTAN. I thank your Majesty. [*To the Queen*] Good evening, maam. I look forward to presenting myself in court dress soon.

THE QUEEN. You will look very nice in it, Mr Vanhattan. Good evening.

The Ambassador goes out with Pamphilius.

MAGNUS [*striding grimly to and fro*] The scoundrels! That blackguard O'Rafferty! That booby bullroarer Bossfield! Breakages, Limited, have taken it into their heads to mend the British Commonwealth.

THE QUEEN [quietly] I think it is a very good thing. You will make a very good emperor. We shall civilize these Americans.

MAGNUS. How can we when we have not yet civilized ourselves? They have come to regard us as a mere tribe of redskins. England will be just a reservation.

THE QUEEN. Nonsense, dear! They know that we are their natural superiors. You can see it by the way their women behave at court. They really love and reverence royalty; while our English peeresses are hardly civil—when they condescend to come at all.

MAGNUS. Well, my dear, I do many things to please you that I should never do to please myself; and I suppose I shall end as American Emperor just to keep you amused.

THE QUEEN. I never desire anything that is not good for you, Magnus. You do not always know what is good for you.

MAGNUS. Well, well, well, well! Have it your own way, dearest. Where are these infernal ministers? Theyre late.

THE QUEEN [looking out into the garden] Coming across the lawn with Sempronius.

The Cabinet arrives. The men take off their hats as they come up the steps. Boanerges has taken advantage of the interval to procure a brilliant uniform and change into it. Proteus, with Sempronius, heads the procession, followed immediately by the two lady ministers. The Queen rises as Proteus turns to her. Sempronius moves the little table quickly back to the balustrade out of the way, and puts the Queen's chair in the centre for the King.

THE QUEEN [shaking hands] How do you do, Mr Proteus?

PROTEUS. May I present the President of the Board of Trade, Mr Boanerges?

THE QUEEN. I remember seeing you, Mr Boanerges, at the opening of the Transport Workers' Summer Palace. You wore a most becoming costume then. I hope you have not given it up.

BOANERGES. But the Princess told me I looked ridiculous in it!

THE QUEEN. That was very naughty of the Princess. You looked particularly well in it. However, you look well in anything. And now I leave you all to your labors.

She goes out along the terrace. Sempronius follows with her knitting.

MAGNUS [*sitting down*] Be seated, ladies and gentlemen.

They take chairs of one sort or another where they can find them, first leaving their hats on the balustrade. When they are seated, their order from the King's right to his left is Nicobar, Crassus, Boanerges, Amanda, the King, Proteus, Lysistrata, Pliny, and Balbus.

A pause, Proteus waiting for the King to begin. He, deep in thought, says nothing. The silence becomes oppressive.

PLINY [*chattily*] Nice weather we're having, these evenings.

AMANDA [*splutters*]!!!

MAGNUS. There is rather a threatening cloud on the western horizon, Mr Pliny. [*To Proteus*] Have you heard the news from America?

PROTEUS. I have, sir.

MAGNUS. Am I to be favored with the advice of my ministers on that subject?

PROTEUS. By your Majesty's leave, we will take the question of the ultimatum first.

MAGNUS. Do you think the ultimatum will matter much when the capital of the British Commonwealth is shifted to Washington?

NICOBAR. We'll see it shifted to Melbourne or Montreal or Johannesburg first.

MAGNUS. It would not stay there. It will stay at a real centre of gravity only.

PROTEUS. We are agreed about that. If it shifts at all it will shift either west to Washington or east to Moscow.

BOANERGES. Moscow thinks a lot of itself. But what has Moscow to teach us that we cannot teach ourselves? Moscow is built on English history, written in London by Karl Marx.

PROTEUS. Yes; and the English king has sidetracked you again. [*To Magnus*] What about the ultimatum, sir? You promised us your decision at five o'clock. It is now a quarter past.

MAGNUS. Are you inexorably determined to force this issue to its logical end? You know how unEnglish it is to do that?

PROTEUS. My people came from Scotland.

LYSISTRATA. I wish they had stayed there. I am English: every bone in my body.

BOANERGES [*vociferously*] Same here!

PROTEUS. God help England if she had no Scots to think for her!

MAGNUS. What does the Cabinet say to that?

AMANDA. All their people came from Scotland or Ireland or Wales or Jerusalem or somewhere, sir. It is no use appealing to English sentiment here.

CRASSUS. Politics are not suited to the English, if you ask me.

MAGNUS. Then I, the only Englishman left in politics, apparently, am to be reduced to complete nullity?

PROTEUS [*bluntly*] Yes. You cannot frighten us out of our position by painting it red. I could paint your position black if I liked. In plain terms we require from you an unconditional surrender. If you refuse it then I go to the country on the question whether England is to be an absolute monarchy or a constitutional one. We are all agreed on that: there will be no resignations. I have letters from the absent members of the Government: those present will speak for themselves.

ALL THE OTHER MEN. Agreed, agreed.

PROTEUS. Now, what is your answer?

MAGNUS. The day for absolute monarchies is past. You think you can do without me; and I know that I cannot do without you. I decide, of course, in favor of a constitutional monarchy.

THE MEN [*greatly relieved and delighted*] Hear! hear!

MAGNUS. Wait a moment.

Sudden silence and mistrust.

PROTEUS. So! There is a catch in it, is there?

MAGNUS. Not exactly a catch. But you have driven me to face the fact that I am unfitted to be a constitutional monarch. I am by nature incapable of the necessary self-effacement.

AMANDA. Well, thats true, at all events. You and I are a pair, sir.

MAGNUS. Thank you. Therefore, whilst accepting your constitutional principle without the slightest reserve, I cannot sign your ultimatum, because by doing so I should be making personal promises which I know I should break—which in fact I must break because I have forces within me which your constitutional limits cannot hold in check.

BALBUS. How can you accept our principle if you dont sign the ultimatum?

MAGNUS. Oh, there is no difficulty about that. When an honest man finds himself incapable of discharging the duties of a public post, he resigns.

PROTEUS [*alarmed*] Resigns! What are you driving at?

CRASSUS. A king cannot resign.

NICOBAR. You might as well talk of beheading yourself. You cant behead yourself.

BOANERGES. Other people can, though.

MAGNUS. Do not let us quarrel about words, gentlemen. I cannot resign. But I can abdicate.

ALL THE REST [*starting to their feet*] Abdicate! [*They stare at him in consternation*].

AMANDA [*whistling a descending minor scale very expressively*] !!!!!!!!! [*She sits down*].

MAGNUS. Of course, abdicate. Lysistrata: you have been a teacher of history. You can assure your colleagues that there is nothing unprecedented in an abdication. The Emperor Charles the Fifth, for instance—

LYSISTRATA. Oh, Charles the Fifth be—be bothered! he's not good enough. Sir: I have stood by you as far as I dared. Dont throw me over. You must not abdicate. [*She sits down, distressed*].

PROTEUS. You cannot abdicate except by my advice.

MAGNUS. I am acting upon your advice.

PROTEUS. Nonsense! [*He sits down*].

BALBUS. Ridiculous! [*He sits down*].

PLINY. Youre not serious, you know. [*He sits down*].

NICOBAR. You cant upset the apple cart like this. [*He sits down*].

CRASSUS. I must say this is not playing the game. [*He sits down*].

BOANERGES [*powerfully*] Well, why not? Why not? Though as an old Republican I have no respect for His Majesty as a King, I have a great respect for him as a Strong Man. But he is not the only pebble on the beach. Why not have done with this superstition of monarchy, and bring the British Commonwealth into line with all the other great Powers today as a republic? [*He sits down*].

MAGNUS. My abdication does not involve that, Mr Boanerges. I am abdicating to save the monarchy, not to destroy it. I shall be succeeded by my son Robert, Prince of Wales. He will make an admirable constitutional monarch.

PLINY. Oh, come! Dont be hard on the lad, sir. He has plenty of brains.

MAGNUS. Oh yes, yes, yes: I did not mean that he is a nonentity: quite the contrary: he is much cleverer than I am. But I have never been able to induce him to take any interest in parliamentary politics. He prefers intellectual pursuits.

NICOBAR. Dont you believe it. He is up to his neck in business.

MAGNUS. Just so. He asks me why I waste my time with you here pretending to govern the country when it is really governed by Breakages, Limited. And really I hardly know how to answer him.

CRASSUS. Things are like that nowadays. My son says just the same.

LYSISTRATA. Personally I get on very well with the Prince; but somehow I do not feel that he is interested in what I am doing.

BALBUS. He isnt. He wont interfere with you as long as you dont interfere with him. Just the right king for us. Not pigheaded. Not meddlesome. Thinks that nothing we do matters a rap. What do you say, Joe?

PROTEUS. After all, why not? if your Majesty is in earnest.

MAGNUS. I assure you I am very much in earnest.

PROTEUS. Well, I confess I did not foresee this turn of events. But I ought to have foreseen it. What your Majesty proposes is the straightforward, logical, intellectually honest solution of our difficulty. Consequently it is the last solution I could have expected in politics. But I reckoned without your Majesty's character. The more I think of it the more clearly I see that you are right—that you are taking the only course open to you.

CRASSUS. I never said I was against it, Joe.

BALBUS. Neither did I.

NICOBAR. I think theres a great deal to be said for it. *I* have no objection.

PLINY. One king is no worse than another, is he?

BOANERGES. Is he any better? The way you fellows scuttle backward and forward from one mind to another whenever Joe holds up his finger is disgusting. This is a Cabinet of sheep.

PROTEUS. Well, give the flock a better lead if you can. Have you anything else to propose?

BOANERGES. I dont know that I have on the spur of the moment. We should have had notice of this. But I suppose the King must do as he thinks right.

PROTEUS. Then the goat goes with the sheep; so thats all right.

BOANERGES. Who are you calling a goat?

NICOBAR. If you come to that, who are you calling sheep?

AMANDA. Steady there, children! steady! steady! [*To the King*] You have brought us all round, sir, as usual.

PROTEUS. There is nothing more to be said.

AMANDA. That means another half hour at least.

BOANERGES. Woman: this is not the moment for your tomfooleries.

PROTEUS [*impressively*] Bill is right, Amanda. [*He rises and becomes the conventional House of Commons orator*].

Ministers compose themselves to listen with grave attention, as if in church; but Lysistrata is contemptuous and Amanda amused.

PROTEUS [*continuing*] It is a solemn moment. It is a moment in which an old tie is being broken. I am not ashamed to confess that it is a tie from which I have learned something.

MALE MINISTERS [*murmur*] Hear hear! Hear hear!

PROTEUS. For my own part—and I think I may speak for

others here as well—it has been no mere political tie, but a tie of sincere friendship.

Renewed murmurs of sympathy. Increasing emotion.

PROTEUS. We have had our disagreements—as which of us has not?—but they have been family quarrels.

CRASSUS. Thats all. Nothing more.

PROTEUS. May I say lovers' quarrels?

PLINY [*wiping his eyes*] You may, Joe. You may.

PROTEUS. My friends, we came here to a meeting. We find, alas! that the meeting is to be a leavetaking. [*Crassus sniffs tearfully*]. It is a sad leavetaking on our part, but a cordial one. [Hear Hear *from Pliny*]. We are cast down, but not discouraged. Looking back to the past with regret, we can still look forward to the future with hope. That future has its dangers and its difficulties. It will bring us new problems; and it will bring us face to face with a new king. But the new problems and the new king will not make us forget our old counsellor, monarch, and—he will allow me to say—comrade. [Hear Hears *ad libitum*]. I know my words will find an echo in all your hearts when I conclude by saying that whatsoever king shall reign—

AMANDA. Youll be the Vicar of Bray, Joe.

Uproar. Proteus flings himself into his chair indignantly.

BALBUS. Shame!

NICOBAR. Shut up, you b—

PLINY. A joke's a joke; but really—

CRASSUS. Too bad, Amanda! Behave yourself.

LYSISTRATA. She has a perfect right to speak. You are a parcel of sentimental fools.

BOANERGES [*rising*] Silence. Order.

AMANDA. Sorry.

BOANERGES. So you ought to be. Where's your manners? Where's your education? King Magnus: we part; but we part as strong men part: as friends. The Prime Minister has correctly represented the sentiments of all the men present. I call on them to express those sentiments in the good old English fashion. [*Singing in stentorian tones*] Fo-o-o-o-r-r-r

MALE MINISTERS EXCEPT PROTEUS [*rising and singing*]

> — he's a jolly good fel-low
> For he's a jolly good fel-low
> For he's—

MAGNUS [*peremptorily*] Stop. Stop.
Sudden silence and misgiving. They sit down furtively.

MAGNUS. I thank you with all my heart; but there is a misapprehension. We are not taking leave of one another. I have no intention of withdrawing from an active part in politics.

PROTEUS. What!!

MAGNUS. You are looking on me, with an emotion which has deeply touched me, as a man with a political past. But I look on myself rather as a man with a political future. I have not yet told you my plans.

NICOBAR. What plans?

BALBUS. A retired king cant have plans and a future.

MAGNUS. Why not? I am looking forward to a most exciting and enjoyable time. As I shall of course dissolve parliament, the fun will begin with a general election.

BOANERGES [*dismayed*] But Ive only just been elected. Do you mean that I shall have to stand two elections in one month? Have you thought of the expenses?

MAGNUS. Surely your expenses will be paid by the State.

BOANERGES. Paid by the State! Is that all you know about electioneering in England?

PROTEUS. You will get your whack out of the party funds, Bill; and if you cant find the extras you must put up with straight votes. Go on, sir: we want to hear about those plans of yours.

MAGNUS. My last act of royal authority will be to divest myself of all titles and dignities; so that I may step down at once into the position of a commoner.

BOANERGES. Step up, you mean. The common man is the superior, not the inferior, of the titled man.

MAGNUS. That is why I am going to make myself a common man, Mr Boanerges.

PLINY. Well, it does you honor.

CRASSUS. Not all of us would be capable of a sacrifice like that.

BOANERGES. A fine gesture, sir. A fine gesture. I admit it.

PROTEUS [*suspicious*] And since when, pray, has your Majesty taken to making gestures? Whats the game this time?

BOANERGES. Shame!

PROTEUS. Shut up, you gaby. [*To the King*] I say, whats the game?

MAGNUS. There is no imposing on you, Prime Minister. The game is, of course, that when I come back into politics I shall be in a better position as a commoner than as a peer. I shall seek a parliamentary seat.

PROTEUS. You in the House of Commons!

MAGNUS [*blandly*] It is my intention to offer myself to the Royal Borough of Windsor as a candidate at the forthcoming General Election.

All the rest except Boanerges and the ladies rise in consternation.

PROTEUS. This is treachery.

BALBUS. A dirty trick.

NICOBAR. The meanest on record.

PLINY. He'll be at the top of the poll.

CRASSUS. There wont be any poll: it will be a walk-over.

BALBUS. This shews what all your fine manners and friendly ways are worth.

NICOBAR. Hypocrite!

CRASSUS. Humbug!

LYSISTRATA. I wish your Majesty every success.

AMANDA. Hear hear! Fair play, boys. Why shouldnt he go into parliament with us?

BOANERGES. Well said! well said! Why not?

THE OTHER MALE MINISTERS. Ya-a-a-ah! [*They sit down in utter disgust*].

PROTEUS [*very sullen*] And when you are in Parliament, what then?

MAGNUS. There are several possibilities. I shall naturally endeavor to form a party. My son King Robert will have to call on some Party leader who can depend on the support of the House of Commons to form a Government. He may call on you. He may even call on me.

AMANDA [*breaks the glum silence by whistling a bar or two of the National Anthem*]!!

MAGNUS. Whatever happens, it will be a great relief to us to be able to speak out quite frankly about oneanother in public. You have never been able to tell the British people what you really think of me: no real criticism of the King is possible. I have never been able to speak my mind as to your various capacities and characters. All that reserve, that tedious affectation, that unwholesome concealment will end. I hope you look forward to our new footing as pleasurably as I do.

LYSISTRATA. I am delighted, sir. You will fight Breakages for me.

AMANDA. It will be awful fun.

BOANERGES. Now, Mr Prime Minister, we are waiting for you. What have you to say about it?

PROTEUS [*rising and speaking slowly, with his brows deeply knitted*] Has Your Majesty got that ultimatum on you?

MAGNUS [*produces it from his breast pocket and presents it to him*]!

PROTEUS [*with measured emphasis, after tearing the paper up into four pieces at two deliberate strokes, and throwing the pieces away*] There is not going to be any abdication. There is not going to be any general election. There is not going to be any ultimatum. We go on as before. The crisis is a washout. [*To the King, with deadly concentration*] I will never forgive you for this. You stole your ace of trumps from the hand I played this morning. [*He takes his hat from the balustrade and goes away through the park*].

BOANERGES [*rising*] That was a very deplorable exhibition of temper on the part of the Prime Minister, sir. It was not the gesture of a Strong Man. I will remonstrate with him. You may depend on me. [*He takes his hat and follows Proteus in a serious and dignified manner*].

NICOBAR [*rising*] Well, I shall not say what I think. [*He is *taking his hat when the King addresses him*].

MAGNUS. So I have not upset the apple cart after all, Mr Nicobar.

NICOBAR. You can upset it as soon as you like for all I care. I am going out of politics. Politics is a mug's game. [*He goes*].

CRASSUS [*rising reluctantly and taking his hat*] If Nick goes, I shall have to go too.

MAGNUS. Can you really tear yourself away from politics?

CRASSUS. Only too glad to be well out of them, if Breakages will let me. They shoved me into it; and I daresay theyll find another job for me. [*He goes*].

PLINY [*cheerful to the last as he, too, goes for his hat*] Well, I am glad nothing's happened. You know, sir, nothing ever really does happen in the Cabinet. Never mind their bit of temper. Theyll feed out of your hand tomorrow. [*He goes*].

BALBUS [*after taking his hat*] Now that theyre all gone I dont mind saying that if anything should ever happen to the throne, and your Majesty should become a President with a Cabinet to pick, you might easily find a worse Home Secretary than me, with all my faults.

MAGNUS. I shall bear it in mind. By the way, if you should happen to overtake the Prime Minister, will you be so good as to remind him that we quite forgot to settle that little affair of the proposal of America to annex the British Commonwealth.

BALBUS. By the Lord, so we did! Well, thats a good one! Ha ha! Ha ha ha ha ha! [*He goes out laughing heartily*].

MAGNUS. They dont take it in, Lizzie: not one bit. It is as if another planet were crashing into us. The kingdom and the power and the glory will pass from us and leave us naked, face to face with our real selves at last.

LYSISTRATA. So much the better, if by our real selves you mean the old English stock that was unlike any other. Nowadays men all over the world are as much alike as hotel dinners. It's no use pretending that the America of George Washington is going to swallow up the England of Queen Anne. The America of George Washington is as dead as Queen Anne. What they call an American is only a wop pretending to be a Pilgrim Father. He is no more Uncle Jonathan than you are John Bull.

MAGNUS. Yes: we live in a world of wops, all melting into one another; and when all the frontiers are down London may be outvoted by Tennessee, and all the other places where we still madly teach our children the mentality of an eighteenth century village school.

LYSISTRATA. Never fear, sir. It is not the most ignorant national crowd that will come out on top, but the best power station; for you cant do without power stations, and you cant run them on patriotic songs and hatred of the foreigner, and guff and bugaboo, though you can run nationalism on nothing else. But I am heartbroken at your not coming into the House with us to keep old England in front and lead a new Party against Breakages [*tears come into her eyes*].

MAGNUS [*patting her consolingly on the back*] That would have been splendid, wouldnt it? But I am too old fashioned. This is a farce that younger men must finish.

AMANDA [*taking her arm*] Come home with me, dear. I will sing to you until you cant help laughing. Come.

Lysistrata pockets her handkerchief; shakes the King's hands impulsively; and goes with Amanda. The King plunges into deep thought. Presently the Queen comes back.

THE QUEEN. Now Magnus: it's time to dress for dinner.

MAGNUS [*much disturbed*] Oh, not now. I have something very big to think about. I dont want any dinner.

THE QUEEN [*peremptorily*] No dinner! Did anyone ever hear of such a thing! You know you will not sleep if you think after seven o'clock.

MAGNUS [*worried*] But really, Jemima—

THE QUEEN [*going to him and taking his arm*] Now, now, now! dont be naughty. I mustnt be late for dinner. Come on, like a good little boy.

The King, with a grimace of hopeless tenderness, allows himself to be led away.

THE END